Colette

GENEVIÈVE DORMANN

Colette
A Passion for Life

ABBEVILLE PRESS · PUBLISHERS · NEW YORK

Acknowledgments

Above all we would like to thank Monsieur Bertrand de Jouvenel and Madame Jannie Malige, without whom this book could not have been written.

We would also like to express our special gratitude to Monsieur Richard Anacréon, Monsieur Jean-Louis Lécard, Monsieur Jean-Pierre Mouchard and Monsieur Michel Remy-Bieth, whose help and cooperation have been invaluable.

Finally, we are greatly indebted to Madame Dominique Aury, Monsieur Alain Bernardin, Madame Yannick Bellon, Madame Sybille Billot, Madame Marguerite Boivin, Madame Helena Bossis, Mademoiselle Maria-Catherine Boutterin, Mademoiselle Yvonne Brochard, Madame Delanoë, Admiral Marcel Duval, the photographic research staff of Editions Flammarion, the Florence J. Gould Foundation, Charles Hathaway, Madame Auguste Hériot, Madame Irène Le Cornec, Madame Denise Tual, Madame Jeanne-Marie Viel, Monsieur Bernard Villaret, the keepers of the Bibliothèque Doucet and the Bibliothèque Nationale in Paris, the Société des amis de Colette in Saint-Sauveur, and all those who have assisted in the preparation of this book.

Original idea and research: Sylvie Delassus
Design: Jacques Maillot
Translated from the French by David Macey (text) and Jane Brenton (captions and chronology)

First published in Great Britain in 1985
by Thames and Hudson Ltd, London

This edition © 1985 Abbeville Press, New York
and Thames and Hudson Ltd, London

© 1984 Editions Herscher, Paris

Excerpts reprinted by permission of Farrar, Straus and Giroux, Inc. from *My Apprenticeships* by Colette. Translated by Helen Beauclerk. Copyright 1957 by Martin Secker & Warburg, Ltd

Inquiries should be addressed to Abbeville Press, Inc., 505 Park Avenue, New York, N.Y. 10022

Printed and bound in France

Library of Congress Cataloging in Publication Data
Dormann, Geneviève, 1933-
    Colette: A Passion for Life
    Translation into English of: Amoureuse Colette.
    1. Colette, 1873-1954—Biography. 2. Authors, French
—20th century—Biography. I. Delassus, Sylvie.
II. Title.
PQ2605.028Z66213   1985   848'.91209 [B]   85-4074
ISBN 0-89659-583-8

Contents

1   Colette as a young woman, dressed in Renaissance costume.

I Her Mother's House

'Madame Willy dragged behind her a plait of hair long enough to lower a bucket down a well. She looked at the mild-mannered Julia and burst out laughing.' This is how Jules Renard described 'the young wife of Henry Gauthier-Villars, who is known in literary circles as Willy' when he first saw her in the glittering crowd at a theatrical première in Paris in 1894.[1]

A long, long plait of ash-blonde hair and a burst of laughter . . . not a bad description, one might think, of Sidonie Gabrielle Colette, a young lady of twenty-three who never lost the accent of her native Burgundy.

Her long hair always caused comment, even at a time when all women wore their hair long, but it was not every day that the young Madame Willy burst out laughing. Most photographs taken at the time show an adolescent with a small face and a dreamy look bordering on boredom and sadness.

In the autumn of 1894, she was still 'Gabri' or 'Minet-Chéri' to her mother, but already 'Colette' to her husband, who transformed her surname into the Christian name she was soon to make famous. She had been married for only eighteen months, but she had already realized that happiness is an illusion and that getting married had been the first big mistake of her life. She was already homesick for the provincial paradise of her childhood, which she had left for a brilliant but suffocating life in Paris, and missed her happy, carefree family, a family as warm as it was eccentric.

Above all, she missed her mother. Madame Colette, Sidonie Landoy or 'Sido', was a grey-eyed blonde and an intelligent woman with a great deal of commonsense. She was the daughter of a quadroon, a chocolate manufacturer known as 'the Gorilla', who had not been a faithful husband. After the death of her parents, Sido was brought up in Belgium by her elder brother and moved in a very lively world of writers, musicians and artists. Her first marriage was a failure. She had met Jules Robineau-Duclos when she went to visit her old nurse in Burgundy at Saint-Sauveur-en-Puisaye. He was known as 'the Savage' – the family had a liking for nicknames – and, unfortunately for Sido, he proved to be a brutal and unfaithful husband. But the Savage was also a man of property who owned farms, land and a large comfortable house. When he had the good taste to depart this world, he left a very wealthy young widow of thirty and two children, Juliette and Achille. Sido finally found happiness with Jules Colette, who came originally from Toulon. He was cheerful, charming, cultivated, and women found him attractive. Whereas the Savage had been odious, Jules Colette was very much in love with his young wife. He was also jealous. Perhaps he had reason to be: Sido had not put up much resistance when he first courted her, though she was still a married woman.

Jules Colette was by profession a soldier. He had graduated from Saint-Cyr at the age of twenty-three and then served with the First Zouaves in Kabylia and in the Crimea. He had been promoted to the rank of captain in 1855 and lost his left leg in 1859 during the Italian campaign, though that seems not to have diminished either his good humour or his flirtatiousness. Since he was unfit for further military service, however, his country granted him the position of tax-collector in Saint-Sauveur-en-Puisaye, where the unhappy Sido was living with her drunkard of a husband.

Jules consoled her. He consoled her so well that it was rumoured in the town that Sido's second child Achille should really have been called Colette and not Robineau-Duclos. But there is always talk in a county town with a population of seventeen hundred; gossip is the only form of entertainment in such places!

Be that as it may, within twelve months of her husband's death Sido had officially fallen into the arms of her handsome veteran. Two more children were born: Léopold (in 1866) and Gabrielle, who is better known to us as Colette. She was born under the sign of Aquarius on 28 January 1873 'in a room which no stove could heat adequately . . . with difficulty, half-strangled, but with a vigorous determination to survive'.[2]

Life in the Colette household was very pleasant. The house was large, with a terrace leading to a double flight of steps, a hugh barn, outbuildings and two gardens. Sido was an energetic, lively mother who was in love with her husband, her children, her animals and her plants. She was a very endearing figure. Saint-Simon's *Mémoires* was her bedside book. Although she was not a believer, she never missed mass on Sundays. During the service, she would read Corneille, concealing the book inside her missal. She quarrelled with the priest when he refused to give her cuttings from his plants. Her daughter may well have painted a flattering picture of her, but she does really seem to have been the mother we all dream of. She was at once traditional and eccentric. Without realizing it, she was a poet. She called her neighbours after the points of the compass, thought that pansies looked like Henry VIII of England, and 'chucked roses under the chin so as to look them full in the face'. She was the kind of woman who would agree to wake her ten-year-old daughter at three in the morning so that she could see the summer sun rise over the countryside. It is not difficult to understand how such a woman produced a daughter who was so in love with life. Nor is it difficult to understand why Colette, who described her so well in *Sido* and *La Maison de Claudine*, treated her as her confidante all her life. They had so much in common and were so alike that Colette always missed her; after her death in 1912, Colette repeated her friend Marguerite Moreno's comment on her own mother's death: 'Now I am no one's little girl.'

It has to be said that Sido's elder children were not her favourites. Juliette was a strange, disturbing child with abnormally thick dark hair who read too much for her own good and whose mongoloid features revealed the heritage of her alcoholic father. Nor was Sido particularly fond of Achille, who became a doctor, or of Léopold, though she had rejoiced in his birth. It was her youngest, Gabri, our Colette, who won her heart. Years later, she was to write to her: 'Yes, you were my golden sunshine . . . and I told you long ago that when you came into the room, it suddenly became brighter.'[3]

Gabri, Minet-Chéri ('dear Puss') or Soleil-d'Or was the youngest member of the Colette family and she was a spoiled child, exquisitely happy during her gypsy childhood in Puisaye. She was pretty, with her schoolgirl smocks, her sea-green eyes and the ribbons Sido put in her hair in the manner of eighteenth-century portraits by Madame Vigée-Lebrun. As a result of playing with her two brothers, she was also something of a tomboy. When she was eight, her ambition was to become a sailor and travel around the world. She was bright, imaginative and sensuous and, like any mischievous little girl, had a taste for melodrama. She would not, for instance, have objected to being abducted. Indeed, she dreamed of it at night.

Then there were the books. Before the days of television children used to read a great deal. Luckily, the Colette family house contained a whole library into which the children could dip any time they liked. Apart from Perrault's delightful tales, there were no 'children's books' in the house; instead, the children had Labiche, Daudet, Hugo and a collection of travel books. Minet-Chéri was not slow to take advantage of them. She did not care for Dumas, but discovered Musset, Voltaire, Balzac and Shakespeare at a very early age. There was only one author they were forbidden to read – Zola, or at least some books by Zola. These were considered to be obscene ('An irruption of mud and filth into French literature', as Léon Daudet was to put it). But forbidden fruit is always the sweetest, and Minet-Chéri read Zola in secret, her cheeks burning. She was both aroused and fascinated by his brutal stories and by certain words . . .

We can picture her so easily: a pretty, precocious girl of thirteen, already curious enough to eavesdrop on what adults were saying and to take an interest in what happened to them. Wild, mocking and yet sentimental, she was in a hurry to grow up and become a woman, to put her hair up and wear a long dress.

From time to time, startling rumours of life in Paris reached the small provincial town. Paris was a world ruled by elegant women dressed in feathers, rustling gowns and precious stones. They were the most beautiful women in the whole world. They were like lionesses, as beautiful as poisonous flowers, and they lived a life of unbelievable lavishness. They were like queens. Men fell madly in love with them, fought duels over them, competed to lay their fortunes at their feet, and blew their brains out at a cruel word. Life in Paris must be wonderful for a pretty girl with a slender waist. Colette could not wait to go dancing at the Moulin Rouge, to show off her black stockings like La Goulue or like Madame Arthur, celebrated in song by Yvette Guilbert.

But Colette was still too young to be abducted and had to be content with playing games and going for walks. Her father, who was 'afflicted with philanthropy', resolved to become a *député*. He took his youngest daughter with him on his election campaigns, but Sido soon put a stop to that; the child acquired a taste for drinking mulled wine with the voters and started coming home tipsy. In those days, Captain Colette courted the muse and would ask his daughter for her advice. If she thought there were too many adjectives in his speeches and poems, he would cut them out.

The good Captain would delight his family with his baritone voice and his southern accent as, with a sidelong glance at Sido, he sang:

> Je pense à toi, je te vois, je t'adore,
> A tout instant, à toute heure, en tous lieux.

(I think of you, I see you, I adore you, Wherever I go, at every moment of every day.) He was indeed very fond of the woman he called 'my dear soul', but he was also a hopeless idealist and simply could not handle money. Within a few years, Sido's fortune was gone. To make matters worse, in 1885 Colette's ugly sister, who had reached the age of twenty-five, finally found a husband in the village. Dr Roché's breath smelled of Vermouth; Sido disliked him and found him very ugly. It was probably Dr Roché who persuaded Juliette to call her stepfather to account for his handling of her share of the Robineau-Duclos inheritance. That finally ruined the family. They had to leave their big house in Saint-Sauveur and its gardens, and say goodbye to childhood memories, to the pretty well-polished furniture and to all their ornaments. The house itself had been left to Achille by his father and remained in his possession, but the entire contents had to be sold at auction, and the family went to live with Achille who was a country doctor at Châtillon-sur-Loing (now Châtillon-Coligny) in the Loiret, forty kilometres from Saint-Sauveur. Captain Colette was granted a licence to run a *bureau de tabac* there.

This was the first great sorrow in Colette's life, and she always regretted having to leave the house and village where she was born. She revisited it once or twice, with the men she loved; and her description is so vivid that one is almost convinced that one lived there oneself.

1. Renard, *Journal, 1887-1910*, Paris, Gallimard, Bibliothèque de la Pléiade, 1960, p. 247 (entry dated 6 November 1894).
2. Colette, *Le Fanal bleu*, Paris, Ferenczi, 1949, p. 102.
3. Letter, 30 December 1911; *Le Figaro littéraire*, 24 January 1953.

2

"Sido" à dix-huit ans

3

4

5

2 Eugène and Jules Landoy, Colette's maternal uncles, were respectively nineteen and twelve years older than their young sister, Sidonie. Around 1840 they moved to Belgium, where Eugène worked as a journalist. When their parents died, Eugène and Jules brought Sido up in Belgium, in a world of journalists, painters and musicians. As a result she was a well-educated girl with a passion for books.

3 A daguerreotype of Adèle Eugénie Sidonie Landoy – 'Sido' – aged eighteen. She was born in Paris in 1835.

4 Sido's mother, Sophie Chatenay, Madame Landoy. This portrait of Colette's maternal grandmother was stolen from the writer's flat; thirty years later, by an extraordinary chance, she found it again at the Marché aux Puces, where she had gone bargain-hunting with Charlotte Lysès, Sacha Guitry's wife. 'The miniature', wrote Colette, 'depicts a young woman with hair arranged in the form of a trefoil – a fat coil on the top and a bunch of sausage curls falling over each temple. She is smiling, well pleased, I suspect, to be restored to my mantelshelf. She died young after countless infidelities by her husband; I know nothing of her beyond her premature death and the silence she kept as a deceived wife – everything that matters, in fact' (*L'Etoile Vesper*).

5 Sido's father, Henry Landoy, known as 'the Gorilla' – 'just a touch "coloured"', as his granddaughter Colette was to describe him – had a chocolate business and a roving eye.

7

6 Sido's first husband, Jules Robineau-Duclos, died in 1865 when she was thirty, leaving her with two children, Juliette and Achille. She soon married Captain Colette, who was deeply in love with her.

7 Achille Robineau-Duclos, Colette's half-brother. He grew up to become a doctor in Châtillon-Coligny, and provided a home for the Colette family when they were forced to leave Saint-Sauveur-en-Puisaye.

8 Juliette Robineau-Duclos, Colette's half-sister, the changeling of the family.

8

9 Colette's paternal grandmother from Provence, whose maiden name was Funel. 'She had gingery eyebrows set low above her green eyes, and a majestic bulk encased in big black taffeta skirts.' Colette called her 'my wicked grandmother'.

10 Her husband, Colette's grandfather, was plagued all his life by the jealous inquisitions of his formidable wife.

11 Colette's legacy from her father: a Crimea ribbon, an Italian campaign medal, the cross of the Legion of Honour and a photograph of Captain Colette, the gallant Zouave.

12 Joseph Jules Colette, Sido's second husband and the writer's father. 'Born to please and to fight, a writer of impromptu verses and a story-teller; it occurred to me later that he might have swayed a Senate as easily as he charmed a woman' (*La Maison de Claudine*).

13

13, 14 Léopold, the first child
of Sido and Jules Colette, born in
1866, was seven years older than
his sister Gabrielle. The Captain
posed proudly with his baby son
perched on his remaining leg.

15 Sido at the age of forty-five,
two years after the birth of
Colette. Devoted to her husband
and children and her garden,
fond of animals, a nature-lover,
she would always respond to
anyone in trouble. Long after her
death, in *La Maison de
Claudine*, Colette tenderly
recalled the warmth and security
provided by her mother, and the
call that would echo across the
garden: 'Children, where are
you?' Sido passed on to her
daughter her love of books, her
feeling for nature and her sense
of humour. Until the end of her
life she remained Colette's
closest confidante.

14

15

17

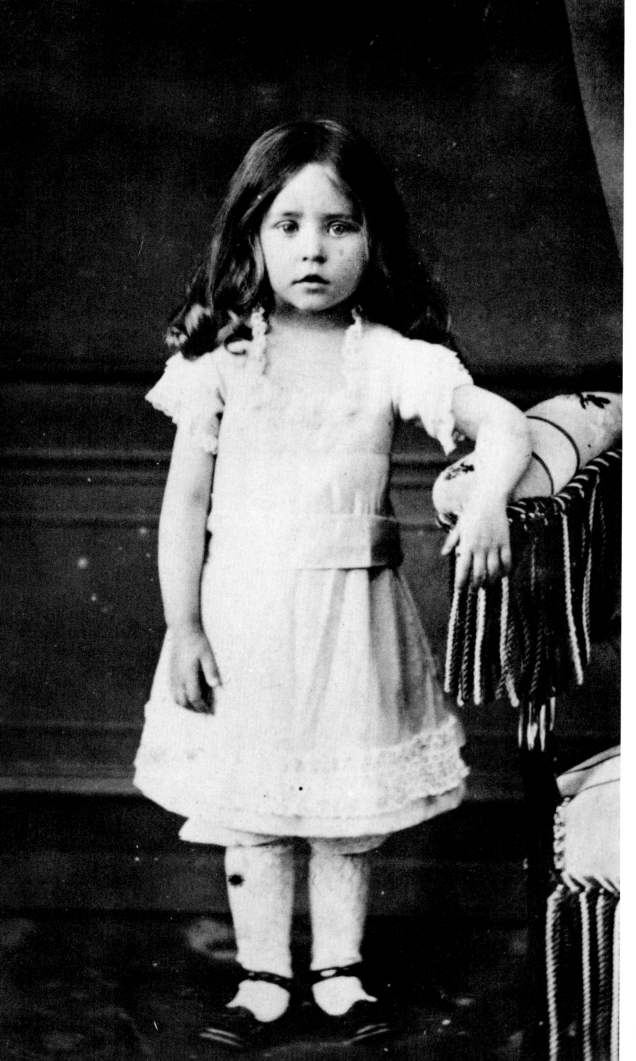

16

18　Gabrielle aged five, wearing earrings, something she later detested. She already has the melancholy look so characteristic of her throughout her adult life.

17

18

19

21

20

19 Colette in 1886, aged thirteen, on her first visit to Paris. Even as a child she loved food and had a sensuous nature, dreaming of being abducted. She was pampered by her brothers, admired by her father – to whom she offered advice on literary style – and adored by her mother, who called her 'Minet-Chéri' or 'my jewel-all-of-gold'.

20 The Colette family. Seated at her parents' feet is the tomboy Gabrielle, her 'two plaits braided behind her ears'.

22

21 The main street of Saint-Sauveur-en-Puisaye as it was in
Colette's childhood; the annotations are hers.

22 The Colette family house in Saint-Sauveur-en-Puisaye, seen
from the rue de l'Hospice, 'a big private house in an old village'. All
her life Colette felt nostalgia for her childhood home.

545 St-Sauveur (Yonne)
Le Château - Le Canal

Blin et Moulliou, éditeurs à St-Sauveur

23

8. St-SAUVEUR (Yonne) — Le Château XVIIe siècle
La Tour Sarrazine XIe siècle (Vue prise des Communs)

Blin, édit. St-Sauveur

24

25

26

27

23, 24 Achille, Léo and Gabrielle roamed the woods and fields around Saint-Sauveur in complete freedom and happiness. When they returned, 'The anxious mother's unerring nose picked up on us the whiff of wild garlic from some distant gully, or mint from the grassed-over marshes' (*La Maison de Claudine*).

25 The market-place in Saint-Sauveur. 'Sundays can be dreamy empty days . . .'

26 The tablet marking Colette's birthplace.

27 'My half-sister's marriage meant that I inherited her bedroom, the one on the first floor.' (See Ill. 22.)

Saint-Sauveur-en-Puisaye

28 The carriage entrance of 'Claudine's house'.

29 A sketch by Colette's friend the painter Luc-Albert Moreau, showing the house and the steps from the upper garden to the lower garden, framed by wistaria and bignonia.

30 Colette in the upper garden with her brother Léo. 'Our boisterousness was oddly silent, voices were never raised.'

28

29

31 'House and garden still exist, I realize, but what does that matter if the magic has left them, if the secret is lost that once opened up [. . .] a world of which I am no longer worthy?'

30

109 — Saint-Sauveur (Yonne) — Distribution de prix présidée par M. Merlou

Blin et Mouchon, éditeurs, St-Sauveur

50

32

114 — Saint-Sauveur (Yonne) — Place de la Mairie

Blin et Mouchon, éditeurs, St-Sauveur

33

34

2ᵉ rang, assises
1 Noémi ?
2 ?
3 Jules ?
4 une Jollet

5 ?
6 Lucie Bellard
7 Hélène Vivien
8 Jules Breuiller
9 Mathilde Boulat
10 Aurélie Ledroit

The real-life setting for *Claudine à l'école*.

32 Prizegiving at the school in Saint-Sauveur, presided over by the Mayor, Dr Merlou, who in the novel became the local government official Dr Dutertre.

33 The new school could not erase memories of the old – 'dilapidated and insanitary, but such fun!'

34 The school Christmas tree. Colette has written in the name of Mademoiselle Olympe Terrain, who in the novel became Mademoiselle Sergent – 'a shapely redhead with a narrow waist and full hips, but with an amazingly ugly face, puffy and always aflame . . .'

35 Colette with her fellow pupils: she is fourth from the left in the front row. At the very end of her life Colette could still recall the names of the other children, and wrote them in beneath the photograph.

11 Arthémise Demon
12 Eugénie Fauconnier
13 ? Breuiller

En bas, assises :
1 Septime Dumoutiers
2 Jeanne Berthier
3 Thérèse Jérôme
4 Gabrielle Colette
5 Camille Jérôme

6 Jeanne Havone
7 Octavie Priaudot
8 Eugénie Peuphely
9 Liline Ballut
10 Camille Havone
11 Jeanne Havone

35

36

37

38

36 Colette as an adolescent, in one of her sailor costumes.

37 The strange Juliette surprised everyone by finding herself a fiancé, one Dr Roché. Sido found him very unappealing, and called him 'le premier chien coiffé'.

38 Captain Colette, the war hero, at Châtillon-Coligny in 1896, after the family's move. 'Shouldn't I, while he was alive, have broken through that wry dignity of his, that simulated frivolity?'

39 Juliette's wedding in 1885. Colette is in the front row, sitting next to the bride. When Juliette subsequently claimed her inheritance the contents of the house at Saint-Sauveur had to be sold, and the Colette family were forced to move to Châtillon-Coligny.

40 A famous photograph of Colette aged fifteen, with immensely long plaits.

40

29

41

42

43

43 Léo, the musician 'with lead-blue eyes' (left), Achille the doctor (standing), and one of their Landoy cousins.

44 Achille and his wife in the woods at Châtillon.

45 Achille sometimes took Colette with him when he did his rounds in the outlying areas. From him she learned how to stitch wounds and make up medicines.

44

45

46 Colette at eighteen, at last old enough to wear her hair up – the great ambition of all young girls at the end of the last century.

47 Captain Colette and Sido, engrossed in a game of dominoes.

48 Jules Colette poses for the camera, ostensibly writing his memoirs. Ever devoted to his wife, he has her photograph on his desk.

49 Sido at sixty, at the time of her splendid letter about a pink cactus, which her daughter incorporated in *La Naissance du jour*.

50 Sido (left) with Achille's wife (centre) at Châtillon.

47   46

48

49

50

51

52

53

51, 52 Colette at twenty in 1893, the year of her marriage. Her little pointed face and childlike features attracted much attention when she arrived in Paris as Madame Gauthier-Villars, Willy's wife.

53 The family on the steps outside the house at Châtillon. On the left are some of Sido's beloved cuttings.

54 This photograph of Colette in the year of her wedding appears in Willy's photograph album with the comment, 'as yet, hiding neither her feelings nor her ears'.

55 Colette as a young woman with her stepson Jacques Gauthier-Villars, who later described her as 'my most seductive stepmother'.

56 Henry Gauthier-Villars – 'Willy'.

II Apprenticeships

It was in about 1891 that young Gabrielle began to show an interest in a family friend she had known for a long time. He was to become her first husband.

Henry Gauthier-Villars (1859-1931) – nicknamed 'Willy' – was then thirty-two. He was the younger son of Albert Gauthier-Villars, a graduate of the Ecole Polytechnique and an important scientific publisher, who had served in the army alongside Jules Colette. Willy himself had received a solid grounding in the classics at the Lycée Condorcet and at the Collège Stanislas, where he won the first prize for Greek composition in an open competitive examination. Although his family would have liked him to go to the Ecole Normale Supérieure, he felt drawn to literature and music. He was an educated but somewhat eccentric man.

He had published a collection of sonnets and had edited scientific texts for his father's publishing house. His rooms above his father's offices on the Quai des Grands-Augustins became a meeting place for writers and musicians. Even some members of the nearby Institut de France were drawn there to enjoy the brilliant wit of their young neighbour.

'Henry Maugis' was the first of Willy's many pseudonyms and it was under that name that his first articles on music and literature appeared in *La Nouvelle Rive gauche*, a review which also published Verlaine, Jean Moréas and Henry de Régnier. He subsequently worked on countless other newspapers and reviews, becoming among other things music critic of *L'Echo de Paris*, where he signed his column 'L'Ouvreuse du Cirque d'été' (the usherette of the Cirque d'été). His unusual style was very different from that of the conventional critics, and the puns and snippets of gossip he included in his articles made him very popular. He was a Wagner enthusiast and did a great deal to popularize the German composer's work in France. He also championed French composers, including Debussy, Chabrier and d'Indy.

Willy was always short of money and he began to produce popular novels, but he did not write them himself. He set up what was in effect a literary factory, using as ghostwriters his friends, some of whom, like Jean de Tinan, Marcel Schwob, Curnonski, Francis Carco and Paul-Jean Toulet, were excellent writers who needed to make a living. The novels were, of course, signed 'Willy'.

Willy rapidly became the darling of Paris. He was much sought after as a dinner-guest. Cab drivers recognized him in the street. His jokes, witticisms and jibes went the rounds at fashionable dinner parties. Women – and Willy had a considerable appetite for women – worshipped him.

He was not, however, handsome. His paunch was already quite pronounced, he was bald, and the wild life he led had already left its marks on him. In 1891, Willy was anything but an Adonis. But he had charm and above all he was funny. What woman, even a young woman, can resist a man who makes her laugh? And Willy certainly made young Gabri laugh. Whenever he came to Châtillon, the young girl's face lit up. Gabri roared with laughter when he called the Princesse de Caraman-Chimay 'le carrément chameau' (a real beast) or described Catulle Mendès, who was very proud of his success with women, as being 'vain du rein' ('loin vain', sounding like 'Rhine wine'). He also amused her by making an anagram of the name of Jules Clarétie, the director of the Théâtre Français and a prolific journalist, as 'Je sue l'article' (I ooze journalism).

His father's friendship with Jules Colette was not Willy's only reason for going to Châtillon so often. In 1889 he had had a son, Jacques, by a young woman he adored, and when she died the boy had been sent to a foster mother in the area.

In Colette's eyes, Willy had all the fascination a womanizer has for sensual girls who know nothing of love. She later explained the attraction very well in *Mes*

Apprentissages: 'In a few hours an unscrupulous man will transform an ignorant girl into a prodigy of licentiousness. Disgust will not deter her; disgust has never been a hindrance. Like morality, it comes later. [. . .] A consuming sensual audacity drives too many impatient little beauties into the arms of Lotharios half spoiled by time.'[1] In short, Willy aroused Colette's sexuality. She was ready for anything and was soon madly in love with him. Willy, for his part, was becoming rather tired of the wild life he was leading and had reached the age when his contemporaries began to think of settling down.

He suddenly found young Colette, whose mouth fell open with admiration whenever he spoke to her, very attractive. Her plaits made her look like a dissolute *ingénue*. They were an incongruous couple and, although their relationship was perfectly legal, Willy had the titillating impression of corrupting a minor. He proposed and was accepted, but his parents asked them to wait two years before getting married. The Gauthier-Villars wanted to make certain that this was not simply another of their son's passing whims. The family were devoutly religious: in 1919 they were to refuse to publish a text by Baudelaire, with the comment, 'Terribly sorry. We are Catholic printers.' They did not approve of their son's wayward behaviour and he had further offended them by having a son by a married woman and then recognizing the child as his. By insisting on such a long engagement, they may also have been trying to discourage him from marrying Colette. Although she came from a good family, she had no dowry whatsoever. There was also a more serious problem: when Willy officially introduced the woman he intended to marry to his brothers and sisters, they were taken aback 'by Colette's language and by the horrifying amount of butter and jam she ate'.[2] In short, they had hoped for something better.

It was at this time that the whiff of scandal that was to remain with Colette throughout her life first arose. By 1892, the projected marriage with Willy was already causing a stir. The Colette family received very malicious letters warning them against their daughter's fiancé. In the fashionable literary circles in which Willy moved in Paris, tongues began to wag when it was learned that this public clown and notorious high-liver had decided to settle down and take a wife from the provinces. On 4 May 1893, a vicious little item appeared in *Le Gil Blas*, a frivolous paper specializing in society gossip:

There is a lot of talk in Châtillon about the passionate devotion with which one of the wittiest of our Parisian *clubmen* [English in the original] is pursuing an exquisite blonde whose marvellous hair has made her famous throughout the region. But there is no talk of the word 'marriage' ever having been mentioned. We would strongly advise the pretty owner of the impossibly golden plaits to follow Mephistopheles' advice and not to give away any kisses until she has a ring on her finger.

Someone sent the cutting to Achille.

Willy was furious, challenged the editor of the paper to a duel and wounded him, an action which won him hearty congratulations from Captain Colette. On 15 May Sidonie Gabrielle Colette and Henry Gauthier-Villars were finally married by the mayor and the *curé* of Châtillon-Coligny. They were so worried that the ceremony might be disrupted that they were married in virtual secrecy. No photographers – not even amateurs – were allowed to be present. One photographer did, however, succeed in taking a picture showing Colette walking beside her father and wearing a white chiffon dress with a train.

As the young couple had no money, they did not have a traditional honeymoon and simply made a short trip to the Jura, where the Gauthier-Villars family owned a chalet. They then went to Paris where they spent a few days in Willy's bachelor establishment above his father's offices on the Quai des Grands-Augustins while they looked for an apartment to rent. According to Colette, the place 'looked uninhabited . . . German postcards were strewn more or less everywhere, celebrating the attractions of underclothes, socks, ribboned drawers and buttocks.'[3] This was what Willy called his 'Venusberg' – two dusty, bleak little rooms painted in bottle green and chocolate brown. There were no cooking facilities and Colette and her husband would cross the river to have breakfast in a cheap *crémerie* frequented by the packers from the Belle Jardinière department store.

All Willy's friends, enemies and acquaintances were eager to see the young woman from the provinces who had become his wife, though some of them were more favourably predisposed towards her than others. In his memoirs, Jacques-Emile Blanche, a fashionable painter who was related by marriage to the Gauthier-Villars, records his first glimpse of Colette in a *brasserie* in the Latin Quarter: 'A little cat-like face . . . a triangular face crowned by a ribbon . . . plaits of chestnut hair [it had darkened since the days when she was Sido's golden sunshine] which came down to her knees, brushing against a lie-de-vin-coloured skirt trimmed with matching braid and a high collar that made her look like a schoolgirl on holiday.' The painter also noted her fresh complexion, her obvious health and those 'long, slanting eyes of an intense blue which changes from grey to green from one second to the next and the long, slanting eyebrows which speak volumes.'[4] Nor did he overlook the young woman's deep, clear voice, with rolled Burgundian 'r's; or her submissive attitude towards her husband.

Colette was indeed submissive. And, with all due respect to the biographers who portray her as the pitiful victim of an old man who was determined to pervert and exploit her, she was passionately in love with her Willy. There can be no denying it. After all, Willy was only thirty-four, and while Colette may well have been naive, she was not exactly a complete innocent. But in later years she herself did paint a grim picture of Willy and of her first marriage. In 1935, four years after Willy's death, her memoirs began to appear in *Marianne* and they were subsequently published in book form as *Mes Apprentissages*. In those memoirs she uses all her lethal talent to annihilate the man she had loved so much forty years earlier. She always refers to him as 'Monsieur Willy'. The character assassination is all the more effective in that Colette cleverly organizes it around details that can be checked against other sources. She is not exactly lying, but she is exaggerating wildly. She paints Willy as a man who was in love with himself and his image, who was desperate for fame. She describes him as part pimp and part torturer, a man who was always ready to exploit the talents of others for his own ends, and a pathetic wretch who could not write and who terrorized her. Not even his physical appearance escapes her venom:

I have known people who were huge [. . .] Monsieur Willy was not huge, he was bulbous [. . .] every one of his features approximated to the curve. [. . .] It has been said that he bore a marked resemblance to Edward VII. To do justice to a less flattering but no less august truth, I would say that, in fact, the likeness was to Queen Victoria.[5]

What can have produced such bitterness, such long-lasting hatred? What caused this incurable wound? Why did Colette's love for Willy turn so sour?

This posthumous attack is shocking, not only to those who had known Willy for the man he had once been but also to those who had known the couple when they were first married, when his young bride was still in love with him, enjoyed being bullied by him and joyfully submitted to his every whim. When he read this venomous account, Paul Léautaud, who deeply admired both Colette herself and her talent, commented: 'She always seemed to me to be a woman whose affairs had left her nothing but great wounds.'[6]

What went wrong between Willy and Colette? What irreparable harm did Willy do her? – Willy, the man who in the spring of 1893 wrote to his friend Marcel Schwob to say how happy he was to be in Châtillon, 'dreaming of marriage and completely besotted with the birdlike grace of my pretty little Colette. . . . Within a month, I shall have married her. Fine. And I won't have a bean. All right! [English in the original]'[7]

Some of his faults were minor, but he did also hurt Colette badly. We have to try to understand her state of mind. In 1893, she was a rather naive girl waiting for her Prince Charming to come along. It did not matter to her then that Willy was fourteen years older or that he was already bald and pot-bellied. She did not even listen to the jibes of her brothers, who were as jealous as only brothers can be and as clear-sighted as only the jealous can be. They did not spare her suitor and said that he must have grown since his last visit because his bald patch had come through his hair.

She definitely loved the first man in her life and was proud to have been chosen by a Parisian whom so many other Parisians found so witty. He truly loved her, and to Colette that meant that he would love her for ever and would love only her, in the same way that her father loved Sido. Since the day she had been born, she had had before her a beautiful example of constant, comforting conjugal bliss. It did not matter to her that her husband had led a wild life. On the contrary, in her eyes that made him even more prestigious and guaranteed that he would always be faithful to her. She was both naive and proud, and she was under the delightful impression that she had supplanted all her predecessors. After all, she was the one and only woman whose hand Willy had ever asked in marriage.

And so, blindly trusting, she followed him into the intoxicating world of *fin-de-siècle* Paris. He was her guide and her mentor.

She was touchingly eager to please her husband in every way. She even took a maternal interest in Willy's son, sixteen years her junior. Willy worshipped his little boy, just as he had worshipped the boy's mother, and would introduce him to his friends as 'My brat. An example to be followed.' The child developed a passion for Colette and called her his 'little mother'. In later years, she went to visit him in England and at his school in Normandy. As an adult, Jacques Gauthier-Villars always spoke fondly of his 'most seductive stepmother.'

Whatever she may have said later, the young Colette was not particularly unhappy in 1893. Willy introduced her into a glittering world that she would not have dared to dream of back home in the country. Willy was proud of his Colette and took her everywhere. He took her to Montmartre, where they met Toulouse-Lautrec, to the Café d'Harcourt and to the Vachette, a meeting place for a group of young writers in the Latin Quarter. There she met Paul Valéry and some of Willy's 'ghosts', including Pierre Louÿs, Paul-Jean Toulet, Curnonski and the frail Jean de Tinan, who was to die young. She joked with Paul Masson, a facetious scholar who signed his work 'Lemice-Térieux'. He was kind to her and she later based one of the characters in *Le Képi* on him.

Willy, who playfully insisted on addressing her as *vous*, whilst she called him *tu*, introduced her to many fascinating people, including Marcel Schwob, author of *Le Livre de Monelle* and translator of *Moll Flanders*, and his mistress, the young and amusing Marguerite Moreno, who became his wife in 1900. The Schwobs and Colette were to become close, lifelong friends. She also met Alfred Jarry, Paul Léautaud, Jean Lorrain, the caricaturist Forain and Marcel Boulestin, a writer from Bordeaux who was later to be better known for the famous restaurant he opened in London.

Colette was seen with Willy at the *soirées* given by the *Mercure de France*, which was edited by Alfred Vallette and his wife, the novelist Rachilde, who would appear with two tame rats called Kyrie and Eleison perched on her bare shoulders. Rachilde was later to give an enthusiastic reception in print to the *Claudine* books.

On Wednesdays Colette attended the literary receptions given in the avenue Hoche by Madame Arman de Caillavet, the formidable mistress of Anatole France. It was at one of her receptions that Colette met Marcel Proust. She visited the poet José Maria de Hérédia and went to the musical evenings given by the Saint-Marceaux, where she made the acquaintance of Debussy. She also met Thadée Natanson and his wife Misia (later Misia Sert), the moving spirits behind *La Revue blanche*. She was received by the Princesse de Brancovan, mother of the poet Anna de Noailles.

Compared with the freedom of her girlhood in the country, she found Paris – which has so few parks – suffocating. The three-room apartment which Willy had rented at 28 rue Jacob was situated between two inner courtyards and was far from palatial. Despite his numerous journalistic and literary activities, her husband was not exactly rolling in money, and Sido had to buy her daughter a coat during the first winter of her marriage. Instead of going to bed at night, she would wait at the *Echo de Paris* in the rue du Croissant for Willy to finish correcting his proofs. Even though she was often exhausted, she then had to go with him on his round of the *brasseries*. Sometimes the young Madame Willy did complain, but she recovered her good humour once they were with friends and Willy soon had her doubled up with laughter at his puns. Once, to the delight of Apollinaire, he transformed the proverb 'Un sot trouve toujours un plus sot qui l'admire' (a fool always finds a bigger fool to admire him) into 'Un sot trouve toujours un puceau qui l'admire' (a fool always finds a virgin to admire him). And he ended a poem dedicated to the dancer Rosita Mauri with the line: 'Mauri, tu ris, tes saluts tentent' – literally, 'Mauri, you laugh and your salutations are tempting', but sounding like the Latin 'Morituri te salutant' (those about to die salute you).[8]

Unfortunately, Willy also indulged in less innocent diversions, and they were to give Colette the biggest shock of her life.

One day in the winter of 1893-4, a few months after her marriage, she received an anonymous note warning her that her husband was deceiving her. It gave a name and an address. Colette took a cab and went and knocked on the door of a minute mezzanine floor apartment. She found Willy with Charlotte Kinceler, a very short dark-haired girl, graceful rather than pretty. The lovers were not in bed, but poring over an account book. Charlotte 'was watching me, a pair of scissors grasped tightly in her hand; a word, a movement, and she would have flown at my face.'[9] There was no need for the girl to fly at Colette, who was petrified with surprise and horror. One can picture the look on Willy's face. The last thing he expected was to see his young wife, and he mopped his brow in amazement: '"You've come to fetch me?" he said. I glanced uncertainly at Mlle Kinceler and at my husband, at my husband and Mlle Kinceler, and found nothing better than to say, in my politest drawing-room manner: "Why yes. Don't you think...?" He could not make out what it all meant, my arrival, my silence, my oddly restrained behaviour. Nor could I.'[10]

For Colette, this scene from a banal farce was a painful tragedy. Broken-hearted twenty-year-olds have little sense of humour. She was all the more hurt in that she was never, by temperament, one to cry: 'I have never been able to cry with ease, decency and fitting emotion. Tears are as grievous to me as vomiting . . . I detest tears – perhaps because I have found them so very hard to conquer.'[11]

But tears held back are an insidious form of poison, and by keeping her grief to herself, Colette made herself ill.

She even refused to unburden herself to Sido. Shortly afterwards, she attended the annual ball at the Ecole Polytechnique with her father-in-law. She wore green, and everyone noticed that she looked almost as green as her dress.

The silent despair that was gnawing away at her forced her to take to her bed. She lost her appetite and became listless. She no longer wanted to live. Everyone thought she was going to die. Her doctor told her, 'Get well, my dear! Help me a little! I am trying so hard to cure you and you do nothing!'[12] Unlike so many young women of the time, she was not tubercular. It was not the change in her life, nor the fact that she could not breathe in Paris that had reduced her to this state. Colette simply had what we would now call a psychosomatic illness, in other words a nervous breakdown.

Sido hurried to her side and did the best she could for her. She had a mother's insight, and suspected that 'Monsieur Willy' – she was the first to call him that – was somehow to blame. Willy, who was far from proud of himself, waited on Colette hand and foot, as did their friends. Paul Masson and Marcel Schwob took it in turns to sit at her bedside and keep her amused. Madame Arman de Caillavet brought her presents.

Colette did not die – Burgundians are tough – but when she recovered two months later, she was a changed woman. She had been tempered like steel in the fires of jealousy and disappointed love.

She saw Charlotte Kinceler again later. She was a minor actress from Montmartre and part-time prostitute; an object of pity rather than fear. Later she became a herbalist and Colette would go to her shop to buy camomile tea. Charlotte committed suicide at the age of twenty-six by shooting herself in the mouth. 'With her came my first doubts of the man I had given myself to so trustfully, and the end of my girlhood, that uncompromising, exalted, absurd estate. From her I got my first notions of tolerance and concealment and the possibility of coming to terms with an enemy.'[13]

Even so, she did not begin to drift away from Willy. No woman stops loving a man merely because he has been unfaithful to her. Colette was mad about Willy who, to make up for what he had done, took her to the sea for the first time. They went to Belle-Ile with Paul Masson. With such jolly companions, Colette soon learned to laugh again. She danced the 'tralala' with Willy. They let the waves knock them over, and went sailing. Colette wrote to Marcel Schwob: 'I am swimming in successive and simultaneous joys.'[14]

In the autumn Jules Renard saw Colette for the first time, at the Théâtre de l'Oeuvre when she attended the opening of *Annabella*, a translation by Maurice Maeterlinck of John Ford's *'Tis Pity She's a Whore*. The premiere was followed by a talk given by Colette's beloved Marcel Schwob.

She went back to her fashionable world. She gave Willy affectionate nicknames like 'La Doucette', 'Le Doux Maître' and 'Le Gros Chat', and he introduced her to his friends as 'Ma Huronne'. But Colette was no longer the little peasant in her Sunday best she had been when she first came to Paris. She had learned how to behave in society and was no longer gauche. Willy – whom Rachilde, despite her affection, somewhat dismissively called 'an almost great man' – was a good teacher.

They visited a lot of *salons* and cafés but, despite all Willy's various activities, funds were low. At the end of 1894, he suddenly had an idea: why not make something of Colette's charming memories of her schooldays, which she had talked about when she was feeling homesick for Saint-Sauveur? 'You ought to put down what you remember of your board-school days. Don't be shy of the spicy bits. I might make something of it.'[15]

At school in Saint-Sauveur, Colette had been a good pupil and at sixteen she passed her *brevet élémentaire*, with no less than seventeen out of twenty for French composition. Now she immediately rushed out to buy exercise books identical to the ones she had had at school. She liked the idea. Deep down inside her, she may also have been flattered at the thought of becoming one of the team of writers who worked for Willy. And so she began to write the story of one Claudine, who might have been her sister. Over the next few months she filled seven exercise books. Writing up her memories of her girlhood made her want to visit her old home again and she and Willy went on a short visit to Saint-Sauveur in the summer, just before they left for Bayreuth. Willy went to Bayreuth every year, but this was to be Colette's first visit.

Willy was not convinced when he read what Colette had written. The memoirs of a little girl were of no interest to him and he stuffed the exercise books into a drawer, much to the relief of his young wife, who consciously at any rate did not feel any vocation for writing and dreamed of becoming a dancer or an actress.

The following year, however, four music reviews signed 'Colette Gauthier-Villars' appeared in *La Cocarde*. Willy had his articles ghosted for him too, and it is possible that Colette agreed to let him use her name. Her account of Madame de Saint-Marceaux's musical evenings in *Journal à rebours*[16] shows that she had certainly learned a lot about music from Willy and his friends.

The century was gradually drawing to a close. The Dreyfus Affair began to divide families and gave society hostesses a great deal of trouble by causing arguments at dinner parties. When Willy, who was no Dreyfusard, refused to sign the petition of *La Revue blanche* in favour of Dreyfus, his friend and collaborator Pierre Véber sarcastically remarked, 'It's the first time he has refused to sign something he didn't write.'

In 1895, when Willy and Colette were on holiday in the Jura, he reached the respectable weight of 105 kilos (231 pounds, or 16½ stone),[17] but even that did not disgust Colette. (The visit to his ancestral region gave Willy the occasion for another of his puns, when it occurred to him that the famous phrase from La Fontaine's fable of the Fox and the Crow, when the penitent Crow 'Jura, mais un peu tard' (vowed, but too late) that he would not be caught out again, could be transformed to mean 'Jura, a little late in the day'.)

In 1896 Willy and Colette moved from the Left Bank to a studio and three small rooms at 93 rue de Courcelles. In December, Colette was seen at the first performance of Alfred Jarry's fantastic and scatological *Ubu Roi*, roaring with laughter. The *bourgeois* in the audience were shocked by what they heard and vociferously expressed their disapproval. The young intellectuals, on the other hand, applauded enthusiastically. The word *merdre* was on everyone's lips, and a mischievous Colette began to wonder if her Willy's paunch would eventually be as big as Père Ubu's. She may well have been twenty-three, but there was still a childish side to her (as when she made sorbets out of jam and snow from the windowsill).

Willy had gone back to his old ways, but if Colette knew about his adventures she pretended to take no notice. She fell in with Willy's mood and put on lively, free-wheeling airs. Respectable people found Monsieur and Madame Gauthier-Villars charming but somewhat 'Bohemian'. They were what was known as a 'modern' couple. In other words, both partners were free to do as they liked. Colette later made use of what her so-called 'freedom' taught her; the couple in *En camarades*, the play she wrote and appeared in in 1909, are easily recognizable as Willy and Colette.

Two years after his decision not to do anything with his wife's memoirs, Willy came across the black-bound exercise books which he thought he had thrown away:

He opened one of the copy-books, turned the pages: 'It's

43

rather nice.' He opened a second copy-book and said no more. A third, a fourth. 'My God!' he muttered. 'I am the bloodiest fool.' He swept up the scattered copy-books just as they were, grabbed his flat-brimmed top hat and bolted to his publisher's. And that is how I became a writer.[18]

Colette was not quite a writer yet, but she soon would be. *Claudine à l'école*, revised by Willy, appeared early in 1900.[19] The fabulous Exposition Universelle had just opened in Paris and Colette was approaching her twenty-seventh birthday. The book was, of course, signed 'Willy'. While this may look like exploitation, Colette was quite happy to have the book published under Willy's name. She says so clearly in a letter to Rachilde, who was preparing to give it an excellent review in the *Mercure de France* and was presumably wondering if she should mention Colette's name. 'I should say not! You must not mention me in connection with *Claudine*! Family reasons, propriety, relations and so on and so forth . . . only Willy. All praise to Willy! Poor Willy-la-Doucette. If only I can pay my shoemaker with the percentage I get . . .'[20]

Rachilde was not the only critic to praise the book. Jean Lorrain saw it as a twentieth-century version of *Les Liaisons dangereuses*. Charles Maurras, who knew both Willy and Colette, greeted the newly-published book with an enthusiastic article in *La Revue encyclopédique*. Although only thirty-two, Maurras showed an unusual critical acumen. He obviously had some idea as to how the book had been written and spoke of 'The astonishing maturity of Claudine's style . . . The most reserved of her confessions reveal unfathomable depths of experience.' Significantly, he subtitled his article 'A mature man's account of a young girl's escapades'.[21]

Willy's reputation as a salacious author was already established and his name alone ensured that *Claudine à l'école* would be an immediate success. The cover

illustration also helped. It showed a schoolgirl in clogs sitting on a desk and looking like a kinky version of Little Red Riding Hood. In the preface, Willy thanked his wife for the help she had given him – a touch which gave a delightfully suggestive flavour to the whole book.

Claudine à l'école sold very rapidly in both Paris and the provinces – forty thousand copies in four weeks. Ollendorf, the publisher, was ecstatic. And Willy, it must be said, was a model for every press officer and sales manager. Eager for publicity, he rushed all over the place, buttonholed booksellers and planted all sorts of rumours in the newspapers. In fact he wrote the 'rumours' himself. He would do anything to have people talking about his book. In order to launch *Claudine* on the grand scale, he produced a mass of images and publicity material. He had a famous *pâtissier* in the rue de la Boétie make Claudine cakes and ice-creams. Soon there were Claudine collars, Claudine perfume, Claudine hats, Claudine cigarettes and even statuettes of Claudine.

The Willys were now in the money. Colette received a monthly allowance of three hundred francs from her husband. At last she could buy dresses for herself and presents for her beloved Sido.

But Willy had no intention of letting things stand still. He planned to exploit this lucrative vein to the uttermost. He put Colette back to work: 'Quickly, my dear, quickly.' Colette did not waste time. 1901 saw the publication of *Claudine à Paris*, which features Henry Maugis, a self-portrait caricature of Willy. *Claudine en ménage* appeared in 1902, followed by *Claudine s'en va* (1903), *Minne* (1904) and *Les Egarements de Minne* (1905). The last two were later republished as *L'Ingénue libertine* (1909).

In order to allow his ghost to work as productively as possible, Willy provided her with a more comfortable working environment. He rented a more spacious apartment at 177bis rue de Courcelles, a pretty town house of two storeys, one of them occupied by Prince Bibesco. Colette had her own study, her green lamp, a chamber-maid and a cook. Willy fitted out one room as a gymnasium, with all the equipment needed for exercise and relaxation. In the morning, Colette would go walking in the Bois de Boulogne with her dogs, and sometimes even with her cat on a lead. The afternoons were devoted to work. Colette worked steadily for four hours a day. Willy would brook no arguments on that score. He would even lock her in and only let her out when she gave him what she had written. Then he would make corrections in the margin, as though he were marking a schoolgirl's homework, and add passages of his own invention. 'Quickly, my dear, quickly.'

Feminists have made a great deal of this period in Colette's life, when her husband locked her up to make her write. As with George Sand and other exceptional women, they try to recruit Colette under their own banner by portraying her as the victim of a ruthless man.

To say that Colette was a victim is simply not true. It has to be remembered that it was by no means unknown for one person to lock another up in order to make them concentrate. The strict Madame Arman de Caillavet locked Anatole France in her apartment in the avenue Hoche to make him write instead of frittering his time away. Lucie Delarue-Mardrus's husband did the same with her because she would do anything rather than settle down to write. Writers often have great difficulty in getting down to work and one can think of several modern authors who might welcome occasional friendly pressure to make them write. Colette's own account must also be taken into consideration. Even when she had turned against Willy, she admitted that

The window, after all, was not barred, and I had only to break my halter. And so – peace be upon the hand, now dead, that did not hesitate to turn the key! It taught me my most essential art, which is not that of writing but the domestic art of knowing how to wait, to conceal, to save up crumbs, to reglue, regild, change the worst into the not-so-bad, how to lose and recover in the same moment that frivolous thing, a taste for life.[22]

Colette was not Willy's victim. She was simply the victim of her own heart.

Ultimately, we ought to be grateful to Willy. He gave us Colette. He not only made her write: he taught her how to write. Willy may not have been a genius, but he was a good professional. Despite her later hostility towards him, Colette herself allows him that:

I still believe that the job of editor on a big daily would have suited him to perfection. He knew how work should be distributed, how to assess exactly the capacities of those about him, how to criticize in a manner that was apt and stimulating, how to judge without praising too highly.[23]

Claude Farrère – another of Willy's ghosts – met Colette in 1902 and fell in love with her. His love for her remained (almost) platonic,[24] but over the years they became close friends. On 23 March 1944, Farrère wrote to his friend Richard Anacréon:[25] 'Colette was a wild foal. Willy was a trainer and he taught her to win by humiliating her. Could she have won the Grand Prix on her own? I am far from convinced. And even if she had done it by herself, it would have taken twenty years instead of two. She would never have succeeded because she is very lazy and hates writing.' He added that Willy taught Colette the value of patient effort. Even Sido, who always resented Willy, agreed. In 1911 she wrote to her daughter: '. . . even so, I often say to myself what you acknowledge to yourself, however vaguely; that if you had not spent some time with that character your talent would never have been revealed.'[26]

Colette spent the early years of the century learning to write, but she also learned how to overcome the torments of heartbreak and jealousy. Willy was an incorrigible libertine as well as an excellent literary adviser. He was a narcissist who loved to be surrounded by portraits, busts and even caricatures of himself. And he could never resist a woman if he saw the slightest sign of admiration or even the hint of an invitation in her eyes. He liked to please and he did please, despite his weight. His facility with words, his gaiety and his success all made him intensely attractive. He always gave the impression of being an available bachelor. The Kinceler affair did not make him change his ways, and he soon put it out of his mind. Society women, women from the *demi-monde*, women writers, actresses of varied ability, young prostitutes, studio models . . . Willy had them all. Although she wanted to be free and although he bullied her and forced her to share certain pleasures she did not really enjoy, Colette was still in love with him and tried to laugh it all off. But she did suffer. And God knows how far a woman in love will go. Her masochism will make her walk through fire if that will bring her any closer to her tormentor.

In 1896, Emile Vuillermoz, at the time an impoverished young composer making a living by playing the piano at fashionable *soirées*, met Colette and Willy at the home of a woman who lived on the avenue Victor Hugo. At her parties, which were restricted to a very small circle of friends, the citizens of Lesbos danced in one another's arms.[27] There Colette first met Mathilde de Morny, 'Missy', who was later to share her life.

Willy was the type of man who is fascinated by such spectacles. He was also fond of what Colette in *Le Pur et l'Impur* calls 'three-part harmony in love'.[28] She adds, 'the shocking variations, the gymnastic side to it and the "human pyramids" soon discourage one from such unstable polygamy.' Willy tried several times to establish this illusory 'three-part harmony' with Colette and another woman. In 1901, he did everything he could to throw her into the arms of a young American woman he had met in Jeanne Muhlfeld's *salon* and whom he met again in Bayreuth. Colette did fall for the charms of Georgie Raoul-Duval, who had become Willy's mistress, but that did not prevent her from caricaturing her as Rézi in *Claudine en ménage* ('a little flashy . . . a liquid Jezebel'). The burning sensuality of these pages shocked the publisher Ollendorf so much that he rejected the manuscript (originally entitled *Claudine amoureuse*), and it was published in 1902 by Mercure de France. Willy constructed other 'human pyramids' with Colette and Missy, Colette and Polaire and finally with Meg Villars, who caused the break-up of their marriage, and whom he later married.

It would, however, be a mistake to believe that Colette's lesbian inclinations were all due to Willy's encouragement. Being blessed with an extraordinary sensuality, she liked men, but she also liked women. But it would also be wrong to say that she preferred women to men. With the exception of a few close friends, Colette was not fond of women. To put it in modern terms, her attitude was that of the typical male chauvinist: she liked beautiful women, and she liked them in bed. In the phrase of François Mauriac, who once said of Drieu la Rochelle that he was 'a homosexual who did not like men', Colette might be described as a lesbian who did not like women. The truth of the matter is that, throughout her life, she was physically and sensually in love with everything delicious, everything good to look at and pleasing to the senses: men, women, the sea, flowers, fruit, fine wines, truffles, succulent dishes, music, birdsong, the soft fur of animals, the satin feel of human skin . . . to say nothing of the infinite range of scents her refined sense of smell allowed her to perceive. In terms of her taste for women, Willy was simply the instigator, the tempter. He provided the opportunity that made the thief.

Colette's sensuality meant that she was extremely attractive to both men and women. Even animals were mysteriously drawn to her. Sylvain Bonmariage, another of Willy's ghosts who fell in love with Colette but whose amorous ambitions were never fulfilled, describes being aroused by the way Colette smelled when she came off stage in a sweat. One of his women friends, who also succumbed to Colette's charms, described it as 'the smell of men. That is what is so exciting about her. It is that smell that gives her her seductive magic.'[29] Paul Léautaud said much the same thing: 'She always gave me the impression of being an extremely sensual woman, even something of a bitch, a woman to whom physical pleasure meant a lot. Physical love was written all over her. She was extremely crude, even vulgar.'[30]

Colette's violent peasant sensuality could at times be subtle and refined, but it also went hand in hand with a joyfully Rabelaisian streak which shocked people with more delicate feelings.

She took a certain delight in tormenting her bashful admirer Sylvain Bonmariage by leading him on and then rejecting him. He gives an account of the visit he paid her in a Brussels hotel when she was on tour. Colette was thirty-three and he was barely twenty. His shyness can be imagined. She received him in bed. And then, taking no notice of him, she got up, crossed the room naked and began to dress behind a screen. From behind the screen, the young man suddenly heard 'the sound of a tyre bursting. Colette laughed and announced: "Un marron" [a chestnut]. More laughter, another noise. "Deux marrons!" . . . and then "Trrrois marrrons!" Finally, there was a gale of laughter. "I can't help it. I'm so pleased to see you again! I just have to fart! . . . Quatre marrons!"'[31] Horrified, the young man left the room before there was time for a fifth *marron*. The mischievous Colette had obviously found a rustic but effective means of getting rid of an admirer who was becoming rather a nuisance. (Her behaviour seems somewhat startling; but at the turn of the century, the famous 'Pétomane' ('Fartomaniac') was acclaimed at the Moulin Rouge by the most refined *bourgeois*, and even the exquisitely-mannered Sacha Guitry indulged in such jokes.)

In 1902, Colette was still passionately attracted to the dissolute Willy. In June of that year, she wrote to Jeanne Muhlfeld: 'As in the past, Willy is still the handsomest and best of men.'[32] He also made her painfully jealous. She did, however, get some respite during their holidays in the Jura. Whenever he was with his prudish family, Willy was always on his best behaviour. In the Jura, Colette again became her normal cheerful self and recovered her sense of fun. In September 1901, she sent Rachilde a very funny letter from Le Chalet des Sapins in Lons-le-Saunier, describing in a few lines the prevailing atmosphere in her in-laws' house:

We have here
  1. the pony,
  2. my mother-in-law,
  3. my sister-in-law. She is so mean that she would skin a flint and then skin it again, just to be certain.[33]

Colette in fact preferred the company of the Gauthier-Villars children, who called her 'Aunt Colette', to that of the adults, unless Willy was in a mood for joking. He was always very good at adapting to his audience of the moment and when he was at home his jokes were perfectly acceptable. He would make his nephews laugh by reciting an hilarious poem he had written in honour of Camille Flammarion, a long-haired astronomer, which ended:

> O savant astronome, ô puissant scrutateur
> Et généreusement, partage ta crinière
> Avec le chauve enfant d'un illustre éditeur!

(O wise astronomer, keen-eyed observer, be generous and share your abundant locks with the balding child of a famous publisher!)

One day, much to Colette's amusement, he began to read out share prices from the newspaper, picking out a funeral march on the piano because the *Rente Française* had fallen, and then breaking into 'Gloire immortelle de nos aïeux', from Gounod's *Faust*, because shares in the Suez Company were rising.

Willy and Colette were a strange couple, at once made for one another and incompatible. Whenever anyone attacked them or ideas they held dear, they always stuck together, as Madame Arman de Caillavet was to learn to her cost. She was a spiteful gossip and once thought fit to tell Colette that Willy was paying a lot of attention to her daughter-in-law, Jeanne Pouquet. Willy and Colette were furious and immediately caricatured her in *Un Vilain Monsieur* and in *Claudine à Paris*, where she became 'Barmann', 'a thickset old harpie, a horrible old mole with a hooked, spotty red nose'. The complaisant husband who allowed his wife to become Anatole France's mistress was dubbed 'le conservateur du collage de France' – not 'the keeper of the Collège de France' but 'the guardian of France's mistress'. Finally, their daughter-in-law became 'Rose-Chou', 'a plump girl with cheeks like the buttocks of a cherub'.

They also took sides together in favour of freedom of worship when Aristide Briand and 'le petit père Combes' began to tear France apart by trying to disband the teaching congregations and to forbid religious education in schools. Although they were not exactly a pious couple, they had both been brought up as Catholics, and would not tolerate this attack on freedom of worship. Fernand Gregh describes a dinner at Madame Caillavet's when conversation became heated as the question of the teaching orders came up:

I was on the side of the anticlericals. I defended my position and Colette shut me up with an unexpected argument. She told me that I was not a true poet because

poets were free, just people. Shortly afterwards Marcel Proust turned on me, arguing that he would rather see monks in the convents than 'liquidators' and that he did not believe in the virtues of non-denominational schools. He wanted the Angelus and processions on Corpus Christi day . . . Basically, I think that is what Colette wanted to preserve too.[34]

Colette did not go to mass. Her life was hardly led in accordance with the teachings of the Church, but she loved and defended the sensuousness of Catholic services, their magic and the pagan poetry of the images, the singing and the incense which reminded her of her childhood. Later in life, she lit candles in Notre-Dame-des-Victoires and Saint-Roch. On her death bed, she would probably rather have seen a priest than a doctor, but her third husband and her daughter would not hear of any such thing.[35]

It is well known that for a woman a change in her hairstyle means a change in her life. In the autumn of 1902, Colette had her magnificent long hair cut, sacrificing her plait, which measured 1.58 metres (5 feet 3 inches). She pioneered the fashion for short hair that was to cause a revolution. It was to be another six years before the couturier Paul Poiret made his models cut their hair, and Chanel did not cut hers until 1917. Who was behind this change? Willy, of course. Colette told her mother that she had been forced to cut her hair because she spilled the contents of an oil lamp over her head, but Sido was not taken in. In 1911, she mentioned the topic again in a letter to her daughter: 'your beautiful golden hair that came down to the ground! I always thought it was Willy who suggested that you should cut your hair, out of jealousy. Go on, you can admit it now, but I was very hurt when you destroyed a masterpiece it had taken me twenty years to create.'[36]

Willy did not in fact persuade her to cut her hair out of jealousy: he wanted her to match little Polaire. Since the beginning of the year, Polaire had been playing Claudine in *Claudine à Paris*, which Willy had adapted for the Bouffes-Parisiens in collaboration with 'Luvey' (a contraction of Lugné-Poe and Charles Vayre).

It was Jules Renard who had introduced him to the young actress. Polaire, whose real name was Emilie Zouzé Bouchaud, was born at Agha in Algeria and still had a *pied noir* accent which contrasted rather oddly with the Parisian slang she used. She had begun singing in *café-concerts* at the age of fourteen and was a great favourite with the students, who would join in the chorus with her to sing *Ta-ma-ra-boum-ti-hé* and *Max, ah c'que t'es rigolo*.

Polaire was thin, highly-strung and shy. According to Jules Renard, she was 'a funny little creature, not pretty. She would give you her hand awkwardly, as though it were a paw, and would raise it to the level of your eyes. She looked like a shy cat.'[37] Jean Cocteau saw her at the Palais de Glace, the Paris ice-skating rink:

The flat head of a snake, yellow, supporting the Portuguese oysters of her eyes, glittering with mother-of-pearl, salt, cool shadows; her features tense, pulled tightly back towards the nape of her neck where her black hair was knotted as tightly as a percheron's tail; a felt hat tipped back above her fringe, a Lalique ring worn as a belt, a foppish skirt which revealed her stockings and her high buttoned boots with their cruel blades – the actress stood at the side of the rink, upright, tense, as aggressive as an insult in Hebrew, and looking as though she was having hysterics.[38]

Polaire was desperate to become an actress, but had failed to get a part in Renard's *Poil de Carotte*. She wanted the part of Claudine and Willy gave it to her because he thought she was such a funny stubborn little thing. As she hopped from one foot to the other in excitement, he would tell her, 'For God's sake, Polaire! Can't you keep still! You look like a flower that wants to do weewee!'[39]

For her part, Colette said later that of all the actresses who had ever played Claudine, Polaire was by far the best.

The play enjoyed a real triumph at the Bouffes-Parisiens. In the meantime, Willy, still hungry for publicity, went around Paris to show off his two Claudines. They were seen in the Bois de Boulogne in the mornings, at the Palais de Glace, at the races and in fashionable cafés and restaurants. He turned Colette and Polaire, who were roughly the same age, into twins, with their hair done in the same way and with identical dresses. He called them 'my kids'. Less charitable souls talked about Willy and his two pet monkeys. The trio obviously attracted gossip and being successful is always the best way to make enemies. But Willy was delighted. So long as people were talking about him, he did not mind what they said.

Colette was not so happy. She was beginning to tire of being put on show with Polaire. She only felt comfortable at Les Monts-Boucons, the estate that Willy had bought in Dauphiné so that she could work in peace. It was a charming old house with a farm and land, woods and an old orchard. She would stay there from June to November, usually alone, as Willy claimed that he could not leave Paris.

Colette lived there with her dog Toby-Chien, an angora cat called Kiki-la-Doucette, her birds and the horse she was learning to ride and which she would sometimes harness to a light trap. She was heartbroken because she did not see Willy as often as she wanted, but she could live in harmony with the countryside, which reminded her of her childhood. Colette was just thirty, and she was learning to live alone. She was also learning to write alone and had fully assimilated all Willy's lessons. She realized that as she wrote her *Minne* stories and *Dialogues de bêtes* (1904), the first of her books to be signed 'Colette Willy'.

When she went back to Paris for the winter, she found her husband busier than ever. He was still actively exploiting the success of the *Claudine* books, but at the same time he was, with the help of his ghosts, turning out other novels with knowing adolescent heroines. Pierrette, Peggy, Jasmin and Mady were Claudine's sisters, but they could never hope to rival the character into whom Colette had put so much of herself.

Willy was drunk with fame and his megalomania was getting out of hand. He was now printing and distributing postcards which showed him lording it over Colette in Claudine costume.

In April 1903, a league for public decency served a writ on Willy and his publisher for publishing his novel *La Maîtresse du Prince Jean* in *La Vie en rose*. The plaintiffs claimed that its immorality constituted an attack on public morals. Willy's notoriety and the case itself attracted a lot of attention and when the trial opened, the 9e Chambre Correctionnelle was filled to overflowing. Willy was defended by Jean-Paul Boncour, a young lawyer later to become Prime Minister, and friends like Renard, Huysmans, Funck-Brentano, Catulle Mendès and Camille Erlanger flocked to testify on his behalf. Willy thought he was Baudelaire. He in fact got off lightly with a fine of one thousand francs. He was also ordered to expurgate his book.

The trial caused such a sensation that the symbolist poet Vielé-Griffin, who knew Willy very well, was convinced that it was yet another publicity stunt and sent him a telegram which read: 'Greatly appreciate your April Fool trick. My compliments to the man who thought it up.' His friend Sacha Guitry wrote the following satirical portrait of Willy for *Le Gil Blas*:

He looks like a well-known man.
The only names that I can think of that are more
   famous
are those of God and Alfred Dreyfus.

He launched a famous hat which suits him perfectly.
Ah! If only this man would publicize himself!
But no, he is inflexible.[40]

Willy, however, was no longer receiving all the credit for his best-sellers, or at least not for the Claudine books. There were so many coincidences between the life and attitudes of Claudine and those of Colette that people were beginning to realize how much Colette had contributed to the novels that appeared under Willy's name. Colette herself had made some revealing slips, perhaps deliberately. Jules Renard urged her: 'Learn to stand on your own two feet.' He was also responsible for a witticism that was circulating in Paris: 'Willy *have* a lot of talent.'

Colette received similar advice from someone who was to have a strong influence on her life: Madame Fraya, the famous clairvoyant whom she consulted for the first time in 1903. Fraya came from the Landes in southwestern France and had taken the name of a Germanic goddess. Her truly extraordinary gifts drew *le tout-Paris* to her ground floor apartment in the rue d'Edimbourg, and when she moved house, her clients followed her to the rue Chardin and went on consulting her until her death in 1954 (she was born in the same year as Colette and they died in the same year). Her clients included monarchs, politicians and writers, many of whom became her friends. Pierre Loti thought that her divinatory gifts bordered on the miraculous and never failed to consult her when he was in Paris. He gave her a two-thousand-year-old necklace from India which was said to be a fabulous talisman. Other visitors included Sarah Bernhardt, Edmond Rostand, Guitry, Gide, Proust, Anna de Noailles, and the prime ministers Poincaré and Clemenceau. Some of her prophecies relate to our own times.[41]

Colette describes her first encounter with Madame Fraya in *Mes Apprentissages*. The clairvoyant looked at the palms of Colette's hands and said: "'It's . . . Oh! it's very odd . . . I would never have thought it. . . . You must get out!" "Of what?" "Of where you are." "The house I'm in?" "Yes, but that's only a detail. You must get right out of it. You've lost a lot of time already.'"[42]

Colette lost even more time. She was still in love with Willy and could refuse him nothing, even though she wanted to escape his stranglehold and was finding it harder to bear day by day.

Long before they actually met, Denise Tual, who was later to be Colette's neighbour and friend in the Palais Royal, was fascinated by the astonishing woman she had heard of in her childhood. Her father, an art publisher, had told her about a scene he had witnessed at the beginning of the century. It took place during a dinner given by José Maria Sert for a number of people from the theatre (including Willy) in a private dining room. 'Colette made a late spectacular entrance with the dessert. An enormous cake was brought in on a silver platter by four liveried valets and from the middle of a mountain of whipped cream two little pointed faces emerged. Colette was naked, clinging to Polaire, screaming with laughter and kicking frothy *oeufs en neige* in all directions with her pink feet.'[43]

1. *My Apprenticeships*, translated by Helen Beauclerk (London, Martin Secker and Warburg, 1957; New York, Farrar, Straus and Cudahy), Harmondsworth, Penguin Books, 1967, p. 53.
2. Sylvain Bonmariage, *Willy, Colette et moi*, Paris, Charles Frémanger, 1954.
3. *My Apprenticeships*, p. 24.
4. Jacques-Emile Blanche, *La Pêche aux souvenirs*, Paris, Flammarion, 1949, p. 288.
5. *My Apprenticeships*, p. 52.
6. Léautaud, *Journal littéraire*, Paris, Mercure de France, 1954-1966, XI, p. 91 (entry dated 24 October 1935).
7. Cited, Pierre Champion, *Marcel Schwob et son temps*, Paris, Grasset, 1927.
8. Guillaume Apollinaire, *Le Flâneur des deux rives*, Paris, Gallimard, Collection 'Idées', 1975.
9. *My Apprenticeships*, p. 26.
10. Ibid., pp. 26-7.
11. Ibid., pp. 28-9.
12. Ibid., p. 35.
13. Ibid., p. 32.
14. *Lettres à ses pairs*, Paris, Flammarion, 1973, p. 13.
15. *My Apprenticeships*, p. 22
16. Paris, Arthème Fayard, 1941.
17. Letter from Colette cited in Gérard Bonal, *Colette par moi-même*, Paris, Ramsay, 1982.
18. *My Apprenticeships*, p. 55.
19. Paris, Ollendorf, 1900; in *Oeuvres*, I, Paris, Gallimard, Bibliothèque de la Pléiade, 1984.
20. Letter, 29 March 1900; coll. Richard Anacréon.
21. Cited, Marie-Jeanne Viel, *Colette au temps des Claudine*, Paris, Les Publications essentielles, 1978.
22. *My Apprenticeships*, p. 65.
23. Ibid., p. 59.
24. As he told Jean de La Varende, he still regretted this in 1942.
25. For Anacréon see below, Chapter VI.
26. Letter, 4 February 1911; coll. Bertrand de Jouvenel.
27. Viel, *Colette au temps des Claudine*.
28. Colette, *Le Pur et l'Impur*, Paris, Armes de France, 1941, p. 199 (first published as *Ces Plaisirs*, Paris, Ferenczi, 1932).
29. Bonmariage, *Willy, Colette et moi*.
30. Léautaud, *Journal littéraire*, XI, p. 91.
31. Bonmariage, *Willy, Colette et moi*.
32. Letter, early June 1902; *Lettres à ses pairs*, p. 53.
33. Unpublished letter; coll. Richard Anacréon.
34. Cited, Viel, *Colette au temps des Claudine*.
35. I am grateful to Marthe Lamy, who was Colette's friend and doctor, for this information.
36. Letter, 30 December 1911; *Le Figaro littéraire*, 24 January 1953.
37. Renard, *Journal*, p. 752.
38. Cocteau, *Portraits-souvenir 1900-1914*, Paris, Grasset, 1935, p. 90.
39. *My Apprenticeships*, p. 80.
40. *Gil Blas*, 4 June 1904.
41. Simone de Tervagne, *Une Voyante à l'Elysée : Mme Fraya*, Paris, Editions Pygmalion, 1975.
42. *My Apprenticeships*, p. 107.
43. Denise Tual, *Le Temps dévoré*, Paris, Fayard, 1980.

57

58

57 Colette and Willy on a visit to Châtillon. On the far right is Captain Colette; beyond him, in shadow, Sido.

58, 59 Colette and Willy were married on 15 May 1893 at Châtillon. Photographers were kept away, but one managed to snap the bridal party on its way to the church, with Colette and the Captain leading the small procession. Among the signatures of the witnesses is that of Willy's friend and ghostwriter, Pierre Véber.

60 Colette on a visit to Châtillon after her marriage, with Sido (far right).

61-63 At the time when photography was still unusual, Colette displayed a distinct flair for self-presentation. Here she poses as a Directoire beauty, pretending to read a book, and in old-fashioned peasant costume – intimations, no doubt, of a future in the theatre.

61

62

64 Colette attempting a smile – something she always found impossible.

63

64

65

66

65 Henry Gauthier-Villars at the age of five.

66 Willy aged twenty, in the uniform of an artillery corporal. As a young man he was slim and reasonably good-looking.

67 The Gauthier-Villars family in their garden in the rue des Vignes, Passy. Willy is standing, left.

68 A tableau of literati. Willy is on the left. On the right is the journalist Léo Trezenik, a friend of Verlaine, who edited *Lutèce* and ran a review for young poets called *La Nouvelle Rive gauche*. He and Georges Rall (centre) shared the nom-de-plume 'Monstrailles'.

67

68

56

Willy   Rote?   Léo
                                                  Tregenik

69

70

71

58

Colette with her husband's relations, on holiday in the Jura.

69 When members of his family where present Willy continued to
make puns, but avoided jokes in more dubious taste. He and Colette
behaved like a conventional married couple.

70 The chalet owned by the Gauthier-Villars family near Lons-le-
Saunier bore the legend 'Small house, great tranquillity' – in Latin, of
course, as was the fashion.

71, 72 Colette with her sister-in-law Valentine, whose meanness
she lampooned.

73 Willy's press card, 1896.

74 A portrait, now lost, of Willy and Colette by Jacques Emile Blanche.

75, 76 Caricatures of Willy with his characteristic flat-brimmed hat and ogling eyes, by Geo and Sem.

77 Willy with Toby-Chien.

74

75

76

77

78 A photograph of Colette dated June 1897, from Willy's album.

79

80

81

82

83

84

Willy's friends and ghostwriters.

79 Marcel Schwob, drawn by Sacha Guitry. Schwob was Marguerite Moreno's first husband and a close friend of the young Colette until his death in 1905.

80 Pierre Louÿs. He wrote the poem *Dialogue au soleil couchant,* which was performed by Colette and Eva Palmer at the home of Natalie Barney.

81 The witty Pierre Véber, a witness at Colette and Willy's wedding.

82 Robert d'Humières, a translator from English.

83 Maurice Saillant, known as Curnonski, Curne or Cur, was a great wit and gastronome and a close friend of P. J. Toulet (Ill. 86). Colette was very fond of him; he outlived her by two years.

84 Jean de Tinan, posing as a monk – 'sensitive, gentle, vowed to literature and to death'; he died at the age of twenty-six.

85 Claude Farrère, sailor and novelist, loved Colette all his life.

86 Paul-Jean Toulet, writer of novels and exquisite poems, reminded his friend Willy of a 'saluki fed on Cubist drawings'.

85

86

87

87 A bust of Colette by Fix-Masseau.

88 Colette aged twenty-seven, with 'ear-phones' hairstyle, in the flat at 93 rue de Courcelles; at this time she was writing *Claudine à Paris*.

89 Portrait of Colette by Ferdinand Humbert. 'I feel quite proud of myself when I think how friends and strangers have fallen under the spell of this profile of a young woman of twenty-five, with her chestnut chignon, and a red poppy tucked under one ear' (*Paris de ma fenêtre*).

88

89

From 1893 onwards, Willy took Colette to the musical evenings held by the sculptor René de Saint-Marceaux and his wife in their flat in the boulevard Malesherbes.

A photograph (**90**) shows Gabriel Fauré at the piano, with Roger Ducasse; standing, left to right, are Louis Aubert, Mathot, Ravel, A. Caplet, Koechlin, Emile Vuillermoz and J. Huré.

Claude Debussy (**92**) worked for a milliner and as a cleaner until his music was recognized, largely through the efforts of a small group of Wagner fans including Vuillermoz, Willy and the Princesse de Polignac. It was at one of the Saint-Marceaux *soirées* that Colette first heard the music of *Pelléas et Mélisande*, hummed by Messager (**93**), who was to conduct the opera at its first performance.

Vincent d'Indy (**94**) was another of the group of Wagner enthusiasts. In 1904 he took over the direction of the Schola Cantorum in association with his friend, the composer Louis de Serres (**95**), to whom Colette dedicated *Toby-Chien et la musique*.

90

91 Willy with Colette, aged twenty-two, at the Cirque d'Eté.

91

92

93

94

95

96

In 1895 Colette went with
Willy to the Bayreuth Festival,
of which she gives a memorable
account in *Claudine s'en va.* She
clearly felt out of place in that
closed, snobbish society. In the
character of Annie she writes: 'I
will tell no one but myself, or
these useless pages, of my
disillusionment with Bayreuth.
There is little to choose between
an interval of *Parsifal* and a
Parisian tea-party.'

96 A postcard from Bayreuth
to her brother Léo.

97 Willy and Colette (left
foreground) exploring Bayreuth.

98 Willy in Bayreuth with
Georgie Raoul-Duval. She was
an American whom he met
through the Muhlfelds, and who
became his mistress. Colette too
was fascinated by her; Georgie
was the model for Rézi in
Claudine amoureuse, which
became *Claudine en ménage*
(1902).

99 Which is Colette, which is
Rézi? Willy was both an
accomplished sketcher and a
willing voyeur.

98

99

100

101

For Colette the 'Belle Epoque' of the turn of the century was a time of public gaiety and private disillusion.

100 A portrait of Colette by the theatrical photographer Reutlinger.

101 Charlotte Kinceler, in a photograph that belonged to her lover Willy. 'From her I got my first notions of tolerance and concealment and the possibility of coming to terms with an enemy.'

102 Outside the Moulin Rouge.

102

70

103

103, 104 Colette in fancy dress
for the Bal Gavarni, in 1904.

104

105 In the summer of 1894, to atone for his affair with Charlotte Kinceler, which had driven Colette to a breakdown, Willy took his wife to convalesce at Belle-Ile-en-Mer. From there she wrote to Marcel Schwob: 'I am swimming in successive and simultaneous joys.'

106

In Paris, cycling was the new craze.

106 *Le Chalet du cycle au Bois de Boulogne,* by Béraud.

107, 108 Bloomers were the fashionable attire, and a boater was indispensable.

107

108

109

110

111

74

109-111 The youthful
Madame Willy expressing her
ambivalent sexuality through
her choice of fancy dress.

112-114 The ideal woman,
with flowing hair, brocade dress,
eyes lowered, bearing a martyr's
palm. ('I was the one who
deserved it', Willy noted in his
album.) Willy captioned the
photograph above 'Colette of the
pampas'.

112

113

114

115

117

118

In the theatres, to which polite society flocked every evening, the fashion was for frills and affectation and languid glances. Extravagance was all. Famous stars were kept by wealthy lovers.

115 Mademoiselle Pierrat of the Comédie-Française.

116 Cécile Sorel, as a humble 'super' at the Variétés – 'where she should have stayed', Willy commented in his album.

117 Georgette Leblanc. For twenty years she was Maurice Maeterlinck's 'muse', and she briefly managed the Théâtre des Mathurins. A friend of Willy and his wife, it was she who gave Colette the part of a little faun in her first mime-show (see Ills. 264-269).

118 The singer Emma Calvé. Colette liked her: 'A signed photograph crossed the seas from time to time . . .'

119 Ellen Andrée.

120 An unknown actress, presumably a friend of Willy's.

121 Colette as a Belle Epoque belle.

119

120

121

122

Colette was a fascinated observer of the demi-mondaines of the day, most of whom used their theatrical career as a cover for more rewarding activites.

122 The beautiful Cléo de Mérode, in costume.

123 The actress Eve Lavallière liked to dress as a man, on stage and off. After an eventful life, she became a mystic and was eventually buried in a robe of sackcloth. Later Colette lived in her old house in the boulevard Suchet.

124 Clara Ward, formerly Caraman-Chimay. It was said of her that she ruined herself by going on the stage.

123

124

125 Caroline Otéro – 'la Belle Otéro' – was known as 'the siren of suicide' because so many men had killed themselves for love of her. She gave her first performance when she was fourteen at the Cirque d'Eté. It was she who told Colette that there was always a moment when even the meanest man would open his fist – when you twisted his arm to get at his gold. And indeed she was known to have acquired fortunes from her lovers.

126 Colette in a theatrical pose.

125

126

Anatole France (**127**) was a
friend, and inscribed an advance
copy of one of his stories, 'For
Madame Willy, before all the
rest' (**128**). His mistress (**129**), on
the other hand, was far from
popular with Colette. The
redoubtable Léontine Arman de
Caillavet, daughter of the banker
Lippmann, was rich, intelligent
rather than beautiful, and bored
with her husband. Jean Lorrain
called her 'a pretentious fat lump
of a woman'. In 1883, in the
salon of the radical Madame
Aubernon, she had met Anatole
France, who was easily led and
unhappily married. After his
divorce they lived together
openly for nearly twenty-five
years, she ruling over his writing
career with a rod of iron. But
Anatole France had the last
laugh. In 1910, soon after her
death, he married her maid.
Colette, who had reason to
dislike her, wrote a vicious
caricature of her as 'la mère
Barmann' in *Claudine en
ménage.*

130 Colette as she looked
shortly after her arrival in Paris.

127

128

129

130

131

132

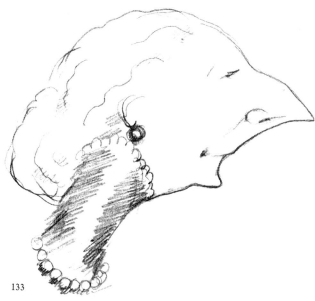

131 Marcel Proust, drawn by Jacques-Emile Blanche in 1891. 'He was a young man when I was a young woman.' Colette met him at the house of Madame Arman de Caillavet, and years later was dazzled by the brilliance of *Swann's Way*.

132 Jeanne Muhlfeld in 1904, by Cappiello. The young writers who attended her *salons* included Gide, Proust, Cocteau, Mauriac and Valéry. It was through her that Willy had met Georgie Raoul-Duval.

133 Caricature of Madame de Saint-Marceaux, hostess of celebrated musical *soirées*, by Georges Lepape.

133

135

134 Colette in a red dress from Old England – 'in the days of my impositions', she noted on the photograph.

135 The novelist and critic Rachilde, born Marguerite Eymery, who was married to Alfred Vallette, founder and editor of the *Mercure de France*. She gave Colette much encouragement in her early years as a writer.

134

138

137

Close friends.

136 Colette with Paul Masson, by Forain. One of Willy's team of writers, Masson was very attached to Colette. With his puns and silly jokes he did much to alleviate her depression over Willy's escapades.

137 The young Sacha Guitry and his first wife, the actress Charlotte Lysès. He was a faithful friend to Colette.

138 The pale, witty Marguerite Moreno, wife of Marcel Schwob, was Colette's lifelong friend, ally and confidante.

85

139 Jean Lorrain, another of Willy's ghostwriters, known for his piercing wit. He preferred young men but had great affection for Colette. She called him 'the Portuguese cat' because of his brindled hair – brown, grey and henna-red.

140, 141 Alfred Jarry delighted his friends Colette and Willy with a reading of *Ubu roi* at one of Rachilde's literary evenings. The stage premiere in 1896 (right, the programme) made Colette roar with laughter.

140

139

141

142 The painter Antonio de la Gandara, a regular attender at
Madame Arman de Caillavet's *salons*.

143 Francis Jammes. 'You are a true poet', he wrote of Colette in
his preface to *Sept Dialogues de bêtes*.

142

143

144, 145 Willy and his wife may have been a bohemian couple, but even they had flashes of bourgeois respectability. The Gauthier-Villars parents could have found no fault with the formal full-length photograph of their son and daughter-in-law, or with the properly submissive attitude of the young wife in another portrait of Willy and Colette.

146

147

148

146-149 A new century had begun. In the autumn of 1902, at Willy's prompting, Colette cut off her long hair – to Sido's great dismay. The character of Claudine was born, and was an instant success in the bookshops. There were whispers that Colette might be the real author. Statuettes, busts and portraits proliferated. Opposite, Colette with bobbed hair, painted by Jacques Emile Blanche.

150

151

150   The far from schoolgirlish creator of 'Claudine'.

151, 153   Before being locked in for an afternoon of writing, Colette would take her dog for a walk. She had a passion for toy bulldogs.

152

153

152, 154 She learned to ride in the Jura – where she was photographed with Willy at the military riding-school of Saint-Claude (opposite, below) – and was proud to be one of the first women to ride astride rather than side-saddle. She and Willy enjoyed riding in the Bois de Boulogne (below), where the fashionable hours were eleven in the morning and five in the afternoon.

154

155

156

157

158

159

155-156, 158 Colette and Willy in the room where she worked, in their flat at 177bis rue de Courcelles. 'And so – peace be upon the hand, now dead, that did not hesitate to turn the key!' In his album Willy captioned the picture of the two of them writing 'Perfect harmony, shared labours, domestic peace – heck!'

157 Willy and Colette eating lunch in the flat. 'What was one supposed to make of the painted wooden balustrade I erected in the middle of the drawing-room?'

159, 160 Colette and Willy in the flesh and on canvas (by Eugène Pascau). At the time she was passionately in love with him, but later she wrote, 'Monsieur Willy was not huge, he was bulbous.'

160

95

161 In an age when disputes were settled at ten paces, Willy was no mean hand with the duelling-sword: whatever his faults, he was not a coward. In 1893 he fought the editor of *Le Gil Blas,* who had impugned his intentions towards Colette; here he is at it again, in 1912.

161

163

164

165

faisant passer pour des fragments du discours académique de M. Rostand. M. Claretie, qui est pourtant un homme au courant des choses parisiennes, se laissa prendre à cette supercherie et publia ces vers dans *le Figaro* du 27 mai 1903.

Dernièrement, Willy a ajouté une palme à sa couronne d'humoriste. Willy aime Londres, et son plaisir familier est d'aller y écouter à Hyde-Park Corner les prédicateurs en plein air ; or, certain dimanche qu'il attendait là son amie, miss Meg Villars, un prédicant d'une secte « wesleyenne » entreprit de convertir cet écouteur si attentif. Willy, sans se troubler, consentit à ce qu'on essayât — il y avait de jolis *girls* dans la confrérie — mais il s'avoua « papiste », et être papiste, là-bas, c'est l'abomination de la désolation. N'importe ! la conversion n'en serait que plus méritoire : on le place donc dans le cercle des choristes, on lui remet un cantique imprimé sur un carton, et le voilà, chantant à gorge-que-veux-tu et avec le plus grand sérieux des strophes protestantes... Vous le voyez !...

Soudain, surgit miss Meg Villars qui n'aime ni qu'on se moque de la religion, ni que son ami s'approche trop des girls : *Vô été un gamin terribeul !* Et, d'autorité, avec une poigne vigoureuse, elle saisit notre Willy ahuri et l'entraîne.

Et tous les prédicateurs et choristes, voyant la belle fille à cheveux courts emmener leur néophyte, de crier avec la plus comique sincérité : « Satan !... Satan !... »

Pauvre Willy, ange déchu ! LOUIS THOMAS.

WILLY, par LÉANDRE

l'on puisse agacer sans dommages. Un soir, dans les couloirs n théâtre, on eut le plaisir d'entendre le dialogue suivant :
Monsieur, disait Willy, je vous ai fait l'honneur de vous ire par deux fois, vous ne m'avez pas répondu, je trouve procédé grossier.
— Hé ! monsieur Willy, que feriez-vous si vous rece- comme moi, chaque jour, de trente à quarante lettres ?
— J'en garderais cinq..... que je m'empresserais de vous voyer. »
ais c'est surtout dans des réponses à des confrères que ly est sublime. Il n'est personne, dans la presse, qui lique avec plus de fantaisie la loi du 29 juillet 1881.
vec *la Croix de Reims* (octobre 1903) il arriva à ce résultat digieux de faire insérer dans ce journal plutôt grave les nions de tous les critiques qui avaient défendu *Claudine*.
vec M. Mangeot, directeur d'une revue musicale, il angea une correspondance foudroyante. Mais M. Mangeot t fort têtu : il ne voulait pas se tenir pour mort. Alors, s voile de l'anonymat, Willy envoya à la gazette enne- un sonnet que M. Mangeot inséra sans défiance. Le son- était acrostiche et les initiales faisaient : MANGEOT EST E !!! De même avec M. Ernest-Charles, directeur du *seur*, qui publia un poème acrostiche de Willy, où on t : LE CENSEUR EST UN SALE CANARD. Mais la plus dé- euse de ses mystifications est celle qu'il fit peu avant la eption de M. Rostand à l'Académie. Willy publia dans *Nouvelle Revue* d'anciens vers de jeunesse de lui en les

WILLY, par LÉANDRE

166

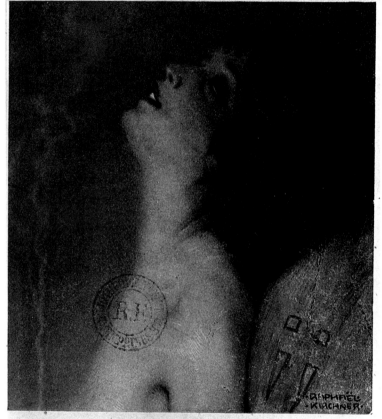

167

162-165 Willy's literary factory was highly productive. His name and picture were seen everywhere. *Le Troisième Sexe* was given an Art Deco cover, but photographs of Willy himself were used to illustrate *En bombe*. *Maîtresse d'esthètes* and *Un Vilain Monsieur* were both actually written by Jean de Tinan.

166 Caricatures of Willy by Léandre.

167 P. J. Toulet collaborated with Willy on the novel *Lélie*, which was a bitter attack on Colette after she and Willy had separated.

168 *A manger du foin*, an anthology of absurd tales, was published in 1925.

169 'St Willy, patron saint of the Claudines.'

168

169

170 A hitherto unpublished photograph shows Colette posing innocently in white ermine: her expression has all the charm and mischief with which she endowed the venturesome young heroine of *L'Ingénue libertine.*

171 Madame Gauthier-Villars as she looked when the writer Claude Farrère fell in love with her. Forty years later he wrote to La Varende: 'In 1902 I met Willy, who introduced me to his wife Colette. She was a *pisseuse* (a Normandy dialect word, you realize) of twenty-nine who looked no more than twenty or twenty-two.' To Farrère's lasting regret, his love remained on the whole platonic.

172 In the flat at 177bis rue de Courcelles.

171

173

174

175

173-176 At 177bis rue de Courcelles. The flat was fitted out by Willy with a gymnasium for Colette. In *Mes Apprentissages* she wrote: 'I used to hang there, I swung round the bar, I strained my muscles without passion or any particular skill . . . Thinking about it later, it seemed to me that I was exercising my body in just the way prisoners do, who are not exactly planning to escape, but who nevertheless cut up a sheet and plait it, sew coins inside a lining, and hide chocolate under the mattress.'

176

177 Colette at the spa of Uriage, near Grenoble, in the summer of 1896. The trip may have been occasioned by Willy's rheumatism. At all events Colette, aged twenty-three, does not appear to be enjoying herself. In *Claudine s'en va* she turned Uriage into Arriège, and described the dreary society life of the resort.

177

178 First page of the manuscript of *Claudine amoureuse,* which was retitled *Claudine en ménage* and published in 1902. Willy's corrections are noted in the margin.

179-181 Covers of the first editions of the *Claudine* books. Colette was amused by the design for *Claudine à l'école,* seeing no resemblance between herself and the Little Red Riding Hood sitting on a table. The melancholy air of the figure illustrating *Claudine s'en va* is much closer to Colette.

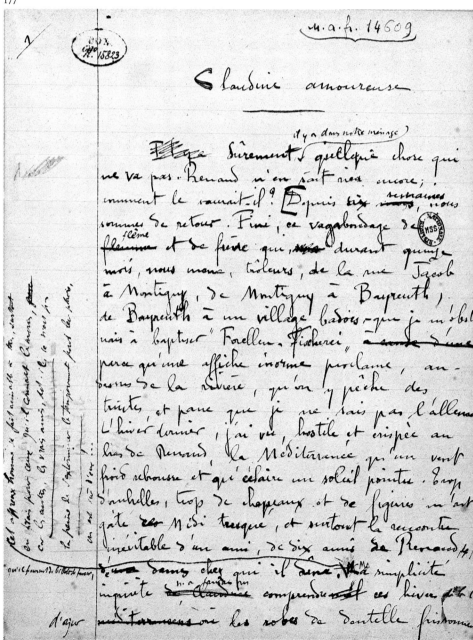

178

179

180

181

182

183

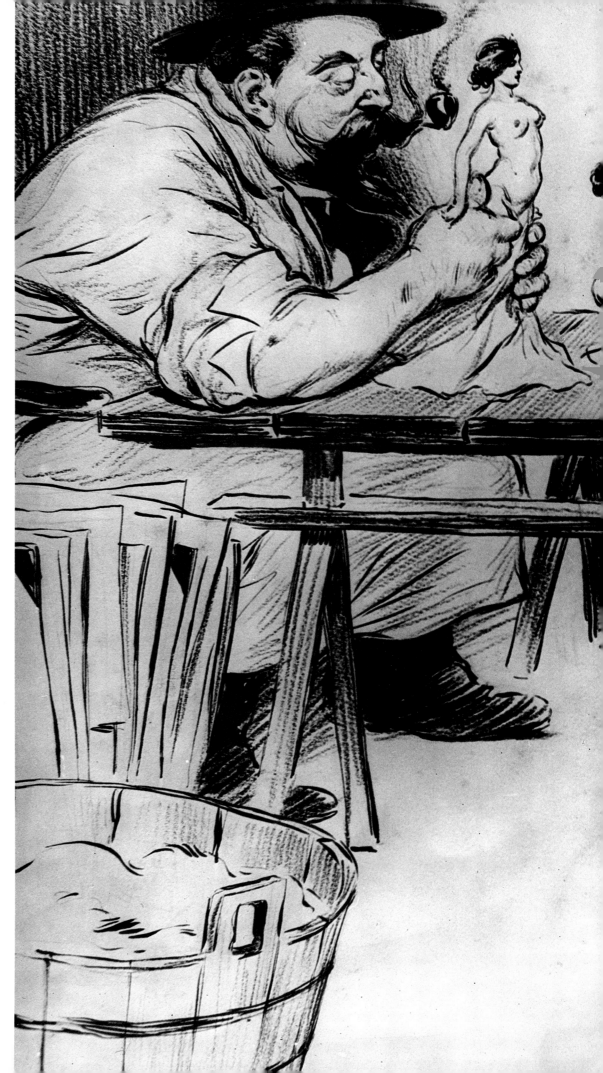

184

HOMMES ET LIVRES

Cliché Nadar.

WILLY

Œuvres principales :

Claudine à l'École. — Claudine à Paris. — Claudine s'en va. — Minne.

182-186 'It's that man's story that ought to be written', Colette said later. Willy had a highly developed commercial sense: he exploited to the last drop the success of the *Claudine* books, promoting sales of Claudine collars and statuettes – an activity caricatured by Bac (**184**) – and even bronze inkwells in the shape of his own famous flat-brimmed hat. Following Jules de Goncourt's dictum that 'Fame is an oft-repeated name', he made sure that his name was on everyone's lips and his picture everywhere to be seen. Never mind if the portraits were unflattering and his physical characteristics grossly exaggerated, as in Rip's cartoons (**182, 183**). No publicity was bad publicity to the man they called, punningly, 'Monsieur Réclamier' ('Mr Advertising'); he could, he punned in his turn, put up with any amount of 'Willyfication'. Of course Colette, as Claudine, was part of the circus, but she was still too much under Willy's thumb to protest.

CLAUDINE et TOBY-CHIEN
Ch. Gerschel, Phot. — Paris

187

COLETTE ET TOBY-CHIEN
Ch. Gerschel, phot.

188

189

COLETTE ET TOBY-CHIEN
Ch. Gerschel phot.

190

COLETTE ET TOBY-CHIEN

Ch. Gerschel, phot. — Paris

WILLY ET COLETTE

191

192

COLETTE WILLY

Ch. Gerschel, phot. — Paris

193

187-193 The sets of postcards published by Willy are now collectors' items. Colette poses as Claudine, the naughty schoolgirl, dressed in the famous collar, neckerchief, black smock and boots. Among her props are Toby-Chien and the flat-brimmed topper. Feminists would be horrified to see Colette kneeling as she sketches the man with whom she was then still in love. True, there is not a trace of a smile in any of the pictures.

194

196

194 Another postcard of Claudine with Toby-Chien.

195 For *En bombe* Willy used as his model Marcelle Rossat, who did her best to look like Colette – 'The poor man's Colette', Willy wrote in his album. On the wall is a picture by Cappiello of the actress Polaire in *Le Petit Jeune Homme*.

195

196-198 *Claudine à Paris* was brought to the stage in 1902, with Polaire, one of Willy's discoveries (see p. 111), in the title role. 'What Polaire made of Claudine was unforgettable', wrote Colette. She was photographed, put on a poster by Lucien Faure, and posed with Colette for publicity in Marseilles, where Willy, Jean Lorrain and Colette went together to watch her triumph at the Variétés Phocéennes. Afterwards whe was mobbed by her fans outside the house owned by the Noailles family, where she was staying, and people came up to her in the street to comment on her slender waist: 'What a thin little thing, you could break her in two!' Willy did not fare too well with the crowds: 'Is he your dad, darling, the fatty with the chimney pot on his head? Ooh, he looks tired!' The florist Poujade offered Polaire his shop and his eternal devotion. Jean Lorrain, on the other hand, eyed the strapping dock-workers. Colette watched it all with amusement.

197

198

Polaire, whose stage name was invented for her by Willy, was born in Algeria in 1877. In *Mes Apprentissages,* Colette recalls seeing her for the first time, 'dressed like a schoolgirl, in navy blue or bottle green. Her famous short hair was longer then and caught back in a bun – not black but a natural chestnut. Apart from the brown on her eyelids, the gloss on her marvellous long lashes and a rather deep red on her lips, her sole aids to beauty were her own flashes of radiance, the light close to tears in the fathomless depths of her eyes, and her sad, drawn smile, the real and infinitely moving attributes that contradicted the message of the diabolically arched eyebrows, the teasing slender ankles and that breathtaking wasp-waist – luminous, dewy, tender, persuasive, announcing to the world that Polaire's soul had ended up in the wrong body.'

199 Polaire seen by Cappiello.

200 A publicity photograph stressing – somewhat beyond belief – her famous slender waist.

201 Polaire as Claudine, holding Willy's belt.

202 Polaire in *Le Friquet,* a play by Willy based on a novel by Gyp.

200

201

202

111

203

204

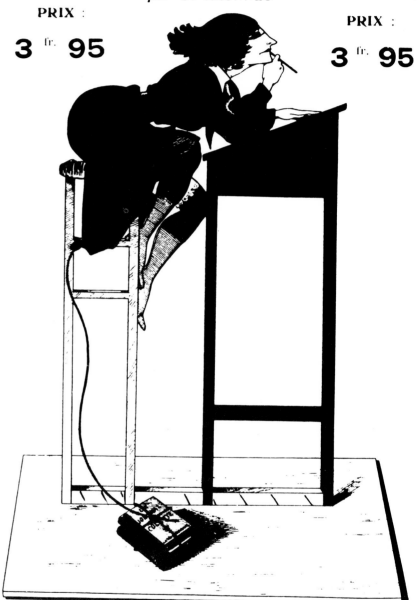
G. Bonnet d'après E. Léonnec

205

112

WILLY et POLAIRE

203-206 'Put on your white dresses', Willy said to Colette and Polaire: 'I shall look as though I'm taking my two daughters for a walk.' He delighted in appearing at all the fashionable places accompanied by his 'twins', with their similar hairstyles and clothes. Naturally the trio was the object of much speculation – all excellent publicity as far as Willy was concerned. Polaire found the gossip hard to take, but Colette was already inured to the caprices of their 'master'. 'Polaire has always showed her soul in her face . . . But on mine you would never have caught such symptoms of honest distress. I was by then over thirty, so I had already had more than ten years' training.' Cartoonists and journalists seized on the trio and everything they did was news. One can imagine the reactions of the strait-laced Gauthier-Villars family to the newspaper articles, or what Sido, in the depths of the country, thought of her exhibitionist son-in-law.

207 A drawing by Cocteau of Willy, Polaire, Colette and Toby-Chien at the Palais de Glace ice-skating rink.

208

209

208, 209 Willy would stoop to anything if it helped the sale of the *Claudine* books – not just statuettes (far left, by Georges Coudray) but even an endorsement for 'Boston Garters'.

210   *Willy.*   *Colette.*   *Polaire.*

210   Sem's view of the controversial trio of Willy and the 'twins'.

211   Poster for the Moulin Rouge production of the operetta *Claudine*, by Willy, 1910.

212-215 Colette in the Jura. In September 1900 Willy purchased Les Monts-Boucons, near Besançon. On this old estate, with its farm and dozen acres of land, Colette was thrilled to recover something of the atmosphere of her childhood. Photographs show her with friends; more usually she was there on her own. Sadly her joy was to prove short-lived, as money troubles forced Willy to sell Les Monts-Boucons five years later.

Les Monts-Boucons.

216   A romantic portrait of Colette by Emilio della Sudda, c. 1900, which still hangs in the house.

216

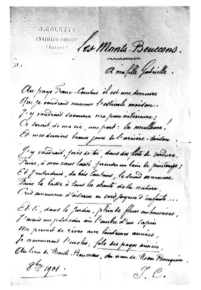

217 The house. 'At the slightest prompting of my memory the house at Les Monts-Boucons stands there before me, with its roof of nearly black tiles and its Directoire façade painted in yellowish-cream and white.'

218 An amateur poet, Captain Colette celebrated the charms of Les Monts-Boucons in verse in October 1901.

219 Colette among the poppies. In *La Retraite sentimentale* (1907), Les Monts-Boucons became 'Casamène'.

220

WILLY

221

WILLY

222

223

UNE VISITE

Un après-midi à Paris, l'hiver. Un atelier tiède où crépite doucement un poêle en forme de tour. Kiki-la-Doucette et Toby-Chien, celui-ci par terre, celui-là sur un coussin sacré, procèdent à la minutieuse toilette qui suit les siestes longues. La paix règne.

TOBY-CHIEN

Mes ongles poussent plus vite ici qu'à la campagne.

KIKI-LA-DOUCETTE

Moi, c'est le contraire.

224

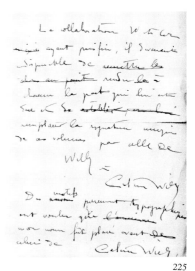

225

Once she was in her thirties, Colette began to achieve independence as a writer. New books started to appear under the name 'Colette Willy', and there was no suggestion that they had been written by anyone other than herself.

220 Colette on the threshold of independence.

221, 222 The last of her novels to be published under the name Willy, in 1904 and 1905.

223 *Minet*, credited to Madame Willy.

224 A page from *Dialogues de bêtes* (1904) – the first book by 'Colette Willy' – with illustrations by Jacques Nam. Francis Jammes wrote in his preface to *Sept Dialogues de bêtes* (1905): 'So it is up to me, who live in Orthez, to introduce you to *le Tout-Paris* . . . Madame Colette Willy is a real, living woman, who has dared to be herself; and she is much more like a country wife than a depraved authoress!'

225 Years later Colette wrote this disclaimer, signed by Willy, and had it printed as a foreword in each of her books.

III The Vagabond

'If you write horrible stories,' says a famous line in the film *Drôle de Drame*, 'in the end they come true.' Writers sometimes appear to be clairvoyants and to have mediumistic powers. The stories they write prefigure the future.

As far as Colette is concerned, *Claudine s'en va*, which was published in 1903, foretold her departure, three years later, for a new life. She had already begun to make her escape. She was soon to separate from Willy and to begin a new career. She was about to enter into the 'vagabond' period of her life.

In 1904 she used her own name to sign a book for the first time. The book was *Dialogues de bêtes*, which was written in the solitude of Les Monts-Boucons. Francis Jammes's preface in 1905 was the first great personal tribute to be paid to her talent as a writer. At the same time, the author of *Deuil des primevères* detected a secret torment in the spiteful comments of Toby-chien: 'I tell you that behind the schoolgirl laughter, I can hear a stream sobbing.'

1905 was a doubly sad year for Colette and the stream became a torrent. At the end of February, Marcel Schwob died at the age of thirty-seven, worn out by illness and morphine. It was the first time that Colette had lost a very close friend. She loathed tears, but when the charming, mocking young man who 'loved her tenderly, teased her without being cruel and admired her unreservedly'[1] was lowered into the grave in Montparnasse cemetery on 1 March, even she must have wept as she recalled the way he had come to see her and looked after her when she was ill or reduced to despair by Willy's escapades, and the jokes, the laughter and the books she had shared with him. In her impulsive letters to him she called him 'mon Chevobe' (playing with the sound of his name), 'a bankrupt', 'a piece of tow' and 'a sea-louse', and threatened to wrap him up in fly paper

when he did not write to her frequently enough.[2] He called her 'Lolette'.

Before the year was out, Captain Colette died in Châtillon. To make matters worse for Colette, September 1905 was to be the last time she would stay at Les Monts-Boucons. Willy was short of money and had sold the house. After a short visit to Châtillon to bury the old Zouave and to be with Sido, who was heartbroken but bearing up bravely, Colette returned to the house in Dauphiné. She had not been given time to learn to love its fields and woods as she might have done. From Les Monts-Boucons, she wrote to Natalie Barney: 'I have brought back my share of the inheritance: a ribbon from the Crimea, a medal from the Italian campaign, the rosette of an Officer of the Legion of Honour and one photograph. I am clinging to my loneliness and to this melancholy sunshine.'[3]

Willy, in the meantime, continued with his womanizing. He did not have to make much effort. 'A whole damned series of crazy little girls with Claudine collars and short hair came running, fluttering their eyelashes and wiggling their hips. They all wish I was dead. . . . So, goodbye to everything . . . Goodbye to almost everything. They can have him.'[4]

But how could she leave when she had no money and no training for a career? It was far from easy for a woman to leave her husband. 'To "desert the domestic hearth" was to us provincial girls of 1900 or so, a formidable and unwieldly notion, encumbered with policemen and barrel-topped trunks and thick veils, not to mention railway time-tables.'[5] Colette was still – and always would be – a provincial at heart. She was bewildered and simply could not behave like those worldly and domineering courtisans who ruled their men with a rod of iron, exploited them and threw them over when they were done with them. She was very unlike the beautiful

226 Colette at the time of *Claudine s'en va*.

society women and *demi-mondaines* she had met with Willy.

To establish financial independence from Willy she went back to her childhood dream: the theatre.

She made her unofficial debut in the spring of 1905 at a 'garden party' (there was already a certain snobbery attached to using English words) given in Neuilly by Natalie Barney. She played one of the parts in an adaptation of Pierre Louÿs' Greek-inspired poem *Dialogue au soleil couchant*. The other role was played by Eva Palmer, another young actress who was just beginning her career. The actresses were both amateurs, and they stammered with nerves when they appeared on the stage that had been erected on the lawn. Eva had an American accent, and Colette had such bad stage fright that her Burgundian intonation sounded almost Russian. Pierre Louÿs never got over 'the unforgettable experience of hearing my work spoken by Mark Twain and Tolstoy'.[6] Fortunately, Eva and Colette were spared further embarrassment by the arrival of the dancer Mata Hari, naked on a white horse, its harness studded with turquoises.

Colette did not give up. Towards the end of 1905, she began to take lessons with the handsome and famous Georges Wague, who had completely revitalized the art of mime by finding a way to use gestures to express emotions rather than just words, as classic mimes like Debureau had done. He was a charming man, two years younger than Colette but already well known, and she worked hard at learning a craft she loved and which would, she hoped, make her independent. She often appeared on stage with Wague, who was to become a friend and, for a while, rather more than a friend. Willy, for his part, watched this new development with interest.

Colette also received encouragement from a very strange character she had met a few years earlier in the company of literary lesbians like Renée Vivien, Natalie Barney and Valtesse de la Bigne. Her new supporter was the Marquise de Belbeuf. Perhaps the reason there were so many lesbians in intellectual and fashionable circles in the France of President Faillières was that many young women had entered into marriages of convenience with unsuitable men, and then turned against men as a race and sought consolation from other women. Others, who were known as 'amphibians', liked both men and women. As Jean Lorrain wrily put it, 'Just because you blow on the fire does not mean that you don't enjoy using the poker too.' Their high priestess was the beautiful Natalie Barney, who lived at 20 rue Jacob. Her *salon* was frequented by all the great literary figures of the day.

The Marquise de Belbeuf who took such an interest in Colette was no 'amphibian'. Nor was she just anyone. Her maiden name was Mathilde de Morny and she was the youngest daughter of the charming Duc de Morny, the illegitimate son of Queen Hortense. Her mother was Princess Troubetskoy, a volcanic Russian. Mathilde de Morny married the Marquis de Belbeuf when she was eighteen, but divorced him in 1903 without ever really having lived with him. Her Sapphic affairs were legendary. The ladies of the circle knew her as Mitzy. Colette knew her as Missy.

Missy was intelligent, educated and refined. Her short hair, plain face and figure were all very masculine. She always dressed as a man and wore boots and a top hat. A cane with a golden handle and a monocle completed the disguise. She was a strange transvestite with a soft, almost shy voice. Her family was very rich. Visitors to her town house often found her in a sort of workshop, dressed up as a mechanic and making brass taps or doorknobs to remind her of an old affair with a factory girl from Charonne. When her coachman was drunk, she was quite capable of taking his place and driving her own team with a firm hand.

This, then, was the strange woman who fell in love with Colette just when she needed someone to take care of her.

Things with Willy were going from bad to worse. He had now fallen for a rather plump twenty-year-old who had come to him for his autograph. Marguerite Maniez was a dancer and singer. Willy allowed her to use part of his name, and she appeared on stage as Meg Villars. Willy tried to establish his normal 'three-part harmony' with Meg and Colette, but the results were inconclusive.

Meg, who called Willy 'Papa' and wanted to become his wife, goaded him into showing Colette the door. He suggested writing a series of sketches for Colette to perform in the provinces, which would at the same time 'provide an excellent opportunity of getting rid of this wearisome flat and of finding an adequate arrangement better suited to a different kind of life – oh! just slightly different. There's no hurry.'[7]

This ill-disguised note of dismissal annoyed Colette. She left the 'domestic hearth' in November 1906. With help from Missy, she rented a small ground floor flat in the rue de Villejust, not far away from her lady-friend's house.

Willy and Colette were both jealous and began to defy one another. Colette appeared in public with Missy, and Willy set up house with Meg.

Colette could not in fact bear the idea of being ousted by Meg, but she tried not to show it. Willy found Colette's attachment to the Marquise exasperating. As usual, he expressed his true feelings by making a joke of it all. When anyone mentioned his wife's affair with Missy he would laugh and say, 'Well, at least I'm not a cuckold.' One day he got into the 'Ladies Only' compartment of a train and when the guard objected, he replied, 'I am the Marquise de Belbeuf.' Their goings-on were the talk of every fashionable dinner party in Paris.

In order to be with her beloved Colette, Missy resolved to follow her onto the boards. She had, on occasion, acted in amateur theatricals in Spain and had even danced the fandango in Tangiers. This time, she wanted to be really up to scratch and took lessons in mime from Wague. She then gave private performances to perfect her art.

In February 1906, Colette made her debut at the Théâtre des Mathurins in *Le Désir, l'Amour et la Chimère*, a *mimodrame* or mime-play by Francis de Croisset. This was followed by an appearance in Willy's *Aux innocents les mains pleines* in March. At the end of the year, she played the part of Paniska in Charles van Lerberghe's mime-play *Pan*. In mid-November *Le Journal* had announced that 'the former Marquise de Belbeuf is to appear in a mime with Madame Colette';[8] in the event Georges Wague played Pan, but the performance was greeted with whistling and with something of an uproar. The audience thought for a moment that Wague was Missy. The critics were not enthusiastic. One newspaper described the play as 'anti-social, anti-Christian and anti-human', adding, 'As for Madame Colette Willy, who was scandalously naked underneath her animal skins, her voice is too lyrical and her strong accent is unpleasant. She cannot dance; she capers.'[9] Colette was in fact the first actress to dare to appear in the nude rather than in the traditional flesh-coloured leotard.

But this was nothing compared to the scandal that was to break in January 1907. Missy had written an outline for a mime-play entitled *Rêve d'Egypte*. It is the story of an old scholar who is interested in the occult and who falls in love with a mummy. The mummy rises up before him, unwinds her bandages – the striptease element is obvious – and dances in order to seduce him. Missy was to play the scholar, and Colette the mummy. The play, directed by Georges Wague and Max Viterbo, was to be staged ten times at the beginning of January as part of the revue at the Moulin Rouge. So as not to shock her aristocratic family, Missy's name was given as 'Yssim' ('Missy' spelled backwards).

On the evening of Thursday 3 January 1907, there was a rush for seats at the Moulin Rouge. Scarcely had the curtain risen on Missy and Colette when the riot started. It was orchestrated by the Morny clan and by members of the Jockey Club, to which the Marquis de Belbeuf belonged. He was furious with his former wife for dragging his name – which she still used – on to the music hall stage. Willy and Meg were in a stage box.

The music was drowned out by whistling, trumpet blasts and shouting. All kinds of missiles – little chairs, lorgnette cases, and symbolic heads of garlic – rained down on the stage.

The long kiss exchanged between Colette and Missy brought the din to a climax and the crudest of insults began to fly. Willy, who was ostentatiously applauding, was picked on by members of the audience who called him a cuckold and a complaisant husband. He was even jostled. For a moment, he fought back with his cane but before long both he and Meg had to leave the theatre to avoid being injured. The auditorium was in an uproar and the police arrived.

The next day, the Moulin Rouge scandal was all over Paris. *Le Figaro, Le Matin, La Libre Parole, Le Petit Parisien* and the other papers were very harsh on the actresses and on Willy. Lépine, the Prefect of Police, threatened to close down the Moulin Rouge if the two women continued to appear in such a shocking production. For the next performance Georges Wague replaced Missy, and the title of the piece was changed to *Songe d'Orient*; but the scandal refused to die down, and attacks and caricatures proliferated.

Sido was not amused. She had come to Paris to see her daughter dance and found the scandal surrounding her name very distasteful. She did not approve of the path she had taken, and on her return to Châtillon she wrote to Colette to say so: 'The perfume you have drenched yourself with does not have the right smell. You are using it to give a false impression. Your short hair, the blue eye makeup and the eccentricities you indulge in on stage are all designed to make people think you are an original spirit independent of convention.'[10]

Initially, Willy defended Colette and Missy, but he soon turned against his wife. For once, the scandal had not worked to his advantage. The staid *Echo de Paris* was shocked to hear that he had gone to the Moulin Rouge and had applauded a performance he should have been the first to condemn, and dismissed him, thereby depriving him of a considerable part of his income. Urged on by Meg, a fortnight later he asked for a legal separation on the grounds that his wife had deserted the conjugal home three months earlier. Colette promptly filed a countersuit instancing his flagrant adulteries.

Despite the separation, the break was not yet final. In 1907, the two couples even went on holiday together to Le Crotoy in Normandy, with Meg and Willy staying in the villa next door to one taken by Missy and Colette. According to Jacques Gauthier-Villars, they were still on excellent terms. A year after Willy and Colette separated, the Marquise invited Willy and Meg to her New Year's Eve party.

The truth of the matter is that Colette still hoped to win back the husband she loved. In the next few months, she did everything she could to get him back. She asked mutual friends to intervene on her behalf and even pleaded with Willy in letters: 'I owe everything to you . . . Oh! the distress that lies behind my mistake. . . . Without you, I am nothing.'[11] She is of course careful to mention nothing of this in *Mes Apprentissages*. But Willy refused to listen.

In the meantime, Colette went on writing. *La Retraite sentimentale* was published by Mercure de France under the name 'Colette Willy', with a note reading 'For reasons which have nothing to do with literature, I have ceased to collaborate with Willy.' *La Vie parisienne* began to serialize *Les Vrilles de la vigne*, and Colette wrote her first journalistic pieces for the same paper.

She now had to make her own living. Missy's family, disgusted with her behaviour, had cut off her source of income and she was having difficulty in helping Colette. Colette took up mime seriously, and went on tour. In March 1907 she performed *Rêve d'Egypte* in Nice. In November she and Georges Wague appeared in *La Chair*, a new mime-play by Marcel Vallée, at the Apollo, which was very successful. In August 1908 she was in Xanrof and Guérin's *Son Premier Voyage* in Geneva. In November, she played Claudine in Brussels. 'So you're taking up the theatre seriously', wrote Sido. 'That must mean you like it, and also of course you must be making money. Well, I confess I never imagined you as having what it takes because you always moved so stiffly – and an actress needs to be so supple, both physically and morally, and I was not sure that you had those qualities. The truth is that you have become more supple in both respects.'[12]

Les Vrilles de la vigne was published in book form. One of the short stories is dedicated to Missy, one to Willy, and a third to Meg. Colette was very jealous of Meg, but she tried to be friendly towards her so as not to lose Willy completely. She was both brave and masochistic, and would rather ally herself with her rival than suffer the agony of exclusion. Towards the end of 1908, she appears to have been completely distraught. While she was on tour in Lyons, a wave of depression overcame her and she wrote to Missy: 'I began to cry like an idiot because I have been so lonely for so long.'[13]

At the beginning of 1909 Colette learned that Willy had sold the rights to the *Claudine* books to the publishers for virtually nothing. As she wrote to Léon Hamel, 'You really would think that he wanted not only to make very little money out of them himself but to be certain that even after his death I would never gain possession of the books, which are mine.'[14] This time, the break between them was final. Getting divorced and coldly settling accounts are very good ways to finish off a love affair that has turned sour.

1909, 1910 . . . Colette was thirty-six and more than ever before, her life was that of a vagabond – the title of the novel she wrote between tours and during holidays at Belle Plage, Missy's villa in Le Crotoy.

Like *Les Vrilles de la vigne*, *La Vagabonde* (serialized in 1910) is a book about pain, loneliness, love and suspicion. The character of Adolphe Taillandy is based upon Willy. 'My God, I was so young and so much in love with that man . . . And how I suffered!' At the same time, there is a boastful note to her misery: 'And when I admit that I was jealous enough to want to kill and then die . . . I sound like the people who say "I ate rats in 1870".'[15] The wild passion she had felt for Willy gradually gave way to the lasting bitterness of *Mes Apprentissages*.

For his part, Willy was content to make digs at his former wife in one or two novels written for him by ghostwriters. In his own way he too was affected by the break-up of their marriage. In a blow which only a writer could give another writer, he killed off the character of Maugis, whom they had created together, so that Colette could no longer use him. And when his son Jacques, who was terribly upset by the divorce, asked what he should call his former stepmother, Willy quipped: 'You can call her cousin. I call her my widow.'

Years later, shortly before his death in 1931, Willy found himself in the company of people who did not recognize him. His fame was a thing of the past, and he was poor and ill. 'Willy?', he said to them, 'He was an old joker, I knew him well. He died twenty years ago.'

His memory was, however, forever linked with the name of Colette. In 1942, Colette's third husband Maurice Goudeket wanted to revisit La Treille Muscate, where he had lived with her a few years earlier. He introduced himself to the new owners as 'Colette's husband'. Flattered at having such a famous visitor, they said, 'Come in, Monsieur Willy.'

Brussels, Grenoble, Lyons, Nice, Ostend, Biarritz . . . in an attempt to make a living, Colette was constantly on the move, appearing in provincial theatres with Georges Wague and Christine Kerf. She gives an account of her exhausting life on the road in *L'Envers du music-hall*. In 1910, she met the young Maurice Chevalier in Lyons; he fell in love with her but was too shy to say anything.

The success of *La Chair* in 1907 and in its subsequent revivals was not unrelated to the fact that Colette appeared half-naked on stage. By baring her left breast she provoked a scandal and caused a lot of ink to flow. In Nice, the prim and proper Prefect of the Alpes-Maritimes made her cover the offending breast. As a result he became the target for *Ruy Blas*'s jibes:[16]

> Le préfet qui Joly se nomme
> N'a-t-il qu'un oeil, n'a-t-il qu'un bras?
> Serait-ce la moitié d'un homme?
> Peut-être même il n'en a pas.

(Has the prefect called Joly / Only one arm, only one eye? / Is he perhaps only half a man? / Perhaps he does not even have one.) In Marseilles, a satirical paper published a caricature of the bare-breasted Colette and a quatrain signed 'Lecochon qui sommeille' (the slumbering pig):[17]

> J'ai vu *La Chair*! Ma foi j'ignore
> Si c'est de l'art ou . . . Mais crénom!!
> Colette a de bien beaux nichons!!
> Et dam! Quand on connaît ses seins on les adore.

('I saw *La Chair*! 'Pon my word, I don't know / If it's art or . . . but damn it all / Colette really does have fine tits / Anyone who likes breasts will love them.)

More distinguished critics praised Colette warmly. *Paris-Journal's* Léon Werth could not speak highly enough of her grace and of the harmony of her gestures: 'Her body has that awareness that plants, animals, children and women who do not curb their instincts never lose.'[18] Sido, however, did not approve of her daughter's exhibitionism: 'How dare you appear half-naked like that?'

But although Colette was daring enough to take off her clothes in public at a time when nudity was tolerated only in private circles, she was still a provincial at heart and she came from a background where women who appeared on the stage – and especially scantily-dressed women – were considered shameless hussies. The provincial Colette was surprised at her own daring. As she put it in *La Vagabonde*, when she looked into the mirror she saw 'a woman writer who has gone to the bad.' Even in 1906, when she had just made her debut on the stage, she felt apologetic towards Francis Jammes: 'I no longer write to you because I have taken up acting and I think that in your eyes that will humiliate me for ever. You see, I know my place. Having played a faun at the Mathurins and a young greenhorn at the Théâtre Royal makes me arrogant with some people and humble with others.'[19]

Colette had absolutely no sense of physical shame (except, as we shall see, about one particular physical blemish of which she was very conscious), but she could be very bashful in other ways. When Rachilde tried to persuade her to approach people who could help her with her career, she replied: 'Alas, you know me, Rachilde. You know I am quite capable of performing in the buff, but not of entering certain houses, flattering people, fishing for introductions, looking for admiration and sympathy . . .'[20]

By temperament, Colette was far too independent to allow herself to be absorbed into any milieu. Through Willy she had met the most fashionable, snobbish and dazzling people in Paris, but she always refused to conform to the rules of society and insisted on remaining an outsider.

She loathed the priggish pedantry of the literati and the society women who devoted one day a week to their meaningless chatter. When she was forced to mix with them, she sometimes reacted with the provocative insolence of a shy woman. At such times, she might do anything. Like Claudine, she was quite capable of asking for cheap red wine at a smart tea party. At one dinner, a delicate young man of letters (Marcel Proust) began to pay her compliments about one of her books and compared her daydreams to those of a young Narcissus whose soul was full of voluptuousness and bitterness. She replied brusquely: 'Monsieur, you are raving. My soul is full of red beans and bacon.'[21]

That is not the way to make friends. Especially when you have sharp eyes and the ability to paint perfectly recognizable caricatures of people in just a few lines.

Colette was not popular with everyone, and certainly not with all women. Women writers tended to dislike her. In the first place, she made them jealous because they did not have her talent. Then she stood out from them by the way she flaunted her freedom. Her daring offended them. Although she made an exception for women like Hélène Picard, Marguerite Moreno and Germaine Beaumont, she felt that she had little in common with most women and despised them. Most were annoyed by her rather masculine attitude to life and by the 'chic type' (good kid) side to her – 'chic type' was in fact the expression she used when she wanted to pay a woman a compliment. They could not forgive her for the scandals she seemed to cause simply for the sake of it, for the friendships she enjoyed with men or for the way she attracted men. So they excluded her or attacked her; and men always stepped forward to defend her. When a certain Madame Faure-Goyau criticized her for attracting 'vulgar publicity that should be reserved for women who have no talent', Franc-Nohain replied in *Fantasio*: 'The real reason why her sisters do not seem to take Madame Colette Willy's books seriously is that Madame Willy never seems to take either her sisters or books seriously.'[22] Sacha Guitry was frank when he published a highly laudatory article entitled 'Colette Willy, danseuse et homme de lettres' in *Comœdia* in 1909. He explained why he called her a 'man of letters' and why she was excluded from all the women's competitions, societies, gatherings, academies and 'talk shops':

By not including Colette Willy in their number, these ladies of letters seem to be suggesting that she really belongs among men of letters.

He goes on,

One cannot pay Colette Willy any of the astonished compliments one normally pays to a woman who writes. She does not spend her time plumbing the depths of her own heart; she writes effortlessly; she is not trying to emulate anyone; and she does not write in order to impress or shock her husband. No, for her writing is neither an assertion of independence nor an 'honourable' way of making a living. Colette Willy is mysteriously gifted.[23]

129

The one good thing about getting divorced is that you find out who your real friends are. When she and Willy officially parted, on 21 June 1910, Colette lost the friends who only smiled at her because she was with him, but some of those who had been her friends when she was married remained true to her: Marguerite Moreno, even though she was constantly on the move between France and Argentina, Marcel Proust, Anna de Noailles, who deeply admired her, Claude Farrère, who was still in love with her, Sacha Guitry and his wife Charlotte Lysès. Then there was Léon Hamel, the man of the world and globetrotter who was to remain a trusted confidant until his death in 1912 (Hamond in *La Vagabonde* is based upon Hamel). She also had Georges Wague, the colleague, friend and occasional accomplice, who probably knew her better than anyone else and who admired the energy she put into her work.

Colette had in fact become a dedicated professional actress. She took great care over her performances and rehearsed thoroughly. She would spend hours with the photographer Reutlinger, holding long, painful poses, standing draped in damp sheets to achieve the look of a statue or wearing rags or animal skins if that was what was needed for the poster of the moment. She listened carefully to the advice of Moreno, who knew all the pitfalls of the business: 'Take care, Macolette, the theatre is a dangerous place.' These were lean years for Colette and she had to learn to look after herself in terms of fees and contracts. She learned to live in the frequently harsh world of the music hall.

She did of course have Missy to look after her, and it was to Missy that she would turn to recover her strength when she was tired. They were now living together, at first in the rue de Torricelli, near the place des Ternes and then in the rue Saint-Senoch. In summer, they would go to Le Crotoy, where Colette delighted in catching flatfish at low tide. She longed, however, to live in Brittany and in 1910 Missy, who could not refuse her anything, bought her a house, Rozven ('rose of the winds' in Breton), outside Saint-Coulomb near Saint-Malo.

But Missy was not enough for Colette who, by temperament, preferred men to women and only turned to Sapphic affairs when there were no men to hand. 'Two women embracing . . . a melancholy and touching image of weak creatures who may have taken refuge in each other's arms to sleep, to weep, to flee from cruel men, or to enjoy something better than pleasure; the bitter happiness of feeling that they are the same, both weak and both forgotten.'[24]

What Colette really liked about Missy was the way she mothered her. Selfishly, perhaps, she took advantage of Missy's maternal instincts. She enjoyed her comforting presence, the gifts she showered upon her and the way she reassured her when she felt lost. But she also found Missy somewhat suffocating and began to drift away from her. She was attracted to a twenty-five-year old who had once been Polaire's lover and who had fallen wildly in love with her.

Auguste Hériot was a superbly handsome young man with an indulgent father (who had once owned the Grands Magasins du Louvre, amongst other things). He was elegant, attractive, very rich, and a bachelor. He was an athlete and was more at home in the boxing ring than in a literary salon. His home in Paris was a vast, luxurious town house filled with rare furniture and tapestries. He had even installed an American bar, with one of the best barmen in Paris. The society pages reported his presence in all the smartest spots. He rode, sailed, motored and gambled. The sumptuous yachts owned by his sister Virginie also provoked considerable comment.

When he saw Colette, Hériot immediately decided that she was the only woman for him. He determined to follow her like a puppy and put his heart and fortune in her hands. Colette, amused and perhaps even a little flattered by the passion she had inspired, let him worship her. She called him 'chérubin' or 'le petit', and he became the model for Max in *La Vagabonde*, and then for Chéri, but she always kept him at a distance because he was not the man for her. She tolerated him as a lover, but made it quite clear that he could never be a husband. Hériot did not give up and spent two years doing everything he could to win Colette. They travelled together. They went to London, to the Côte d'Azur – which she had yet to learn to love – and to Naples, which she disliked. He reserved her the best sleepers on trains, the most reliable boats, the finest cars and the most comfortable rooms in the best hotels. He helped her discover the luxury that only money can buy. But she did not give in. 'This adventure is more serious for him than for me,' she wrote to Hamel in February 1911. 'I am in no moral danger.'[25] She also said, 'He is a sweet child when he is alone with me. He will never be happy; his whole character is based upon an underlying sadness.'[26]

Missy was far from delighted at having a rival, but she rapidly realized that young Hériot was no serious threat to her. She gave Colette a free rein and busied herself with furnishing the house in Rozven. When she came back from her travels, Colette always went to Missy in the same way that a cat goes back to its favourite cushion when it is tired after having been out too long. 'I was anxious to get back to Missy to be scolded, looked after and warmed.'[27]

Missy knew that she had another trump card in her hand: Colette's beloved Rozven.

I wish you could see Rozven, with its cove and the green sea, its complicated rocks, its little wood, the trees, old and new, the warm terrace, the rose trees, my yellow room and the beach where the sea casts up its treasures – mauve coral, polished shells and sometimes barrels of whale oil or benzine from some far-off shipwreck. I have a rocky perch between sky and water. We catch bright blue lobsters, agate-coloured shrimps and crabs with backs of woollen velvet.[28]

1. Marguerite Moreno, *Souvenirs de ma vie*, Paris, Editions de Flore, 1949, p. 80.
2. Colette's letters to Schwob are included in *Lettres à ses pairs*.
3. Unpublished letter; coll. Richard Anacréon.
4. 'Toby-Chien parle', in *Les Vrilles de la vigne, Oeuvres*, I, p. 995.
5. *My Apprenticeships*, p. 105.
6. Ibid., p. 113.
7. Ibid., p. 115.
8. Fernand Hauser, 'L'Ex-Marquise de Belbeuf joue la pantomine en L'Hotel de la Marquise', *Le Journal*, 17 November 1906; reprinted in Colette, *Lettres de la Vagabonde*, Paris, Flammarion, 1961, pp. 287-9.
9. Albert du Moulin in *Paris-Lumière*, 5 December 1906.
10. Cited, Viel, *Colette au temps des Claudine*.
11. Unpublished letter; coll. Michel Remy-Bieth.
12. Letter, 31 July 1908; *Le Figaro littéraire*, 24 January 1953.
13. Unpublished letter; coll. Michel Remy-Bieth.
14. Letter, 28 February 1909; *Lettres de la Vagabonde*, p. 30.
15. *La Vagabonde, Oeuvres*, I, p. 1083.
16. *Ruy Blas*, 1909.
17. *Théatra*, 9 May 1911.
18. *Paris-Journal*, 2 May 1911.
19. Letter, April 1906; *Lettres à ses pairs*, pp. 113-14.
20. Unpublished letter, 2 January 1909; coll. Richard Anacréon.
21. *Claudine en ménage, Oeuvres*, I, p. 428.
22. *Fantasio*, 1 November 1906.
23. *Comoedia*, 21 May 1909.
24. *La Vagabonde, Oeuvres*, I, p. 1207.
25. Letter, 14 February 1911; *Lettres de la Vagabonde*, p. 46.
26. Letter, 19 November 1910; ibid., p. 45.
27. Letter to Louis de Robert, April 1911; ibid., p. 49.
28. Ibid., pp. 49-50.

227 After her separation from Willy, Colette learned to enjoy her own company. In *Bella Vista* she later wrote: 'it is folly to believe that times when love is absent are "blank pages" in a woman's existence.'

228 Colette in her 'bachelor flat' in the rue de Villejust. 'From the very first night I spent in this ground-floor flat I forgot the front door key in the lock on the outside.'

229 Colette in men's clothes –
perhaps a way of boosting her
self-confidence?

229

230

231

232

230-235   The man in the bowler hat, with cropped hair, dressed as an Arab sheik, wearing a false moustache (made of hairs from a dog's tail), posing as a Roman emperor and as a monk – all these are none other than Mathilde de Morny, the former Marquise de Belbeuf, known as Missy, who was in love with Colette and became her protector.

233

235

236 A rare photograph of Mathilde in feminine dress, taken when she was a girl.

234   236

135

237

238

239 'L'Avenue du Bois', a cartoon frieze by Sem. Willy drives the carriage in which Colette and Mathilde de Morny are passengers.

237 Colette and the Marquise de Belbeuf, caricatured by Sem.

238 The couple in 1910. In *Le Pur et l'Impur*, Colette wrote about Missy in the guise of the character called La Chevalière.

239 'L'Avenue du Bois', a cartoon frieze by Sem. Willy drives the carriage in which Colette and Mathilde de Morny are passengers. The two women were labelled 'The "mornigatic" marriage', and Willy 'the coach driver-usherette' (a reference to an early pseudonym: see p. 37).

241

242

243

244

Holidays in Le Crotoy, Normandy, 1907.

240, 244 Colette, Missy and three friends.

241 Colette and Missy on the steps of the Villa Belle Plage.

242 Colette doing her exercises, supervised by Missy. Willy captioned this photograph 'Dislocated aristocrats'.

243 Colette on the swings.

245 'The Execution of Mary Stuart', a tableau-vivant created by the poet Renée Vivien. Missy is the executioner, Léon Hamel plays the monk, and Renée Vivien is Mary Stuart.

245

Colette with Missy, and Willy with his mistress Meg Villars, took villas at Le Crotoy for a joint holiday.

246, 247   Colette and Meg Villars, rivals in gymnastics as they were for Willy's love.

246

247

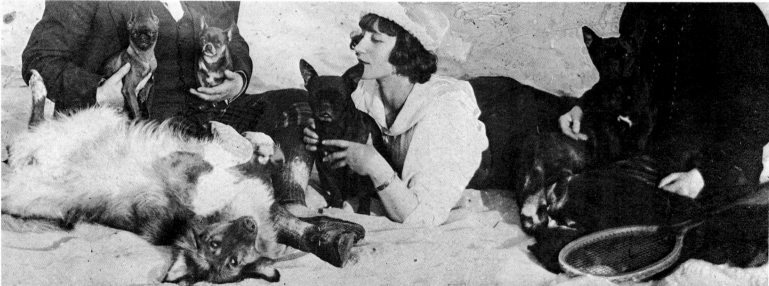

248

140

248 Colette with her dogs.

249 Colette's daring on stage was not reflected in her choice of beachwear.

250 Colette's style of dress clearly owes much to Missy.

249

250

251

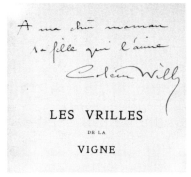

252

253

254

255

256

251, 252   First edition of *Les Vrilles de la vigne* (1908), inscribed for Sido.

253-255   Colette was in Nice on tour in March 1908. She and Willy had been legally separated just over a year, and he was living with Meg Villars, but they still saw each other (**253, 254**). Also in Nice was Renée Vivien (**255**, centre).

256   Colette in an orchard.

257, 258   Meg Villars, the cause of the separation. Willy had hoped to make a threesome with her and Colette, and made them pose together as friends; but the coolness between them is clear. Not until much later were they reconciled.

257

258

143

260

261

259 Colette as Paniska at the Théâtre Marigny, late 1906; the mime-play *Pan* was devised by Charles van Lerbergue, with music by Robert Haas. It was planned that the Marquise de Belbeuf should play the part of Pan, but at the last minute she was replaced by Georges Wague (**260**). This unannounced substitution caused some confusion among the audience, who murmured, 'She certainly does look like a man.'

261, 262 *La Vagabonde* was published in serial form in *La Vie parisienne*, the first episode appearing on 21 May 1910.

263 Colette in her mid-thirties, from Willy's album.

259

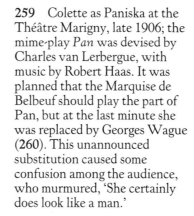

262

263

- L'Amour, le Désir, la Chimère -

Mes impressions de première ? Attendez.

Derrière un rideau baissé, au centre d'un jardin de toile peinte bordé d'un mur en carton, s'agite un petit peuple désespéré... On crie, on pleure, on menace, on court et on se heurte... Georgette Leblanc vole de l'un à l'autre, éblouissante et nue dans sa robe du dernier acte de *Tintagiles*, et ses cheveux d'or la suivent, soulevés par l'élan.

Sous mon costume de faune, je cours aussi, les mains écartées, afin de ne pas écailler leur fard écru... Et je crie, pour faire comme tout le monde :

— Mon arc !... Mon arc, je vous dis ! Il était là, qu'est-ce qu'on en a fait ? Et ma flûte ? Flûte, on a marché dessus, c'est du

propre ! Ah ! mon Dieu, j'ai une corne qui ne tient pas. Oh ! que j'ai soif ! Et ce sale public qui trépigne ! Nous ne sommes pourtant que de trois quarts d'heure en retard... Et où a-t-on mis la colophane pour mes semelles ? Georgette, mon maillot plisse au genou !... Willy, va-t-en dans la salle, tu ne tiendras jamais dans les coulisses...

Inès Devriès passe, joli Tanagra paisible, sous des crêpes immaculés. Miss Borrowdale frissonne dans ses voiles verts, son cou frêle plie sous la tour somptueuse de ses cheveux roux. Ça sent la poudre de riz, la toile peinte et le machiniste affairé.

— Nouguès, y êtes-vous ?

— Je vous attends, ma chère amie.

— Oh ! ce musicien, ce qu'il m'agace avec sa politesse !..

Rageuse, je vais me hisser sur mon mur, d'où j'épierai les nymphes, quand un cri d'angoisse, un vrai, m'échappe : le mur ne tient pas ! Voyez-vous mes débuts, les quatre fers en l'air ?

— Vite, des machinistes !

Il n'y a plus de machinistes, ils ont fui comme des ombres vaines. Enfin, Mathilde Deschamps, secrétaire à poigne, les ramène par l'oreille et je les invective :

— Qui est-ce qui m'a planté ce mur-là ? En quoi avez-vous les mains, ce soir ?

Ils ronchonnent et tendent une corde qui assurera l'équilibre du mur vacillant... Et la corde casse... Et le public trépigne d'impatience, et les violons grincent, et Georgette Leblanc secoue ses cheveux d'un geste tragique. Il faut prendre un parti. Je colle les deux infâmes machinistes derrière le mur, qu'ils étaient de leurs dos accroupis, et je leur promets le gril et la corde s'ils bougent...

D'un saut, je bondis sur l'édifice instable, pendant que le rideau déjà, s'enroule en grinçant.

Et, pendant que j'assure, faune guetteur, mon pied sur une épaule de machiniste invisible, le public sourit au calme jardin fleuri, à la trompeuse perspective, à la musique voilée, à tout ce petit Eden que tout à l'heure balayait la tempête...

Colette WILLY.

268

269

266

267

264-269 On 6 February 1906, Colette made her first professional appearance as a mime-artist, at the Théâtre des Mathurins, playing the little faun in *Le Désir, l'Amour et la Chimère* by Francis de Croisset and Jean Nougues. Her props consisted of a bow, pan-pipes, and two little horns on her head. Nearly half a century later, Georges Wague recalled Colette's vitality as a theatrical performer; she never complained and allowed nothing to dim her high spirits.

Rêve d'Egypte caused a sensation in 1907 when it was performed at the Moulin Rouge.

271 On the poster Missy was billed as 'Yssim' – her name spelled backwards – in an attempt at disguise.

272, 273 Letter from Colette to Georges Wague, asking him to give mime lessons to Missy.

270, 274 Colette as the mummy who is brought back to life.

275 The mummy and the scholar just before the kiss that scandalized the audience. The De Morny family were not amused by Mathilde's transvestism and her public exhibition with Colette.

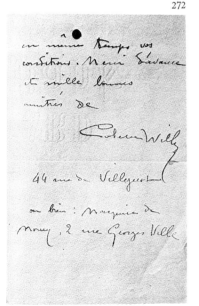

276

277

276, 278 Colette – from Burgundy to the Cairo of *Rêve d'Egypte*, via mime, dance and nudity.

277 The dancer and spy Mata Hari, whom Colette saw at Natalie Barney's: 'exotic' costumes, mimes and ballets were the order of the day.

278

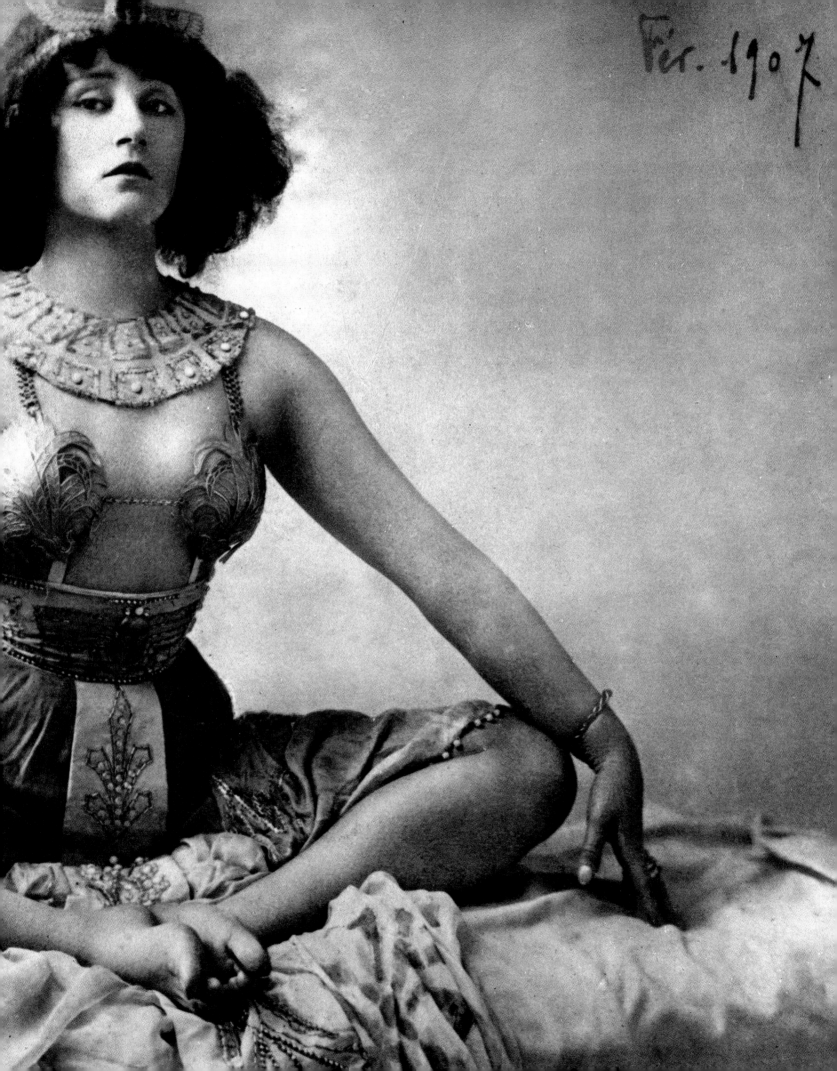

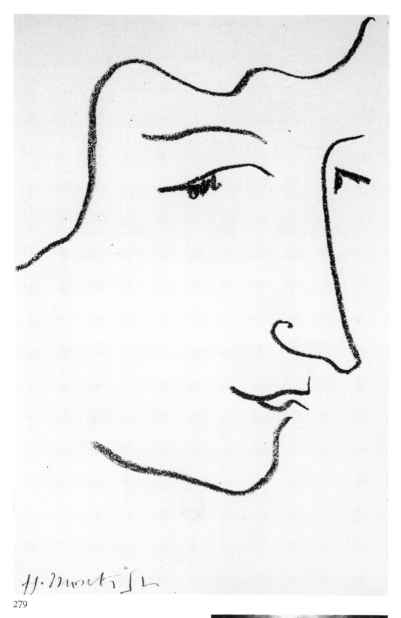

279

280

281   282

152

COLETTE WILLY

Danseuse et Homme de Lettres

(Dessin de Sacha Guitry).

283

279 'La Vagabonde', by Matisse.

280 Colette as a music-hall artiste, by Marcel Vertès.

281 The young Maurice Chevalier, in love with Colette but too shy to declare himself.

282 The beautiful Breton singer Marguerite Boulc'h, who achieved fame as 'Fréhel'; she was the model for 'la petite Jadin' in *La Vagabonde*.

283 Illustration by Sacha Guitry to his article celebrating Colette in *Comœdia*.

284, 286-288 It was this bared breast that audiences flocked to behold in *La Chair* (see Ills. **289-295**), that inspired the newspapers to such flights of fancy, and that so shocked a prudish prefect of the Alpes-Maritimes that he demanded the offending object be covered when Colette performed the play in Nice.

285

Lâchez un sein !...

Derniers échos d'une Wague querelle

284

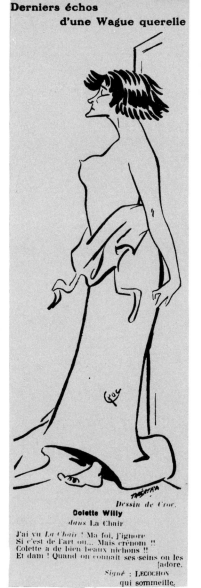

Dessin de Cruc.

Colette Willy
dans La Chair

J'ai vu *La Chair* ! Ma foi, j'ignore
Si c'est de l'art ou... Mais crénom !!
Colette a de bien beaux nichons !!
Et dam ! Quand on connait ses seins on les
[adore.

Signé : LECOCHON
qui sommeille.

287

Before 1906, nudity in the French music-hall was inconceivable. Artistes wore a flesh-coloured leotard to give the illusion of exposure. Colette was the first to bare her own skin, in the mime-plays *La Romanichelle* and *Pan*. Theatre managers were eager for something controversial that would boost the audiences for their shows, and it did not take them long to realize that the unconventional Colette Willy was exactly what they were looking for. But if they 'used' her, she also used them, as objects of satire in her writing. In *Les Vrilles de la vigne* (**285**) she introduced the character of an impresario who undresses an actress by having her costume progressively torn off in the course of a rehearsal. 'Inspired, the impresario stepped back three paces, threw out his arm, and in the voice of a balloonist taking off shouted: "Release one breast!"'

La Chair

LA CHAIR... DE POULE !

286

288

289

290

291

292

293

294

289-295 *La Chair*, by Georges Wague with music by Albert Chantrier, was first performed on 1 November 1907. Colette played the beautiful but inconstant Yulka, who deceives her lover Hokartz (Georges Wague) with the youth Yorki (Christine Kerf). Hokartz flies at her in a passion and slashes her clothes – 'Release one breast!' – with his dagger (see Ill. 288). Evidently, in 1907 love was a somewhat tormented affair. The critics noted unkindly that, although Colette was skilful at expressing emotion, her capers on the stage were less than sylph-like. Certainly her main concern as a mime-artist was to earn a living (292).

295

296

297

298

296-299 In 1912 Colette appeared at the Bataclan in *La Chatte amoureuse,* a mime-sketch by Roger Guttinguer, produced by Georges Wague, which formed part of the revue *Ça grise.* A critic in *Comœdia* praised 'the supple, lascivious and teasing sensuality of her original and varied talents'.

300 Colette in 1908, borne in triumph at the Théâtre des Arts.

Colette WILLY, Christine KERF, Georges WAGUE dans "L'OISEAU DE NUIT" Musique de A. CHANTRIER

301

4_ Colette WILLY et Georges WAGUE dans "L'OISEAU DE NUIT" Musique de A. CHANTRIER.

302

5_ Colette WILLY _ Christine KERF dans "L'OISEAU DE NUIT" Musique de A. CHANTRIER.

303

304

301-305 Colette herself thought up the title of the mime-play *L'Oiseau de nuit,* in which she appeared in December 1911 at the Gaîté-Rochechouart, together with Georges Wague and Christine Kerf. The production was revived in September 1912 at the Bataclan. 'This time I put into it more effort than real enthusiasm, and it would be no sacrifice on my part to give up the *café-concert* altogether.' She did not give up her part, however, in spite of her grief at the recent death of her mother, and the fact that she was in the early stages of pregnancy – 'amid the stage-managed fights, the stabs with a pitchfork and the hand-to-hand clinches on the table and under the table'.

L'OiSEAU DE NUiT

ATELIER BERNARD. PARIS. 44 Rue de Lancry.

MUSIQUE de A. CHANTRiER

COLETTE WiLLY.
CHRISTINE KERF.
GEORGES WAGUE

DANSES
RÉGLÉES PAR
CERNUSCO

306

308

307

L'Oiseau de nuit.

306 Christine Kerf, Georges Wague and Colette, as seen by René Martel.

307 The cast pose for the photographer in Colette's dressing-room.

308 Colette as the pathetic orphan from the storm, the 'night-bird'.

309 Before going on stage. If Colette is even less inclined to smile than usual, it is because of Sido's recent death.

309

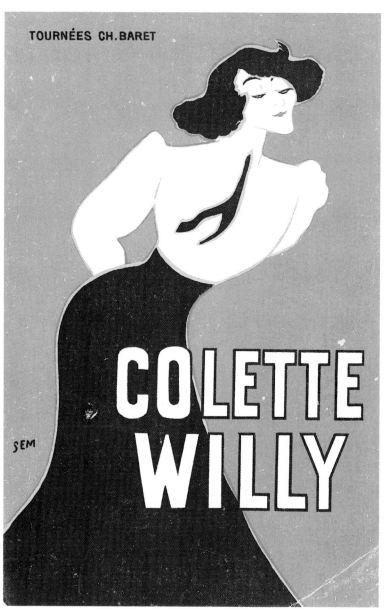

EN CAMARADES

311

310   Poster by Sem for a tour organized by Baret.

311   Colette and Georges Prieur in a scene from *En camarades,* a two-act play by Colette, first performed on 22 January 1909 at the Théâtre des Arts. Léon Blum reviewed it favourably the next day in *Comœdia.*

312   Colette revived the role of Fanchette in 1912, at the Théâtre Michel.

313   Colette and Saint-Mars in *Son Premier Voyage,* by Xanrof and Guérin, first performed in Geneva on 29 August 1908.

314-317 *(following pages)*   As a professional actress Colette knew the importance of publicity photographs, and was prepared to pose for hours for the photographer Reutlinger, who wrapped his models in damp sheets to achieve dramatic effects of drapery.

318

168

319

The inspiration for the character of Chéri was Auguste Hériot, a rich young man who loved sport and the social whirl. He was madly in love with Colette, but she wrote: 'this adventure is more serious for him than for me'.

318 Hériot adopts a boxing stance. 'Intoxicated with his new-found strength, Chéri flew into a passion, sneaked in unfair punches and reddened with anger.'

319 Hériot during the First World War. Paul Morand met him while he was on leave after receiving a minor wound – 'the elegant wounded hero type, perfect for the cover of *La Vie parisienne.*'

320

322

325

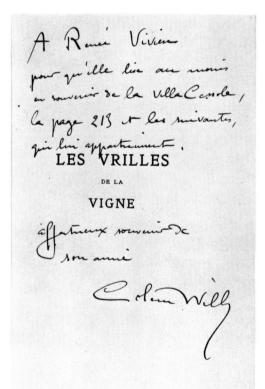

321

323

324

326

Ladies literary and scandalous.

320 The poetess Renée Vivien, whose real name was Pauline Tarn. She was gifted and charming, and a lover of women. Charles Maurras compared her poetry to the works of Verlaine and Baudelaire.

321 Inscription from Colette to Renée Vivien.

322 Anna de Noailles. When she published her collection of poems *Le Coeur innombrable*, her husband's mother was mortified: 'People will think I have written this filth.'

323 Liane de Pougy, friend of Natalie Barney and Renée Vivien; her success in the demi-monde was comparable with Otéro's. She eventually married Prince Ghika and ended her days as a virtuous wife performing good works.

324 Baroness Ilse Deslandes. She never forgot that Barrès had been her lover and simply refused to acknowledge that she was no longer young. This amused Colette, who wrote to Annie de Pène: 'She is fifty-four, but she doesn't let that stop her.'

325 Lucie Delarue-Mardrus, from Normandy, a poet, friend of Natalie Barney and Baroness Deslandes. Her husband used to lock her in a room to make her get down to writing.

326 Renée Vivien in Directoire costume.

327 Colette with a muff.

327

328 Henry de Jouvenel – 'Sidi'.

IV Fetters

This period of wandering was to be the least settled in Colette's life. She had not yet got over Willy and avoided emotional entanglements but, not having the temperament of a nun, her affair with Auguste Hériot was not the only one. None of them came to anything and Missy did not take offence.

Things were to change in 1911, when the second important man in Colette's life appeared on the scene. His name was Henry de Jouvenel and at thirty-five he was three years younger than Colette. He was an educated member of the bourgeoisie and had a charm that most women could not resist. 'Dark hair, velvety eyes, a superb build, no money, and luxurious tastes.'[1] Colette found him quite irresistible.

As a young man, Jouvenel had been private secretary to a Minister for Justice and he was now one of the three editors-in-chief on *Le Matin*, an important newspaper owned by Bunau-Varilla. He had an eight-year-old son named Bertrand from his first and short-lived marriage to the beautiful daughter of Alfred Boas, a rich Jewish industrialist, and a second son – Renaud – by his mistress Isabelle de Comminges. He was unable to marry her because she could not divorce her insane husband Pillet-Will (who thought he was a dog). It was at the home of Isabelle de Comminges, who was known as 'the Panther', that Colette met the handsome Jouvenel. It was love at first sight.

In December 1910, Colette, who had become something of a celebrity as a result of the success of *La Vagabonde*, which obtained three votes when it was short-listed for the Prix Goncourt in November, began to write both for *Le Matin*, which had agreed to publish her short stories, and for its rival *Le Journal*.

Initially, she and Jouvenel kept their affair a secret, but rumours began to leak out in the spring of 1911 and before long the scandal broke.

In February, Colette went to Nice on tour with a friend called Lily de Rême and Auguste Hériot: there, she gave Auguste the slip and took a boat from Marseilles to Tunisia with Lily. Hériot fled to Rozven to seek solace from Missy, who was beginning to suspect that something disastrous was about to happen. Although Colette went back to her in April, their relationship was rapidly turning sour. Missy made scenes. Hériot left for Morocco and sent telegrams in which he pleaded with Colette. In May, she asked Georges Wague to provide her with an alibi by saying that she had a rehearsal to attend and went to Paris to meet Jouvenel. She could no longer live without him. Leaving Missy 'using a riding crop and ants' eggs to bring up a five-day-old crow and a two-week-old chaffinch',[2] Colette left to give a series of performances in Geneva, where Jouvenel had arranged to meet her. Matters then became more complicated. Hériot did not know that Jouvenel was with Colette and wanted to go to Geneva. She sent telegrams forbidding him to do so. Jouvenel was, like Willy, a formidable swordsman. He had recently fought a duel with the editorial secretary of *Le Journal*, who had insulted him in his paper. The duel ended with both men wounded in the forearm. As Colette's letter to her dear friend Léon Hamel shows, events now began to move very rapidly:

Do you know that, the day after his duel, Jouvenel turned up in Lausanne, wounded and with his arm in a sling, declaring that he neither could nor would live without me? Do you know that at the same time Hériot wanted to join me in Switzerland and that I stopped him by sending mad, lying and contradictory telegrams? Do you know that when he returned to Paris, Jouvenel admitted to the Panther that he loved another woman? She immediately swore that she would kill the other woman, whoever she was. Jouvenel, who was quite distraught, told me of this threat, and I said, 'I'm going to see her.' And I did go to see her. And I told her, 'I am the other woman.' She collapsed and pleaded with me. But her moment of weakness did not last long, and two days later she announced to Jouvenel that she intended to kill me. Distraught again, Jouvenel had Sauerwein [another editor of *Le Matin*] pick me up and the three of us drove to Rozven. We found Missy icy and disgusted as she had just heard the news from the Panther. Then my two guards left me and Paul Barlet[3] mounted guard, revolver at the ready. Still icy and disgusted, Missy decamped for Honfleur. Shortly afterwards [three days later] Jouvenel telephoned to tell me to go to him, and Sauerwein came to fetch me because the Panther was still prowling around with a revolver and looking for me. That was the beginning of a period of semi-incarceration in Paris, where I was guarded by the Sûreté as well as by Jouvenel, Sauerwein and Sapène, the three pillars of *Le Matin*,[4] as though I were a precious reliquary. Believe it or not, that period has just ended, thanks to a magnificent, providential and quite unexpected event. Tired of practising shooting at Gastinne-Reinette's [*sic*], Monsieur Hériot and Madame Panther have gone off together on his yacht the *Esmerald* for at least a six weeks' cruise after having astonished their home port of Le Havre with their spectacular drunken parties. Isn't that fine? Isn't it theatrical? Really too much, don't you think?

In the meantime Jouvenel distinguished himself by his honourable actions, which earned him little esteem from Missy. Basically, Missy adores Hériot; she prepared a room for him here and intended to force him on me in quasi-conjugal style. That was more than enough to put me off that young man for life. Jouvenel has had his house made ready for me. He has no fortune, but he does have *Le Matin* (about 40,000 francs a year) and, as I make my own living, we'll get by. Do I need to tell you again that I love this man, who is tender, unsociable and incurably honest? No need to. . . .

Missy has bought Princesse, a villa three kilometres from here. That snippet of information sounds like an epilogue, doesn't it? The day after tomorrow, I will be leaving for Castel-Novel, Jouvenel's château in the Corrèze. Missy is still icy and disgusted, and I can't get a sensible word out of her, no matter what I do. I assure you, it's not malice on my part; I feel very sad about it.[5]

Playing the femme fatale was a new role for Colette, and she obviously enjoyed it. At last something interesting was happening. At last she was the centre of attention. At last she was the heroine of the play. This was just what she had wanted when she was a girl in Saint-Sauveur and dreamed of being abducted.

Exit Missy, who left Colette the house in Rozven to remember her by. Colette rarely saw her after this, and Missy never recovered from the blow. Poor Mathilde de Morny ended her life in poverty at the age of eighty-one, alone, ruined and half mad. She died in June 1944 as a result of a terribly botched suicide attempt. Her only friend was Sacha Guitry, who looked after her until the end and who was her chief mourner.

When a woman falls in love again, she recovers her virginity. 'I have a new heart,' wrote Colette in 1911. At the age of thirty-eight, she was rediscovering all the excitement of adolescent passion with Henry de Jouvenel. It was no accident that she should call him 'Sidi' ('lord', in Arabic), 'the Pasha' or 'the Sultan'. Jouvenel's every wish was indeed her command.

Although she continued to make her living on the stage – in the summer of 1911 she was rehearsing *Bat' d'Af*[6] for the Bataclan and in December she appeared in *L'Oiseau de nuit* at the Gaîté-Rochechouart – Colette followed Jouvenel's example and became a journalist. His friends became her friends. She did everything with him and went everywhere with him – when she could, that is, for Sidi proved to be an errant as well as a jealous husband. He took every possible opportunity to be off: his paper, a war, diplomacy, the demands of his social life . . . and of his love life. He had a great appetite for women, and as a result he was known in Paris as 'il vit au grand air', an allusion to *La Vie au grand air*, a mass-circulation weekly [and an obscene pun: 'il vit au grand air' means 'he lives in the open air', but *vit* also means penis].

The coming months and years were to be the 'bourgeois' period in Colette's life, but she also experienced the torments of waiting and those of jealousy. *L'Entrave* (1913), *Les Heures longues* (1917) and the letters she wrote to various people all reflect the sufferings of a woman who is anxiously waiting for the man she loves, while he seems to have been 'born to please effortlessly, to seduce and then vanish' like Jean in *L'Entrave*, of whom May says, 'He is an expert at running away, and you can never get him back.'[7]

Once again, Colette was in love. And once again, she trampled her own dignity underfoot. In order to keep 'the avid vagabond she wanted to be tied to', she committed a man's mistake. She has one of her characters say, 'There are two kinds of love; the love that is never satisfied and makes you hateful to everyone, and the love that is satisfied and turns you into an idiot.'[8]

In the autumn of 1911, she and Jouvenel moved into a bungalow in the rue Cortambert in Passy. It was a wooden, Swiss-style chalet, old and fragile but charming. It had nearly an acre of garden, 'given over to old trees, wild roses, hazels and free-ranging cats.'[9]

For the first time since her arrival in Paris, Colette was living in a house surrounded by trees, with dogs scratching at the door and logs burning in the hearth.

I owe a great deal to the chalet in Passy. Beneath its balconies and trefoil fretwork, I lived the life of a real woman, a life interspersed with ordinary pains that could be cured, rebellions, laughter and acts of cowardice. It was there that I acquired a taste for decorating and for destroying. There, I worked, spurred on by the need for money. I enjoyed hours of laziness there.[10]

Despite her fame, the hint of scandal that had clung to Colette since the *Claudine* books and the scene at the Moulin Rouge meant that not everyone would receive her. Before she could write regularly for *Le Matin*, Jouvenel had some sharp words with his fellow editor Stéphane Lauzanne, who even threatened to resign if 'that acrobat' joined the paper.

Sido too was dubious about her daughter's new career, but for different reasons. 'So you're going to write an article for *Le Matin* every week. It's a lot, and I deplore your decision, because journalism spells death for a novelist. It's a pity as far as you are concerned. Don't squander your talent, my darling, it's worth more than this.'[11]

Sido was also worried about Jouvenel, as she suspected that he was becoming more and more important to Colette. Like any mother, the ageing Madame Colette, who was soon to die in Châtillon, was always worried about her children. And it has to be said that Colette's life was not designed to reassure her mother. In her letters, Sido was always concerned for her daughter's health. She was afraid that she would catch cold as she came off stage, that she was not getting enough sleep, and so on. That was why she had not objected to Colette living with Missy. For Sido, the care with which Missy looked after her daughter was more important than any moral consideration. 'Oh! so you are going to visit opium dens? That should be interesting, provided that you don't sample anything. It reassures me to know that Missy will be there, because you are not like your mother: I resist my passions.'[12] She realized that Missy was far from being a threat to Colette. For similar reasons, she had also tolerated her daughter's relationship with young Hériot, whom Colette described as a charming and harmless 'imbecile'. But Sido was not certain what to make of Jouvenel. The famous letter from Sido that opens *La*

Naissance du jour is not the real one. The real letter she sent to Jouvenel to accept his invitation contains a phrase which sums up all her doubts: she only agreed to meet him 'to get to know you and to do my best to find out why she has so enthusiastically kicked over the traces for you.'[13] The dialogue with Sido which Colette reproduces in *La Naissance du jour* is also significant:

'Are you very fond of this Monsieur X? [Jouvenel]'
'But, *maman*, I love him.'
'Of course you love him, of course you do.'
She thought again, making an effort to hold back the words her celestial cruelty was dictating.
'No, I'm not happy.'
I pretended to be shy, lowered my eyes to concentrate upon the image of a handsome, intelligent man who was envied and for whom the future shone brightly, and softly replied:
'You are hard to please.'
'No, I'm not happy. I prefer the other one, that boy you are treating like dirt [Hériot].'
'Oh, *maman* . . . he's an imbecile.'
'Yes, he's an imbecile. . . . That's the whole point. [. . .] You wrote such beautiful things when you were with him, Minet-Chéri [. . .] You're taking an interest in this other man and giving him the most precious thing you have. And then to top it all, he may make you unhappy. That is probably what will happen [. . .] If I told you everything that I can foresee [. . .] Luckily, you are not in very great danger.'[14]

The beginning of an affair is always wonderful. Colette and Jouvenel were always together. At the beginning of 1912, they went to Grenoble and visited the Grande Chartreuse. In April, Colette was applauded at the Bataclan. She played 'The Cat in Love' in *Ça grise*, and *Comœdia* praised 'the supple, lascivious and teasing sensuality of her original and varied talents'.

In May Jean Sapène invited them to his home in Normandy and Jouvenel took her to Trouville. This was Colette's first experience of the 'funereal charms of that elegant necropolis.'[15]

In the same letter, she adds: 'We are eating a lot and eating well. I have only to look at garlic to put on weight' (Colette loved garlic and raw onions). When Colette was happy, she ate even more than usual, and that is saying something. The delight she took in food went hand in hand with her extraordinary sensuality. Food, like scents, played an important part in her life and she describes food so well that it is impossible to read certain passages in her books and letters without a feeling of arousal similar to that provoked by erotic literature.

Colette's love of food, which she called *gueulardise*, was quite in keeping with the mood of the times. As we can see from contemporary menus, the pleasures of the table were of considerable importance in French society. Unfortunately, Colette's liking for food had harmful physical effects. She had been putting on weight for some time. Although Natalie Barney was always a friend to Colette, she also had a sharp tongue (though Colette gave as good as she got), and in her *Souvenirs indiscrets* she notes: 'When I first met Colette at the turn of the century, she was no longer the slender adolescent with plaits lying in a hammock [a reference to a photograph: see Ill.40] but a well-built young woman with sturdy legs, a thickening waist and a rounded bottom.'[16] Which is not surprising, if we recall that in 1902 she told a friend, 'I have made a bet with myself that I can eat four hundred hazelnuts between lunch and dinner.'[17] In 1922, she weighed over 80 kilos (176 pounds, or 12½ stone), which is a lot, given her height.

Gradually, she fell into the habit of not taking exercise. When Christiane Mendelys (Georges Wague's wife) criticized her for this, she replied: 'And who told you that I am not taking enough physical exercise? I've discovered a new method, that's all. The Sidi method. Excellent. No public classes. Private lessons – extremely private lessons.'[18] But a few lines later she adds: 'We've been wolfing *brandade* at Blanc's'.[19]

Her natural inclinations aside, Colette's love of food went back to her childhood in Puisaye. She was a Burgundian and inherited her taste for food and wine from her parents. In *Prisons et Paradis*, she tells us that her father taught her to appreciate the taste of Muscat de Frontignan when she was three. In order to build up her strength when she was an adolescent, Sido would bring up bottles of Château-Larose, Château-Lafite, Chambertin and Corton from the cellar, where she had hidden them during the Franco-Prussian war of 1870 for fear of looting. 'I drank my way through my father's cellar, daintily, glass by glass. My mother would recork the half-empty bottle and observe the effects of the finest of French vintages on my cheeks.'[20]

She also learned to enjoy the delights of cheese as a child: camembert, roquefort, *fromage à la cendre* and *fromage à la claie* served with a dandelion salad dressed with walnut oil and washed down with Treigny. She went to the market with Sido to buy cheese and delicious butter wrapped in chestnut leaves.

All women are fond of cheese, and the only reason they have stopped eating it is that their lives are governed by a dreadful neurosis about being slim. Women used to be better at choosing cheese than any man. Feeling the rind, gauging the elasticity and softness, and guessing what a cheese will be like is rather like the art of water divining . . . If I had a son who was looking for a wife, I would tell him never to trust a girl who doesn't like wine, truffles, cheese and music.[21]

Colette never forgot the tips on tending fires that were handed down from mother to daughter in her native province. She never lost the art of keeping the embers glowing, the embers which 'make everything you entrust to them taste so succulent' – apples, pears, potatoes, truffles, slow-cooking *daubes* and beef stew with carrots. It was as a girl in Puisaye that she first acquired her immoderate and lyrical taste for truffles. For the rest of her life she sang their praises, caressing them with the words of the gourmet. Down in central France she even went out one day with a little black sow to look for truffles. One could almost say that the scent of the black truffles of Périgord perfumed all her loves.

Although she was immensely and flamboyantly greedy, Colette was no *cordon bleu* and rarely cooked, unless, as we shall see, she did so out of love or friendship. Nor, of course, did she care for elaborate, sophisticated dishes: she liked good things, things full of flavour, stimulating to the taste buds, the stomach and the soul, the kind of food that helps one live through sorrow and pain, which warms one and which transforms life at the most difficult moments. 'A nice little country *terrine*, Monsieur! You are kind! I've been eating sweet things for two days now, and I know that tomorrow smoked herring and cod with potatoes or a garlic salad are the only things that will make life worth living', she wrote to Charles Saglio, the editor of *La Vie parisienne*, in 1907.[22] She also sang the praises of the flatfish, shrimps and lobsters of Le Crotoy and Rozven: 'No one can resist a dish of fresh shrimps as an hors d'oeuvre. . . . Oh, what a delicious little rosé wine!' Then there were the joys of Marguerite Moreno's *confit d'oie*, Annie de Pène's beef in red wine, and raw onions at every meal at Castel-Novel: 'I am going to bed stuffed with hot girdle cake, and raw chives and garlic – it's already quarter past nine.'[23] 'I smell of garlic, sausage, *fromage blanc* mixed with pepper and raw onion . . . yesterday we ate pine kernels, making the nuts pop in the fire.'[24]

All this obviously had certain disadvantages in terms of her health, not to mention the weight she was putting on.

Continued on p. 182

The 'café au lait' in Chéri

There is in *Chéri* a reference to a 'café au lait de concierge' that has aroused – and I choose my words advisedly – a hungry curiosity, which I have until now left unsatisfied. A concierge once gave me this recipe for a breakfast guaranteed to dispel the shivers on winter mornings.

Take a small soup tureen – the individual soup tureen you would use for a *soupe gratinée* – or a sturdy bowl in fire-proof china. Pour in your milky coffee, prepared and sugared according to taste. Cut some hearty slices of bread – use household bread, refined white will not do – butter them lavishly and lay them *on* the coffee, ensuring they are not submerged. Then all you have to do is place the whole thing in the oven and leave it there until your breakfast is browned and crusty, with fat, buttery bubbles sizzling here and there on the surface.

Before breaking your raft of roasted bread, sprinkle on some salt. Salt counteracting the sugar, sugar with a faint taste of salt, that is one of the great principles of cooking that is neglected in a number of Parisian puddings and pastries, which taste bland simply because they lack a pinch of salt.

(Marie-Claire, 27 January 1939)

330

331

329-331   Colette the gourmet.

Milk of fresh almonds

To make two litres of almond milk you will need rather more than a kilo of fresh, blanched almonds in perfect condition. Pound them in a marble mortar with a small quantity of sugar. Add, drop by drop, sufficient water to make a liquid paste. Cover with a cloth and leave the mortar and its contents overnight in a cool place. Next day, strain through a bag of cambric or fine muslin. Test, add a little more sugar, make up the quantity to two litres with water [. . .] Never beat almond milk, just place a green leaf of lemon balm on the creamy blue-tinged surface, so that it floats on top, tapered like a Chinese junk . . . And do not forget – if you do all is lost – a single drop of rose water, just one drop . . .

(Prisons et Paradis)

179

Truffles, in the style of Colette

. . . you have purchased your truffle, now eat it on its own, all pungent and grainy, eat it like the vegetable it is, in generous helpings. Once it has been pared, it will not give you much trouble; its incomparable flavour disdains elaborations and combinations. Cover with a good white wine, very dry – keep your champagne for parties, truffles don't need it – salt lightly, pepper sparingly and cook in your black covered casserole. Keep at a constant boil for twenty-five minutes, adding to the swirling foamy liquid [. . .] twenty or so cubes of bacon, half-fat, half-lean, to enrich the sauce. No other spices! [. . .] Your truffles should be brought straight to the table in their liquor. Serve yourself without stinting; truffles stimulate the appetite and they aid the digestion . . .

Always drink wine with truffles. In the absence of a full-blooded burgundy of illustrious vintage, choose a robust but smooth Mercurey. Don't drink too much. In the part of the world where I come from, they say that during a good meal you are not thirsty, but 'hungry for a drink'.

(*Paysages et Portraits*)

332-334 The pleasures of bread and wine.

332

Chicken baked in embers

To make chicken in embers you must plaster the unplucked bird all over with wet clay of the kind potters use. You need do no more than clean it carefully beforehand and sprinkle pepper and salt in the cavity. The natural juices trapped inside will do the rest. The lump of clay with its gallinaceous contents should then be baked for a longish period in a thick heap of glowing ashes, surrounded on all sides by hot embers which you must keep fanned and stoked. After three-quarters of an hour the lump of clay will have turned into a big terracotta egg. Break this open: all the feathers and part of the skin will come away with the potsherds, and the mild perfection of the tender fowl will encourage you to a faintly savage and prehistoric enjoyment of your food . . .

(*Prisons et Paradis*)

333

334

Orange wine

This dates back to a year when the oranges around Hyères were particularly fine and had ripened until they were red. I took four litres of dry yellow Cavalaire wine and added to it one litre of good Armagnac, making my friends exclaim: 'What a tragedy! Fancy sacrificing the best brandy to an undrinkable ratafia!' Amid the protests I cut up and dropped in four thinly-sliced oranges, a lemon which a moment ago had been hanging from its tree, a vanilla pod silvery as an old man, and six hundred grammes of cane sugar. A large jar was pressed into service, stoppered with a cork and cloth, and it was left to steep for fifty days; all I had to do then was strain and decant it into bottles.

Is it good? Parisiennes, you arrive home at the end of a bitter winter afternoon, or after one of those deceptive spring days lashed with rain and hail and whipped by piercing sunbeams, your shoulders are shaking, you blow your nose, you feel your forehead, examine your tongue, and you moan, 'I don't know what's the matter with me . . .'. Well, I know. You need a little glass of orange wine.

(Prisons et Paradis)

Colette paid for her greed with indigestion, liver trouble and bouts of intestinal inflammation that left her prostrate. In the summer of 1908 she speaks of being 'laid low by eating contaminated mussels'. She also suffered from violent indigestion and kidney trouble. But, to her mother's regret, she never did resist her passions, and two days later she was at it again: 'I feel a little better, though a delicious stuffed cabbage with cider and currant tart provoked a slight but well-merited relapse.' Two days later, she had another relapse: 'I rather overdid it with the tomatoes and the apricots, not to mention the cider.' Colette clearly had a lot in common with Louis XIV's sister-in-law, the truculent Princess Palatine, who ate black pudding with cabbage to cure her indigestion. Compulsive eating is a form of emotional compensation, to use psychoanalytic jargon, but a taste for good things can also be the sign of a conscious wish to keep sadness at bay.

Colette was too intelligent and too clear-headed to have the gift of contentment. But at the same time, she had an instinctive horror of sadness. Eating was one way to fight it off, and she was convinced that an empty stomach is an invitation to despair. If need be, she would go to extremes. The champagne, the foie gras, the oysters, the Château d'Yquem and the truffles, which she would have liked to eat as generously as potatoes – 'If I cannot have too many truffles, I will do without truffles'[25] – represented a form of exorcism, defences that were more effective than artifical tranquillizers, which she never trusted.

In a radio interview, Germaine Beaumont once said that when her mother Annie de Pène died in 1918, Colette refused to join in her tears and told her that physical pleasure could overcome even the worst grief. To prove her point, she immediately took Germaine to Prunier's and ordered a dish of prawns. Much later,

when Colette herself was going through a period of depression, her daughter Colette de Jouvenel reminded her of her own principles in a letter: 'I would remind you of an excellent old piece of maternal advice: "The stomach comes first."'[26]

What was going on between Colette and her Sidi in the early summer of 1912? She told her confidant Léon Hamel that there had been a 'singular crisis'. Jouvenel and Colette had suddenly decided to separate, but they did not actually do so. Perhaps Jouvenel was involved with another woman. Colette was obviously hurt, but as usual she put a bold face on it. 'I do not despair of treating him as casually as I treated Hériot', she told Hamel.[27]

The problem was that she was much more attached to Jouvenel than she ever had been to Hériot. A trip to Tours to cover a trial for *Le Matin* did nothing to take her mind off things. 'Alas, I miss the presence of an unworthy creature, I miss his warmth, the sound of his voice, his lies, his ridiculous childish tricks.'[28]

She was also having money problems, as her fees were not being paid on time. Colette took refuge in writing, and began *L'Entrave*. She was still living in Jouvenel's chalet in Passy. Before he left, he asked her to take charge of some interior decorating, 'as though I were to end my days in this house', she said sadly in an attempt to ward off bad luck. In order to raise some money, she asked Auguste Hériot – of all people – to pawn her pearl necklace. He still adored her, even though she had thrown him over, and despite his affair with the Panther.

L'Entrave is a bitter book and reflects Colette's feelings as she waited for Sidi in the gloomy summer of 1912, a woman in love and in despair. She was so much in love with Jouvenel and so miserable at being separated from him that she swallowed her pride and was ready to do anything to get him back. 'I heard two assertive young women saying, "When it comes to love, my motto is all or nothing." That's all very well, but a little bit of nothing is quite something, if it is wrapped up nicely.'[29]

But on 17 August, her mood suddenly changed. Sidi had come back. The nightmare was over. Colette was ecstatic. 'I am letting myself enjoy an ephemeral, animal happiness, and I will have to pay the price for it.'[30] She compared herself to a pear that has been bruised by hail.

Her troubles were not, however, over. A letter summoned her to Châtillon; Sido was very ill and was asking for her. She died a month later, on 25 September, at the age of seventy-seven.

Colette announced the news in a short letter to Hamel. The more than controlled emotion anticipates the beginning of Camus's L'Etranger:

Dear Hamel, *Maman* died the day before yesterday. I do not want to go to the funeral. I have told almost no one and I am wearing no outward sign of mourning [this was in accordance with Sido's wish, as recounted by Colette in La Maison de Claudine: 'I never want to see you in mourning. You know very well that I only like you in pink and some blues'[31]]. For the moment, things are not too bad. But I am tormented by one silly idea: never again will I be able to write to my mother as I used to do so often. . . . I am still appearing in L'Oiseau [de nuit] and carrying on with life as usual, that goes without saying. But it is the same whenever I am hurt . . . I have an attack of internal inflammation which is very painful.[32]

Eleven years later, in a letter to Marguerite Moreno, she recounts opening a drawer and finding, purely by chance, one of her mother's last letters:

It is so strange, you successfully fight back tears and bear up well at the most difficult times. And then someone gives you a friendly wave from behind a window [. . .] a letter falls out of a drawer – and your whole world falls apart.[33]

Now that she could no longer write to her beloved Sido, to whom she told everything (or almost everything), Colette's main confidantes were to be Marguerite Moreno, Annie de Pène and her daughter Germaine Beaumont, and Hélène Picard, a young poet.

Annie de Pène, whose real name was Désirée Poutrel, was a writer and journalist. Between 1910 and 1918, when she died of Spanish influenza, she published several novels and two collections of poetry. She wrote for both L'Eclair and L'Oeuvre, whose editor Gustave Téry was her lover. It was through Henry de Jouvenel's brother Robert, an editor on L'Oeuvre and probably a former lover, that she first met Colette. The two women became close friends. Annie was pretty, shrewd and amusing, and an excellent cook. She had previously been married to a man called Battendier, and in 1890 she had a daughter, who was to become Germaine Beaumont, the well-known novelist and member of the Prix Fémina jury, and who died in the spring of 1983.

Colette was now working as a reporter and on 13 June 1912 she made her first flight in a dirigible.

Shortly after Sido's death, Colette found that she was pregnant, and on 19 December 1912 at 4.30 p.m. she married Henry de Jouvenel. Léon Hamel was her witness. Colette thus became Madame la Baronne de Jouvenel. (She was later to say that being a Baronne did her as much good as having a feather on her backside.)

She greeted the news that she was definitely pregnant with 'a considered suspicion.' Contrary to popular belief, not all women are fitted to have children and Colette had no maternal streak. It was no accident that she waited until she was forty to have her one and only child. She was more surprised than anyone at the state in which she found herself in the autumn of 1912. Indeed, she was almost embarrassed. She said nothing and went on appearing in L'Oiseau. One day, Sauerwein said to her,

'Do you know what you are doing? You're reacting to the pregnancy like a man. A pregnancy should be more cheerful than that. Put your hat on and come and have a strawberry ice-cream at Poirée-Blanche's'.[34]

In view of her love of life, plants and animals, Colette's attitude to motherhood was somewhat strange. It may have been a reaction against the climate of her late-nineteenth-century childhood, which required women to conform to the image of the 'angel bending over the cradle'. It may also have been that it is difficult to become a mother when you have been the daughter of someone like Sido for so long and have enjoyed being a daughter so much. Perhaps we are born parents or children.

Colette's maternal instincts usually took on a sexual aspect and found expression in her relationships with young men and women. But she was certainly not enthusiastic about real children. She thought of them as animals. During her pregnancy she described herself as 'a swollen she-rat', and said things like 'the complacency of a pregnant she-animal is overcoming me' and 'My litter is stirring inside me.' She would have none of the usual sentimentality or the classic silly prattle. It was as though she mistrusted mother love and its dangerous excesses.

For Colette, children were always 'fruit' or 'products'. And they were always in the way. In 1924, she wrote to Marguerite Moreno from Rozven: 'There is a child cluttering up the caretaker's lodge. He was born prematurely at seven months and he cries weakly; he is probably asking to leave this world.'[35] In 1939, she tried to help a typist who had 'a backward child twenty-three months old with rickets, which can neither walk nor talk' and wrote to Lucie Saglio: 'I would like to take the child off her hands (it is with a nurse). What can one do for a baby of that age? He is alive, but only just, and goes on living at his mother's expense. Aren't there homes for subnormal children? Homes that cost nothing or almost nothing?'[36]

Colette's black sense of humour could at times border on the surreal: 'Dr Marthe Lamy [Colette's doctor] delivered a poor creature of a fruit that had been growing for ten months and was threatening to suffocate her; a child as big as a sheep, complete with hair, moustache and everything.'[37]

At times one would swear that she fully agreed with her old friend Alfred Jarry's comment on seeing a square full of children: 'How painfully one feels the absence of an ogre!'

Once she became reconciled to being a mother, however, she decided to make the best of it and turned her 'man's pregnancy' into 'one long party'. Ever watchful, she observed the 'state of pride or banal magnificence I enjoyed as my fruit ripened.' And she went on joking: 'Towards the end I looked like a rat rolling away a stolen egg.'[38]

On 3 July 1913, she gave birth to a daughter, Colette de Jouvenel. 'I have a little she-rat, and I paid the price for her: thirty hours without *any* respite, chloroform and forceps. She is well-shaped and pretty.'[39] She called her daughter Bel-Gazou (in the patois of the Nevers region, *gazoute* means 'little girl'). She often described her, but she did so as though she were describing a plant or an animal. Sometimes she writes of the wonder of a human being taking shape. She watched her grow up, blossom and 'open out'. She watched her, but only intermittently. Colette soon found an English nurse for Bel-Gazou and only saw her during the holidays at Rozven or Castel-Novel. Three months after the birth of her daughter, she wrote: 'I have experienced agony, worry, boredom and intense irritation, and I am writing to you as last time, on one hand shouting "Whew! I've found a nurse!", and with the other hand mopping my brow.'[40] Bel-Gazou was later sent to boarding school. Colette liked children, but not too close to her.

I met Bel-Gazou when she was sixty. I am sorry that I did not get to know her better, as she was a lively, intelligent woman who had inherited her mother's sense of humour. When anyone mentioned Colette to her, she remained strangely silent. One day, however, she told me, 'I found my mother very intimidating.'

Neither the assassination that took place in Sarajevo that June nor the political upheavals that shook Europe as it teetered on the brink of war disturbed Colette's holidays in Rozven in July 1914. It was a happy summer: Sidi was there, swimming nude or larking on the beach, and Bel-Gazou, now one year old, according to her mother looked 'superb, golden brown as a pie-crust'. Colette also had a friend at her side: Musidora, the beautiful actress who was to play the Vagabond when the book was filmed in Rome. They went fishing, caught butterflies and went into raptures over the rainbow-coloured jellyfish. As always, the sea brought Colette back to life, and she was tireless. She would swim for hours and do gymnastics. When she was not romping in the waves, she was working on the villa. She painted, polished and moved furniture. At the same time she was beginning to plan a new novel. A few years later, it was to be published as *Chéri*.

There was also time to discuss a political event that had become the talk of the whole of France: the trial of Madame Caillaux. Joseph Caillaux, a former Prime Minister and Minister for Finance, had been criticized for his anti-war stance and for his ambiguous links with Germany. Robert de Jouvenel had attacked him in *L'Oeuvre* and *Le Figaro* had launched a particularly violent campaign against him. Outraged at the attacks on her husband and at all the revelations about his private life, Madame Caillaux focussed her anger on *Le Figaro's* editor: on 16 March she went to see Calmette at the paper's offices in the rue Drouot and shot him with a small Browning – which she had learned to use at Gastinne-Renette's range – concealed in her muff. (In 1914 it was not unusual for delicate little revolvers to nestle in reticules and muffs next to embroidered handkerchiefs and powder compacts. Colette herself later had one, but never used it.) When the police came to arrest her, Madame Caillaux cried, 'Do not touch me. I am a lady.' Women still had considerable prestige in the early years of the century. At the trial much play was made of *crime passionnel* and 'frayed nerves'. Whatever the reasons, Madame Caillaux was acquitted on 28 July. Some judges are extraordinarily susceptible to tears.

But in both Rozven and Paris, there were more serious matters to worry about than the fate of Madame Caillaux: war.

During the last week of July, troops were beginning to be gathered and officers were recalled from leave. On 31 July, Jaurès, who had persuaded the 'national' congress of the PSU to call a general strike in the event of a general mobilization, was assassinated in the rue du Croissant. At 3.45 p.m. on 1 August, Viviani gave the order for general mobilization. War broke out on 5 August. Colette, who had gone to Saint-Malo to find out what was happening, heard the news amid the sound of the tocsin, of the town drum, and of shouting, weeping crowds. This time, the holiday was over.

They returned to a dead city. Trams, cabs and buses had mysteriously disappeared from the streets of Paris. The only pedestrians were women rushing out to buy provisions. Older women still remembered the famine of 1870 and were besieging grocers' shops, hoarding tinned goods, flour, sugar and pasta. Fear of food shortages made the whole of France panic.

The heat was terrible. All the smart shops in the rue de la Paix were closed; the only one that remained open was staffed by cocottes in all their finery selling tricolour rosettes they had made to benefit the Red Cross. Maps showing the countries to which troops had been committed were on display in public buildings to allow passers-by to follow the course of operations.

Marguerite Moreno lived in the rue Jean de Boulogne, two minutes from Colette's house, and they began to discuss pooling their resources. This was the beginning of the *phalanstère* or commune which Annie de Pène and Musidora, who lived nearby in the impasse Herran and the rue Descamps respectively, also joined.

Second Lieutenant Henry de Jouvenel was called up and joined the 29th Territorial Infantry. On 12 August, he departed for Verdun. 'Colette's husband left yesterday', wrote Marguerite Moreno. 'As soon as he put on his uniform, he was miles away from her and everything else.'[41] Before he left, he sent a letter to his friend Anatole de Monzie: 'I am leaving. I expect to come back, of course, but you never know. If I don't, please look after my family.'[42]

'Colette is trying to be brave', wrote Marguerite Moreno. 'At the moment, women are keeping a stiff upper lip.' Colette tried to get by as best she could. Jouvenel no longer had his salary from the newspaper and could not help her. She had barely enough to live on. She left her daughter in peace in Rozven, where her nurse could look after her, and wrote articles for *Le Matin*.

She tried to be brave, but she was worried about Jouvenel, who wrote to her from time to time, but not often enough for her liking. The post was in chaos and no private telephone calls to the East were allowed. The news from the front published by the newspaper was either censored or too optimistic to be believed.

Fortunately, she had her friends in the *phalanstère*. Musidora often slept at Colette's because she was afraid of the zeppelins that were floating over Paris. The four women shared the shopping, cooking and cleaning.

We were a good squad of women. We washed the sheets by hand and wrung them out by twisting them on a big brass tap. Marguerite Moreno presided over the housework with a cigarette between her lips, pouring out a cheerful stream of news – true and false – anecdotes and predictions [. . .] Moreno would have no idlers in our sixteenth-*arrondissement phalanstère*, and tirelessly sowed the miraculous seed of laughter, the nervous, compulsive laughter of women in wartime, the insolence that comes out when danger is near, the wordplay which is as intoxicating as a draft of spirits.[43]

Annie de Pène enjoyed her food greatly and was an expert cook; even during the war she knew where to find the tenderest chickens and the freshest vegetables.

France was in patriotic mood. As a child, Colette had been influenced by the anti-German spirit of *revanchisme* that followed the defeat of 1870, and she shared that mood. Like many women who had been left behind, she wanted to make herself useful, and in October 1914 she worked as a volunteer night nurse in the Lycée Janson de Sailly, which had been turned into a military hospital. 'This is a terrible job and I am not surprised that it is not very popular. What with alerts that last thirteen hours, and caring for the men, when morning comes we are somewhat haggard.'[44]

Bel-Gazou and her nurse left Rozven for Castel-Novel, and in December Colette went to join her husband in Verdun. This was not easy, as civilians could not go into the frontier area without special permission. Colette wanted so much to be at Sidi's side that she used a false name and papers to deceive the police. After thirty hours in a blacked-out train which slowly crawled from Châlons to Verdun, she finally reached her husband. In Verdun, the Jouvenels lived at 15bis rue d'Anthouard. Colette could not show her face or even go to the window for fear of being seen by the neighbours. She became a voluntary prisoner, and only ventured out for a breath of fresh air at night. She was not the only woman in this position. Many wives and mistresses had gone secretly to Verdun and were living there as recluses. 'There is talk of one woman who has not crossed the threshold of her prison for seven months. The only human face she sees is that of the man she loves. They say, she writes to distant friends that she is the happiest of women.'[45]

Colette described her days in Verdun in *Les Heures longues* (1917), but she also wrote letters to Annie de Pène in Paris. In the following extracts from those letters, which have never been published before, she gives a vivid account of her day-to-day life in Verdun.[46]

My dear Annie, I was terrified. Beautiful frost flowers on all the train windows. Relative solitude, no difficulty in getting here, an indifferent *gendarme*, in short the best of journeys. Sidi ... very much to my liking, although the business about the uniform caused us to fall out immediately and we exchanged such insults that I dare not ... I do believe that one of us went so far as to say, 'You are absolutely unbearable.' Rows between married couples are dreadful. . . .

I do the housework. The way I clean lettuce would horrify Maurice Leblanc: I throw away all the green bits, like the rich. Lots of guns. Lots of Taube [German aeroplanes] yesterday. Sidi wanted me to go down into the cellar! A cold is a lot more dangerous than gunfire . . .

I am leading a strange existence, my dear Annie. Sidi is careful not to take all his meals with me – in fact I only see him at one meal in four. But he is here from 9.30 in the evening onwards. As Louis XIV used to say to Madame de Maintenon, I won't go into that in any detail. He is woken at 7.30, but only so that he can enjoy breakfast and then go back to sleep until 8.45. Then life becomes serious. He belongs to the citadel and I belong to the broom, the slop pail and the bath tub.

Sidi reappears at about 2.30 – like an ephemeral star that shines for an hour and then vanishes. After dark I have the right to take a short walk along the Meuse – for my health. It is strange, Annie, to walk beside water I cannot see, on a river bank that I cannot see and that I will never see. In the distance, the reassuring sound of the guns. During the day, our men order us to stay on the ground floor when it's time for the Tauben. And that's it.

Colette had lost none of her interest in food, and wrote to Annie to thank her for sending a home-cooked stuffed chicken:

What a monster, and how wonderfully scented with cognac! It had the thighs of a woman, and the wings of an angel. Strictly between us, Annie, I will tell you that Sidi exclaimed: 'She mustn't marry Téry! He will get all the stuffed chickens!' There you have the egoism of the true artist and the fanatical gourmet. [. . .] Everything around us is peaceful. But then you suddenly hear that eight hundred wounded have just been brought in.

Colette returned to Paris, and then left once more for Verdun, again travelling clandestinely. There the correspondence continued.

[*Verdun, 1914 (written in pencil)*]
I've not seen a lot of Sidi, but I have seen enough of him to say that he is just as 'very handsome' as a first class pharmacist and that he finds me not unattractive. He will be back for dinner soon – and will stay for dinner until tomorrow morning, if I can put it that way.

I had such a fright at Verdun station! The *gendarme* wanted us to get back on the train – just like that. He threatened to come looking for us in four days' time, but we will take precautions. I am more stupid than words can tell. But Sidi is not all that much more intelligent, you know.

I am living in a cell. I am writing in pencil because the electricity is not working. The first words we exchanged on seeing each other were so stupid! I told Sidi, 'By the way, Annie is coming'. 'Why?' 'To make beef in red wine.' I didn't think I had said anything particularly funny, but Sidi gave me the giggles and I could not stop laughing. [. . .] I forgot to mention that the railway line was being shelled as we went along. Beautiful flashes in the night sky and beautiful dull 'booms'. Don't be alarmed. There was only one shell all day, and that fell beside the line. Sidi tells me there is very heavy fighting a few kilometres away – and I can hear it very clearly.

[*Verdun, Monday, 2 December 1914*]
. . . Apart from that, they say that there is a general offensive on and it sounds like something special. What a fine cannonade, Annie! It is magnificent. The house shakes, the windows rattle. You feel a gong beating in your stomach and the sound of tom-toms in your ears. No news, but I hope we will have some tomorrow or tonight. Hamel will tell you how I went to 'watch the battle' from the place de la Citadelle. It is beautiful to see from so close at hand the source of the pink glow and the circular aurora borealis lights which appear and disappear in the mist in the space of a tenth of a second. The noise is magnificent and as varied as the noise of a storm, now close at hand, now in the distance, now sharp, now dull. Apart from 'that', the only thing is that no one here talks about the war or takes any notice of it. [. . .]

When are you coming? There are only two *gendarmes* at the station. Pick out the better-looking one, the very good-looking *gendarme*. And then go to it! 'Screw up your eyes, let your jaw drop, and follow your nose', as Wague would say [. . .]

[*27 December 1914*]
I spent the day 'at the front', like everyone else. I will tell you about it [. . .] I am dead tired tonight. I set off at 8 for Clermont-sur-Argonne and other places that have been reduced to rubble.

[*Henry de Jouvenel to Annie de Pène. Verdun, 26 December 1914*]
I hold out little hope of seeing you here because all the soldiers in Verdun feel that they have to take themselves very seriously, particularly as they have nothing to do. I have to admit that Verdun is the biggest flop of the war.

They promised us that we would be at the centre of everything, but here we are in a forgotten corner. Our commanders are disappointed, and you can imagine the mood they are in. Because of all that, they are being very strict.

[*Undated letter*]
Do you know who I met on the train between Paris and Chalons? Madame du Gaste. She was wearing a hat with cherries on it, made up like an August peach, wearing a low-cut dress, and dripping with imitation pearls. I immediately realized that she was travelling incognito.

[*Verdun, 1914*]
I have to tell you about a great upheaval in my life. I am learning to play chess with Sidi. This is the only remaining pledge of love that I can give him; I am giving it to him.

[*Verdun, Saturday (early 1915)*]
Everything has changed. I leave on Monday evening.

I'm coming home, my dear Annie. I am not complaining, as I am coming back to you and my daughter. In any case, Sidi assures me that I will be able to come back to Verdun in three weeks – So, I leave on Wednesday evening and arrive on Thursday morning . . . and go to bed [. . .]

Annie, the black pudding!!! The black pudding and the butter!!! If the same craftsman made them both, blessed be the womb that bore him. I have yet to sing the posthumous praises of the truffles, those beautiful, noble truffles, black, no holes, no white spots. Would you believe that in their honour I became a cook? Since my first success, I dream of nothing but having lessons from you. Tell me, will you teach me to make beef in red wine, and *craquelins* [biscuits]? If you are willing, I will have hours of fascinating lessons with you . . . I am already planning mad evenings at the cinema and incomparable hours at the Petit-Casino.

Colette was obviously enjoying a rare period of happiness. Back in Verdun, she wrote to Annie on 14 May 1915:

I am all in favour of life. (Why are you laughing?) I simply mean that I am passionately in favour of life. Horror of horrors, I have to live behind shutters. But I am very well. I am enjoying the calm that comes to people who have achieved their aim in life. The guns mark the seconds with a good reassuring beat. Below me, there is a very pretty garden with birds in the chestnuts and the lilacs. The bitch is also fat through being kept indoors. The cat has two kittens. Everything is charming. I have not yet said anything about Sidi, but when it is light, you do not spend all your time saying, 'It is light', and I do not need to talk about him for you to know that he is the light of my life.

The journey via Bar is torture.

[21 July 1915]

I am working for *Le Matin* and *Le Flambeau*. I am limbering up with a few exercises. I am doing the cooking. As Robert de Jouvenel says, I do not like work, Annie . . . I will be back on 1 August, the day before or the day after. Make ready the garlands of beef in red wine, and let the chopped onion flow! You see, I am as stupid as ever. Your godson [Jouvenel had adopted Annie as his 'godmother' for the duration of the war] will be there too, thank God. You will see how cute he is when you put him through a little oral exam:

'What are you?'
'A darling girl.'
'And what else?'
'A sort of beauty, etc. etc.'

And when Sidi shows any sign of understanding literature or strategy, your pest of an Abramibarbusse won't miss the opportunity to say, very solemnly:

'He's a perfect example of a darling girl.'

[. . .] I have finished today's melancholy task for *Le Matin*. I am going to do some pastel work.

In 1915, Colette began to travel widely. She went to Italy initially as a journalist and then with her husband, who was posted there on a diplomatic mission. For the next two years, she lived alternately in Paris and in Italy, spending the holidays with her daughter at Castel-Novel.

Travelling for *Le Matin*, she reached Rome towards the end of June 1915, having journeyed via Turin and Modena. She tried to register at the Excelsior under the name 'Baronne de Jouvenel': there was considerable confusion, and the hotel refused to give her a room. It transpired that Claire Boas, who was divorced from Jouvenel but still used her married name, had stayed at the Excelsior a month earlier, and had not gone unnoticed. Claire Boas was not exactly the retiring type. She kept open house for the cream of the political and diplomatic world in her luxurious apartment on the boulevard Saint-Germain. Despite rationing, she also kept an excellent table. Claire was still young, rich and beautiful, vibrant in her feather boas and with violets in her hair. The circles she moved in included Anatole France, Philippe Berthelot (the charming secretary general to the Minister for Foreign Affairs, who was often the guest of honour at her dinner parties), Henri Bergson, Paul Claudel and Gabriele D'Annunzio.

Gabriele D'Annunzio, the prince of Monte Nevoso, was then at the height of his literary fame. His novels and poems were to be found in every self-respecting home. At the age of fifty-two he was still as dashing as a young man. Although he was bald and ugly, he was a breaker of hearts and had had countless love affairs. A few years earlier, he had eloped with a Roman princess and had been sentenced to five months in prison for adultery. The famous actress Eleonora Duse, who had created many roles in his plays, had been madly in love with him. Yes, he was ugly, but he was so charming, and so good with words . . . He was also an active politican. He had been elected to parliament and was regarded as the spokesman for nationalism. But his expensive lifestyle had ruined him, and to escape his creditors he had fled to France, where he was being kept by a Russian princess, and divided his time between Paris and Arcachon. In May 1915, shortly before Colette's arrival in Rome, D'Annunzio had gone to Genoa to exhort the people of Italy to join the allies. He was accompanied by Claire Boas, who was also devoted to the cause. She had had a huge Italian flag made in Paris, with a staff engraved by a Parisian jeweller. Louise Weiss travelled with them. Whenever the train stopped, they were acclaimed by crowds who showered them with lilies of the valley. Finally, they reached Rome.

It is not, then, difficult to understand why Colette was greeted with suspicion when she claimed to be the Baronne de Jouvenel. The hotel management thought that she was simply an adventuress. 'What do you think of that?' she wrote to Léon Hamel: 'This may be too much for my forgiving nature.'[47] Colette and Claire Boas were obviously not on friendly terms, though they did normally treat each other fairly diplomatically.

Colette moved to another hotel, where Gabriele D'Annunzio was staying in the room next to hers. Boni de Castellane was also there and acted as Colette's courier, taking her letters to Paris to avoid the censor.

Colette wandered around Rome and was particularly impressed by the gardens and fountains. 'It is very hot', she wrote to Annie de Pène. 'I am looking around, sight-seeing. I store up memories until I am exhausted, so how do you expect me to work? I'm scribbling down lots of rough notes, but I don't think I'll be able to work until I get home.' Venice she found 'very different from all the descriptions I have read.'[48] Despite the 'Asiatic heat', she was delighted when she finally received a telegram from Sidi, who had yet again been called away.

It was not until September that he joined her in Cernobbio on Lake Como. She waited impatiently for him, playing bezique with her brother-in-law Robert de Jouvenel and his mistress Zou. The two brothers were overjoyed at being together again. Ever since boyhood they had been close and their love of laughter made them good company. Both men were handsome and brilliant. Henry was a diplomat and Robert a businessman and a formidable pamphleteer, but they still enjoyed childhood games: Henry's son Bertrand de Jouvenel recalled how, as an adolescent, he watched his father and his uncle playing a form of cowboys and Indians at Castel-Novel.[49]

Colette remained in Cernobbio until the end of the year and stayed at the Villa d'Este while Jouvenel came and went. The hotel was extremely smart: 'People (other people) change three times a day, and then change again for the evening. The Jouvenel brothers love that.'[50] While Sidi was away, she wrote,

I console myself by looking at the lake, which is beautiful without being too picturesque or too blue. I go rowing, Annie. My strong arms are just what's needed. After only two lessons, I can row fairly well. And what energy! I cross the lake and recross it with Zou as though it were a mere puddle. I could take you to Como, and that means three hours at the oars. I am as proud as a flea that has learned to walk on its hind legs.[51]

At the end of 1916 Colette was back in Paris and was soon moving house again, to 62 boulevard Suchet in Auteuil, a town house with gardens at both back and front, which the Jouvenels took over from the actress Eve Lavallière.

I didn't touch the things she left behind. A black and ochre batik fabric covered the bedroom walls, and a red and white batik generously curtained three windows. There was a carpet patterned to look like a black and white marble pavement. A very low divan covered in tarnished gold lace offended one's sense of touch and, on wet days, one's sense of smell.[52]

During the war, she was alone in the house whenever she was in Paris.

I was alone in the house, with my man in the East and my child in the country. When the bombers flew overhead, the house echoed around me like an empty barrel. I was amazed to see that my old cat, a big blue Persian, seemed to be able to see them and follow their flight path through the ceiling.[53]

All men old enough to be conscripted were at the front and Paris had become a city of women. The women waited, hoped and wept. Others took advantage of their temporary celibacy, decided that half a loaf is better than no bread, and discovered the charms of very young men. (This was the theme of *Le Diable au corps*, which caused such a scandal in 1923.) Needless to say, there were a lot of divorces after the war. Many of the women were in mourning, but all busied themselves: some replaced men in the factories, while wealthier women devoted their time to nursing the wounded. Nurses' uniforms were all the rage. Hemlines began to rise and feminism was growing stronger. The absent are always in the wrong.

Although the guns were roaring less than a hundred kilometres away, in Paris itself the only warlike sound was that of the engines of the Zeppelins on night bombing raids. The Prefect of Police had ordered all windows to be blacked out as soon as it was dark.

It was impossible to ignore the war. The newspapers were carrying advertisements for artificial limbs. A wooden leg was as acceptable a gift as a tennis racket had once been. At Christmas 1915, sweets came in boxes shaped like *képis*, mess tins and drums. The traditional *bûche de Noël* Christmas log-shaped cake was replaced by a miniature trench made of chocolate. An anti-alcohol

campaign was launched, but with little success. Propagandists argued that President Poincaré drank nothing but water, much to the amusement of the *poilus* of Verdun. The campaign did not stop Colette drinking to the French advance.

The wave of patriotism affected every facet of life. The most fashionable name for little girls was Joffrette (after the military commander, Joffre) and at the Folies Bergères the girls kicked their legs in a revue entitled *En Avant!* The Touring Club de France sent a circular to hoteliers in coastal resorts warning them not to employ Austrians or Germans if they wanted to remain on its list of recommended hotels. It is true that before the war 75% of all hotel staff on the Côte d'Azur were German. Two new colours featured in the fashion collections, trench grey and *poilu* blue, which looked particularly well on blondes. *Embusqué* – shirker – became a deadly insult. Even children were affected by the prevailing mood: at school, they pinned little flags on maps to mark the French advance on the Eastern Front; Colette's daughter spotted *Tauben* and cheerfully sang patriotic songs.

The postmen's bags were full of love letters for men at Verdun, the fort of Douaumont and Le Chemin des Dames, letters from Lou to Apollinaire and from Colette to Henry de Jouvenel . . . Melancholy songs like *Roses are blooming in Picardy* and *La Valse bleu horizon* replaced the cheery *Madelon*. Pierre MacOrlan later wrote of the days when the women waited so anxiously:

> J'ai dans la mémoir', un' chanson qui bouge
> Le nom des pat'lins où t'as derrouillé
> Carency, Hablin, le Cabaret Rouge
> La rout' de Bapaum' où tu es resté. . . .

(A song is stirring in my memory – The names of the villages where you limbered up, Carency, Hablin, the Cabaret Rouge, The road to Bapaume, where they finished you off.)

In Paris, the Prefect banned the tango, which was thought to be unsuitable for such dramatic times. Conventional people began to wonder if it was quite the done thing to go to the theatre. On the other hand, society life continued to some extent and the theatres did not close. The cinemas were crowded and reserved free seats for the wounded. They showed military subjects and the first Charlie Chaplin films. Parties were still given, despite the food rationing. There were still plenty of people making the most of life behind the lines: men on leave, men who had succeeded in avoiding active service, serving diplomats and foreigners. On 28 December 1916, Paul Morand, who was then a young attaché to an ambassador, met Auguste Hériot at a luncheon given by the Baronne de Rothschild at the Ritz. Chéri swaggered in, fresh from the front with a clean bandage – 'the elegant wounded hero type, perfect for the cover of *La Vie parisienne*', noted Morand, 'wearing an identity bracelet from Cartier's, and saying things like "I will be wounded again in March", "I never ask for convalescent leave", and other boasts.'[54]

In 1917 Colette returned to Rome with Henry de Jouvenel, who had been appointed principal private secretary to his friend Anatole de Monzie, the Under-Secretary of State for the Merchant Navy. Temporarily released from military service, he was France's delegate to the Entente conference in Rome. They stayed at the Palace Hotel:

We have a little suite on the roof all to ourselves. The terrace is as big as my back garden in the boulevard Suchet. We have a breathtaking view over Rome and beyond. On clear days we can see the snow on the mountains. When it is cold, and it is often cold, we use an oil stove. No coal in the hotel; they keep it for heating the bathwater, thank God.[55]

In 1917, Rome, with its mild climate and its calm, was the playground of Europe. People took every possible political or diplomatic pretext to go there and to forget the horrors of war for a while. 'Between sittings, Berthelot comes to Rome and goes with Gonse to the Pincio in the pouring rain to haggle over a Venetian cage for 7,000 francs.'[56]

Society life was in full swing and Colette, at Jouvenel's side, was at the heart of it. She describes her life in her letters to Annie: 'Ah, my dear Annie. The number of people who arrived today! Briand, Lyautey, Thomas, and more Berthelots than I can count.'[57] The Jouvenels also became friendly with Pierre Laval, the militant socialist who had just turned down the post of Under-Secretary of State for the Interior at the request of his party, which refused to collaborate with Clemenceau.

Colette avoided the politicians because they bored her, and went for walks with her dog Gamelle, 'A model of tact. The perfect dog to travel with.'[58] She preferred the quieter areas of Rome: the garden of the Knights of Malta, and the area around the little church of Santa Maria in Cosmedin. She went to buy flowers from the Trinita de' Monti market. During Holy Week, she tells Annie, 'I was surprised to see scenes of what I can only call Catholic savagery: people climbing holy staircases on their knees, people licking the shape of the cross on pavements covered with spittle and mud and other filth, confessions going on every ten paces inside St Peter's.'[59]

In order to make up for the shortage of food in the hotel – no more than two dishes, and no butter or cheese on the table – Colette went to the markets to buy

A kind of cream cheese called 'buffalo's eye', which they sell in stoneware pots sealed with interwoven fresh iris leaves. There are ten soft, firm cheeses crammed into each pot. In the afternoon and the evening, I eat them as they come, as though they were sweets. I know how much you would enjoy the life I am leading here – it's almost like being in Auteuil.[60]

She was busy writing *Les Heures longues* – she later used the royalties to furnish the house in Rozven more comfortably – and waiting for Musidora, who was due to begin filming *La Vagabonde* in Rome.

If I started a chapter on high society in Rome, I would never get to the end of it. There are hordes of Roman aristocrats living in palaces that they cannot heat because the rooms are eight to ten metres high, shivering and coughing over little oil stoves. It is both comic and sad. There are also hordes of Teutonic ladies, divorcees who used to be married to Prussian generals and Polish ladies who were born to be something. Both comical and worrying.

Sidi came back this morning. I am delighted, but in moderation, as I have only seen him for three quarters of an hour since he got back. We had a quick lunch together and since then he has been showing twenty-four French parliamentarians around!!! Rather him than me.[61]

'I am seeing a lot of people,' she writes to Annie, 'but I will not let myself be invaded.' Colette was not, however, averse to society gossip, provided it was amusing, and delighted in exchanging choice morsels of scandal with Annie. They told each other about their friends' affairs and gleefully demolished reputations whenever they had the chance. Baronne Deslandes was a well-preserved former beauty. She originally came from Germany and used to be known as 'the little girl from Cologne'. She was a writer, and Barrès had once been in love with her. She gave Colette the material for a masterpiece of catty humour.

Annie, you know Baronne Deslandes, don't you? The ex-wife of Robert de Broglie; it was a morganatic marriage and she could not inherit the title. Before that she was Comtesse Fleury and, in literary circles, she was 'Ossit'. She is here, and there are some juicy stories about her. She is fifty-four, but she doesn't let that stop her. Far from it. She's been playing the trick she tried on young Broglie, but this time her quinquagenarian fires are singeing a young Duke of Galese, who is seventeen and a half.

She told him that she was twenty-five and a virgin (of course). [. . .] She calls him 'my little page' and drives him mad (the job was already half done). Intrigues, moonlight strolls, letters, bribes to servants. Old Galese learns everything; he puts the young man in a monastery, as though he were still living in the days of Louis XIV. Our sweet fiancée demands justice, pours out her grief and turns to the Count of Cossato, a sinister old Roman who lives in a gloomy palace. 'Look what they have done to me. They have locked up my fiancé in a monastery', and so on. Old Cossato listens, glowering from under his white eybrows without saying a word. Then he explodes: 'You've come to tell me that? You've come to find out what I think? I think Galese should have given his son a hundred *sous* twice a week, a hundred *sous*, do you hear, so that he could go to the whores. At least he would have learned what a woman is and wouldn't have fallen into the clutches of a mad old thing like you. A mad old thing, do you hear?' It's even better in Italian; you can hear the chink of money – '*cinque lire, cinque lire*'. And he went on shouting at her like that in the stairway. It's a good story, isn't it?[62]

Both Colette and Annie, in Rome and Paris respectively, were making plans on behalf of Musidora, who had been unlucky enough to fall in love with a pimp. Colette was even thinking of introducing her to Auguste Hériot as a distraction.

Musidora (whose real name was Jeanne Roques; her pseudonym came from a romance of the time of Louis-Philippe) was a superb brunette of twenty-eight with dark eyes and a pale skin. She had begun her career as a scantily-dressed singer and dancer in small theatres in Paris. She later appeared half-naked in an adaptation of *Paul et Virginie* at the Folies Bergères which must have made Bernardin de Saint-Pierre turn in his grave. As a result of that, Gaumont had approached her and asked her to play the Virgin in a film they were planning to shoot in Palestine. The project came to nothing, as Musidora innocently asked for one hundred francs a day. She made almost twenty-five films before she had her first real success – in the twelve episodes of Louis Feuillade's *Vampires* (1915) and then in the same director's twelve-part *Judex*. She then made four other successful films. Musidora had persuaded the producers to accept Colette's screenplay for *La Vagabonde*, and it was due to be filmed by Eugenio Perego and Ugo Falena in Rome in 1917. Musidora was more than just a beautiful woman: she was both talented and intelligent and wrote two novels, a play, a volume of memoirs and numerous articles on the cinema. But she had an unfortunate tendency to fall in love with men who were unworthy of her.

The previous autumn, Colette had been putting off signing the contract, worried about finding the right actress for *La Vagabonde*.

It's raining here, but it's not cold. A thousand cinemas, a thousand films, a thousand actresses; it is so stupid that it is frightening. So here I am, stuck again. The contract is fine, but the actresses! I tell you, Annie, it is impossible. Genuine *marquises* fighting to be on the screen, each one of them more stupid and more gauche than the next. At the opposite extreme, we have the professionals, who try so desperately to express emotion through their faces, their hands, their stomachs and their toes that the debauchery of expression makes you feel seasick. What a position to be in! We wanted to have Musidora; she has made a brilliant start, but won't leave her shark. Damn it all![63]

On 20 April 1917, Colette had the shock of learning that her beloved Léon Hamel was dead. 'I feel that I will miss him much more when I come back to Paris than I do at the moment; he was a transparent, fragile friend, who seemed to need only the bare necessities of life.'[64]

Lack of money eventually forced Colette to sign the contract to adapt *La Vagabonde*. The Jouvenels were finding it difficult to make ends meet. Life in Rome was expensive and Madame de Comminges, who was already receiving 6,000 francs a year to bring up Jouvenel's son, had demanded another 1,700, making it difficult for them to pay the April rent on their apartment. Colette wrote to Annie in Paris to ask her to sell the manuscript of *L'Ingénue libertine*, for which she hoped to get 3,000 francs from someone who had already bought other manuscripts from her.

Musi finally reached Rome, where Colette was working on the adaptation of her novel, at the end of April.

We are shooting *La Vagabonde*, sometimes (mostly) in a glass-roofed hall where you die of heat and thirst, and sometimes outside. We have been lent the gardens of the old Sciarra palace, and if you saw them, you would never want to leave them. A deluge of heavy flowers, of apple trees, double pink flowering plums, black, white and blue iris, paeonies, cascades of roses, torrents of wistaria, red lilies, early roses – I can't begin to describe it all. The gardens are magical. Giant trees, umbrella pines, the pure waters of Rome burbling in antique fountains. Two hundred dazzling peacocks roaming free; some are blue and some are snow white, and they have serpents' necks and trains like queens. The terraces are given over to the old, old flowers of our childhood, to bright green lizards and lilac bushes, big and blue as storm clouds.

I cannot tell you enough about the Sciarra gardens.

Musi is working hard at her thankless task and never complains. Sometimes she is on the set from 9.30 to 6.30 and has no time for lunch; she just bolts down some eggs and coffee. In the evening she either collapses with exhaustion or goes out to dinner with film people – and makes some very useful conquests amongst the directors. For the last three weeks, I have been making a film. ('Three weeks!', exclaims Annie) Oh yes. I am making it image by image and I am more than a little proud of being one of the first writers to make a film that way unaided. As you can guess, this has nothing in common with literature. It requires extraordinary agility, and you ought to learn how to do it; it might be useful to you. Do you understand? I am doing what would normally be done by a professional director after the writer (me) had supplied the short story or the screenplay. You would find it fun.[65]

It would be a mistake to believe that wartime rationing did anything at all to curb Colette's greed. The letters she wrote to Annie de Pène from Rome in 1917 are adequate proof of that. In one letter she speaks of feasting on 'grilled haunches of lamb – lambs so young they should be sacred – with the skin and fat crackling and the tail nicely browned. Wonderful.' In another she describes going to a market and gorging herself on fritters fried in oil, fish, raw artichokes and grilled almonds.

In the company of Katia Barjansky – a young sculptress – she discovered a 'waggoners' inn' on the outskirts of Rome, and they would go there to eat pasta with cheese, artichoke omelettes and Parma ham. She even sent Annie a recipe for a delicacy:

Something to eat that comes only from Sicily. In July, when they are harvesting the grapes – I am talking about Sicily – you take a handful of muscat grapes and wrap them in a handful of green chestnut leaves. You roll them up, one leaf at a time, until you have a little packet that is tightly closed, and then tie it up with a long stalk of grass. And then? That's all. You leave it in the sun. When the little *pochetto* is dry and crackles between your fingers, and when the leaves fall apart if you roll them in your hands – it takes . . . ? weeks for that to happen, from one August to the next – you have a very unusual dish, a dessert cooked by God. When you open the *pochetto* and

unwrap the leaves – which smell very good in themselves – in the centre you will find a handful of crushed, candied grapes swimming in a divinely juicy fermented mush. It has the musky smell of a grape press and is dripping with black syrup. Oh, Annie, a dessert sticky with natural sugar, which can make you drunk!

I am going into raptures like this over a delicacy that costs nothing because you only make two or three such gastronomic discoveries in any one country.[66]

Back in Castel-Novel, the banquet continued. Bel-Gazou's nurse Miss Draper was also a good cook, and Colette sings the praises of her inventions, especially the 'wonderful cognac-flavoured meringues filled with cream'. In an attempt to persuade Annie to come to Castel-Novel, Colette intersperses her descriptions of Bel-Gazou running around with hay on her clogs, chasing the cockerels, speaking patois and improvising a song about a cat sitting on four big cat's eggs ('Her father finds Colette II delightful, and her little shadow is always dancing at his feet') with accounts of all the good things she was eating. 'Salad with garlic twice a day. Fresh onions the rest of the time. Frothy milk whenever you want it.' She boasts that when Sidi had to go away, for two days beforehand she stuffed him to bursting point with 'hare, fruit, garlic, onions, cream cheese, blackberry jam, cherries in eau de vie . . .'[67] Colette obviously enjoyed the country life she led in the Corrèze; it reminded her of her happy childhood in Puisaye and she wanted so much to have her friend share it with her.

Sidi arrives, and then goes off again. Less than forty-eight hours . . . I miss you, Annie, and this house without a man was made for you. No stockings, no shoes, no curlers. They are bringing the hay in. The byres are full. Three hundred and sixty fowl, turkeys, little guinea fowl. Toulouse geese. Six calves this month. The stud bulls look so beautiful with their curly hair on their foreheads. And above all, beautiful countryside all around us.[68]

Colette always found it difficult to write, and work was obviously the last thing on her mind. From time to time she did force herself to it: 'I have just written, with great reluctance, my article for *Excelsior*.' But it was much more fun to do things like 'Washing the dog in the river. The method is as follows. I take off (1) my shoes, (2) my stockings, (3) my knickers, (4) my skirt, (5) my pullover, (6) my shift and (7) I wade into the water up to my waist and then dry myself on Sidi's handkerchief – there was nothing else to hand.'[69]

She also enjoyed making her own butter and claimed that it was 'as good as Normandy butter . . . I made a kilo this morning . . . we make it in the house with the whisk we use for beating egg-whites. It's exquisite.'[70]

Unlikely as it may seem, Colette also began to deal in apples. In a letter written to Annie in the autumn of 1917 she sounds like a peasant woman getting ready to go to market. But this peasant was also a good businesswoman.

Do you think any of your society friends would like to stock up with Canada pippins? I still have two or three hundred kilos to sell; I've already sold the rest. I send them by post in ten-kilo packages, the customer returns the basket and the hay, pays 1 franc 50 postage, and I sell the apples at seven *sous* a pound. A word to the wise. Big Charles has bought one hundred kilos, and someone else will probably buy the same quantity. I've reached an agreement with Mirmont, who runs the station buffet, and I sell him everything the crazy old agent used to send to market at a low price. Once transport improves, I will sell apples in Paris, Annie. Annie, do come, and we can set ourselves up as farmers. We will live splendidly. And a six-day spree in Paris every two months. Why not?

Living in the country was Colette's constant and unattainable dream. Being a diplomat and politician, Sidi could not live far from Paris, and, as always, Colette went along with the man she loved, even though she did not want to. 'If there were no love in my life, no damned pig love to get in the way, I would never again live in Paris.'[71]

At the end of the war, Colette engaged Pauline Tissandier, a thirteen-year-old servant girl from the Brive area, near Castel-Novel, who was to remain at her side until Colette's death.

After the summer holidays at Castel-Novel, Sidi was called back to active service. Left alone in Paris, Colette went back to work. *Les Heures longues* appeared in the bookshops, and she began to write *Mitsou*, a novel which also deals with the war.

As Colette was not rolling in money, she went on working for the newspapers, reviewing films for the weekly *Film* and plays for *L'Eclair*, the newspaper for which her beloved Annie worked. It was through *L'Eclair* that she met Francis Carco when he returned to Paris on leave.

In 1917-18, Colette was still in love with her husband, but that in itself did not make for a peaceful life. Sidi was by nature polygamous. He was very successful with women and kept flitting from one to the next. Once again, Colette suffered the sharp pangs of jealousy. She may have inherited her jealous streak from her Provençal paternal grandmother, who was so jealous and suspicious that even when she was over sixty she would follow her husband to the privy and wait outside the door, telling her horrified daughter, 'Get on with you, child. A man who wants to deceive you can escape through smaller gaps than that.'[72]

Colette made an admirable analysis of her jealousy in *Le Pur et l'Impur*: 'a gymnic purgatory that affects all the senses one by one. [. . .] I mean, of course, the kind of jealousy that is motivated, that you can admit to [. . .] your hearing becomes sharper, your sight becomes keener, you move quickly and silently, your nose becomes attuned to particles left in the air by hair, perfumed powder, the passage of an indiscreetly happy being.'[73]

She could in fact be homicidally jealous. Colette was a medium and everyone who met her speaks of her magnetism. She was superstitious and fascinated by clairvoyants, used a pendulum to detect 'vibrations', and lit candles in churches. She was a woman and therefore a witch, and she admitted to having cast spells: 'Like everyone else I have at times wished for a woman, or two or three women to die . . . I am talking about spells which do no real harm to anyone, not even to the woman who casts them, if they are cast on robust people.'[74] But in *Lune de pluie*, she tells the story of a spell that went disastrously wrong.[75]

Such practices are not without their dangers. 'During one particularly acute fit of jealousy, I myself took risks. A rival concentrated all her thoughts on me, and I concentrated mine on her.'[76] But Colette was busy with her journalism and put off her spells until later. The other woman was not so busy and had more time to weave spells. She did not have long to wait for the outcome: within the space of a few days, Colette fell into a workmen's trench in the road, caught bronchitis, lost a manuscript in the metro, had some money stolen, and lost three of her angora kittens in a mysterious epidemic. 'I only had to re-establish a balanced exchange of trajectories between Madame X and myself to put an end to this evil series of events. And then we lived happily on mutually bad terms.'[77]

Colette does not say who the mysterious Madame X 'with the sea green eyes' was, but some years later they made things up and discussed the results of the spells they had cast on one another. She may have been Jouvenel's mistress, the Roumanian novelist Princess Marthe Bibesco. Colette described her to Marguerite Moreno: '*Rouma* is an anagram of *amour*. Add *nia* and what you get is a woman with the bones of a horse who churns out two-volume novels. Our Sidi has no luck.'[78] Alternatively, she may have been Germaine Patat, a blonde who ran a fashion house, and another of Sidi's mistresses. Colette eventually became friends with her and used her as the basis for 'Jane', a character in her novel *La Seconde*, which appeared in 1929.

We can, however, date the beginnings of the fit of jealousy and the spells. At the beginning of September 1917, Colette wrote to Georges Wague and mentioned going through a crisis she was trying to 'conjure away' and losing a manuscript – *Mitsou* – in the metro: 'I didn't have a rough copy of even a single line'[79] (the ultimate nightmare for any writer!).

Mitsou, a minor music hall artiste, is very like Colette herself, and *le lieutenant bleu* has some of the characteristics of Jouvenel. Reading between the lines, it is obvious that the novel is about the end of their love. The final pages reduced Marcel Proust to tears.

Although Colette was finding it more and more difficult to tolerate Sidi's absences and escapades, they were still fairly happy together. In June 1918, he wrote:

My dear love, I am writing another short letter because I have just been mentioned in the divisional orders of the 125th Division and I thought that would mean a lot to you, being the daughter of a soldier. The full text reads: 'De Jouvenel, Henry, lieutenant in the 10th Company of the 29th R.I.T. [Territorial Infantry Regiment]. A brave, devoted officer with remarkable sangfroid. He particularly distinguished himself on 11 June 1918 when he went out alone and under fire to meet an enemy patrol which was thought to be about to surrender. His complete disregard for danger is an example to all.'

It gives me great pleasure to copy it out, my darling. I am thinking of you, and of Jeanneney, who tried to make out that I was a coward. Remember what I told you, 'I need to be mentioned in a dispatch.' But I never expected that fate would be so providential as to bring me this, which, fortunately, is something out of the ordinary.

You are the daughter and the wife of a soldier. Don't forget that when my next furlough comes through I will have an extra two days. Let's be practical; come here, and let me give you a kiss. Your Sidi.[80]

It was Henry de Jouvenel who suggested in 1920 that an unknown soldier should be buried beneath the Arc de Triomphe to perpetuate the memory of the war and, it has to be admitted, to get publicity for his newspaper.

Autumn 1918. The great epidemic of Spanish influenza struck Paris, and Colette lost another friend. It was while she was on what she called 'agricultural leave' in Castel-Novel with Sidi and her daughter that she learned of the death of Annie de Pène. Never again would the joyful, pretty little woman from Normandy come to tell Colette about her varied and short-lived love affairs. Never again would they exchange gossip or recipes, tell each other the names of flowers or collapse into giggles together. Never again would they go to the flea market to drink lemonade and haggle for opaline lamps, Rubelles plates or sulfur glass paperweights. Annie de Pène, 'la bougresse', as Sidi called her, 'better than the best',[81] was dead. For the rest of her life, Colette would mourn 'Annie's subtle ear and her bright reddish-brown eyes'. She had her own explanation as to why Annie had fallen victim to influenza. 'She would forget to have lunch or dinner and would skip meals so as not to get fat, and the 'flu caught her with her defences down, with an empty stomach.'[82]

Two years earlier, Annie had asked her daughter Germaine to take a letter to Colette. It was almost as though she knew that she was nearing the end, and wanted to ensure her succession.

Germaine Battendier, later Germaine Beaumont, was twenty-five at the time. She admired Colette, but did not really know her and found her intimidating. Years later, she recalled how she curled her hair so as to look her best when she went to see her mother's friend. When, trembling with excitement, she reached the rue Cortambert, she found Colette making preserves. 'You've arrived at just the right moment, daughter of Annie,' Colette told her, 'you can help me to finish topping and tailing the green beans.' Then, eyeing the girl's curled hair, she added, 'It looks like a brain!'[83]

Germaine remained under Colette's spell for a long time. For years she never left her side, became her unpaid secretary on Le Matin, and shared holidays with her at Rozven. Along with Marguerite Moreno and the poet Hélène Picard, she became one of her trusted correspondents. Colette called her 'daughter' in remembrance of the affection she had felt for her mother. She encouraged her with her writing and journalism and comforted her during the difficult moments of what was to prove a stormy emotional life.

Colette was beginning to become something of an expert on emotional upsets. It was as though she took a delight in attracting fickle men like Willy and Henry de Jouvenel in order to suffer. On both occasions she trustingly entered into a passionate love affair; on both occasions she was disappointed.

Colette and Jouvenel began to drift apart in 1919. He was now a diplomat and often had to go away. His love affairs also took up much of his time. At the end of the war he was a member of the French delegation to the disarmament conference and he was soon to become senator for the Corrèze and then a delegate to the League of Nations.

Colette was not sufficiently self-effacing, patient or fond of society to be the ideal wife for a politician. Independence of mind and outspokenness are not the qualities required in a political wife. She felt, and indeed was, an outsider in the circles in which Jouvenel moved.

Although Paul Claudel was a poet as well as an ambassador, and although Berthelot, who later became Prime Minister, was a friend to writers, the world of politics and that of writing really belong to different spheres and they rarely meet. Politicians see writers as performers and writers find politicians boring, though they may well take advantage of the temporary protection they can afford them when they are in power.

Colette was recognized as a talented novelist and she was officially the Baronne de Jouvenel, but the scandals of the past had not been forgotten. While Jouvenel was campaigning for the senatorial elections in the Corrèze, one of his political enemies sneered at him for having married 'a dancer'. Colette dined with President Poincaré in the Elysée Palace, but only because her husband had been invited and insisted that she be at his side. The politicians' wives were not fond of Colette either. They were either secretly jealous of the way she flaunted her freedom or shocked by her tempestuous love life. Needless to say, they had a somewhat exaggerated notion of how tempestuous her life was. Certain politicians were even afraid that she might seduce their wives.

Colette was too sensitive not to be upset at being the object of their scorn. She also found politics and the frequently pointless debates it gave rise to extremely boring. 'If a woman has not been bitten by the politics bug by the time she is forty-five, she is highly unlikely to develop a taste for politics in later life.'[84]

Sidi's new position meant that Colette had to do a lot of entertaining, and she did her best to organize dinners – occasions which she enjoyed only for the chance they gave her to observe these busy, talkative men who absent-mindedly ate her legs of lamb, her foie gras and her tarts as they settled the re-ordering of the world. She studied them as though she were an entomologist:

Before going up to the little room I kept for myself on the first floor, with my dog at my heels, I would spend a while pretending to listen to them, but it was merely an excuse to watch them at leisure. [. . .] A sudden violence would appear on the faces I thought I knew and would wipe out the familiar desire to please. Forgotten and silent, I felt vaguely guilty at watching a spectacle that I was not meant to see. Then an instinctive realization that I was about to get up and leave recalled me to the attention of these men who were in love with something that no one can embrace with impunity.[85]

It is not that Colette was totally indifferent to the brilliant and privileged circles to which her marriage had admitted her – and, as we shall see, she was by no means indifferent to official honours – but her sensual love of life meant that she could not tolerate the constraints of high society. She even made arrangements to avoid the chore of attending official dinners. On such evenings, she would meet Francis Carco, who lived by night and who enjoyed taking her to the dubious but picturesque places he frequented. In his company, Colette haunted the cabarets of Montmartre and the cafés of Montparnasse, the *bals musette* of the rue de Lappe and the *caf' conc'* of the working class areas, discovering the secrets of Paris by night and enjoying the strange festivities that ended at dawn over a bowl of onion soup in the Halles.

Colette and Jouvenel no longer worked together and they no longer had the same friends. They met less and less frequently in the house in the boulevard Suchet. Each found the other's habits more and more intolerable. Colette found Jouvenel's ambition irritating: 'When a public figure leaves the obscurity in which he used to live, he enters into a very dangerous period of his life.'[86]

Jouvenel was increasingly annoyed by his wife's love of animals and the menagerie in which she had made him live for the last eight years. In addition to the many cats and dogs that shared her life, she brought home tortoises, squirrels, grass-snakes, lizards, a serval and even a little panther called Bâ-Tou, who ended her days in the zoo of the Jardin des Plantes.

At this point, it has to be said that Colette's love of animals, which for a long time reduced her reputation to that of a writer of animal stories, was mainly a literary device. She certainly liked animals better than children, but the way she treated them would have shocked any real animal lover. Paul Léautaud, for instance, who greatly admired Colette's talent, nevertheless conceded: 'What she liked was luxury pets.' He was shocked that she enjoyed watching cats and dogs fight, and that she disposed of the mortal remains of her beloved Kiki-la-Doucette by throwing the body into the ditch surrounding the fortifications of Paris. His conclusion was: 'She seems to love animals rather as a lion-tamer does.'[87] When Annie de Pène wrote to say that she was upset because her cat Musette was ill, Colette replied: 'If Musette is that ill, have her put down. Don't prolong her agony; it is causing you as much pain as it is her.'[88] Colette had the harsh outlook of a peasant, and a physical horror of emotional suffering that made her react brutally when either people or animals threatened to cause her grief. Nor did she like to be disturbed or tied down by animals. Simone Berriau's daughter Héléna Bossis recalls seeing Colette in Provence get very angry with a puppy which was making too much noise in its game of fetching pebbles.

Was it a mistake for Colette and Henry de Jouvenel to have married? Natalie Barney was later to claim that it was, though one suspects that she saw the failure of the marriage as proof that she herself had been right to stay single.

It was not without apprehension that I saw Colette fall in love with Henry de Jouvenel, marry him, and lovingly, bravely, move into a real house with a handsome husband, a baby, a nurse, servants and so on. Although they had many tastes in common, including the table and the bedroom, and shared interests through their work on Le Matin, I saw nothing to convince me that their marriage would last, even though they seemed happy. [. . .] What could make this tall dark man in the prime of life, intelligent and vain, and so attractive to women – whom he found so attractive – stay with one woman, even Colette, and even if she did bring him not only all her love but the originality of her spirit and of a whole new environment?[89]

It was in fact Henry's constant womanizing rather than their different life styles which eventually drove a jealous Colette away from him. Even Henry's mother (whose verbal tics Colette could imitate so well: see p. 202), who had looked favourably on Colette when she married her son, finally turned against her and encouraged Henry's amorous exploits. The thought that he might marry Princess Bibesco certainly appealed to her sense of snobbery.

1. Louise Weiss, *Mémoires d'une européenne*, I, Paris, Payot, 1968.
2. Letter to Georges Wague, late May or early June; *Lettres de la Vagabonde*, p. 54.
3. Barlet had been Willy's secretary, and remained a faithful friend to Colette. He owned a publishing house in the rue Ségur and published *L'Entrave* in 1913.
4. Jean Sapène was the advertising manager.
5. Letter, 31 July 1911; *Lettres de la Vagabonde*, pp. 55-8.
6. A mime-play by Georges Wague, based on a novel by Aristide Bruant.
7. *L'Entrave*, Paris, Librairie des lettres, 1913.
8. Ibid.
9. Colette, *Trois . . . six . . . neuf*, Paris, Corréâ, 1944, p. 54.
10. Ibid., p. 57.
11. Letter, 27 October 1911; *Le Figaro littéraire*, 24 January 1953.
12. Letter, 8 January 1911; coll. Bertrand de Jouvenel.
13. Undated letter; *Le Figaro littéraire*, 24 January 1953.
14. *La Naissance du jour*, Paris, Flammarion, Collection 'J'ai lu', 1968, pp. 39-40.
15. Letter to Léon Hamel, 13 May 1912; *Lettres de la Vagabonde*, p. 66.
16. Barney, *Souvenirs indiscrets*, Paris, Flammarion, 1960.
17. Letter to Jeanne Muhlfeld, August 1902; *Lettres à ses pairs*, p. 55.
18. Letter, 29 August 1911; *Lettres de la Vagabonde*, pp. 59-60.
19. A restaurant near the Opéra Comique, famous for its southern cuisine.
20. *Prisons et Paradis*, Paris, Ferenczi, 1932, p. 96.
21. *Paysages et Portraits*, Paris, Flammarion, 1958, pp. 174-75.
22. *Lettres à ses pairs*, p. 119.
23. Letter to Hélène Picard, June 1920; *Lettres à Hélène Picard*, Paris, Flammarion, 1958, p. 33.
24. Letter to Hélène Picard, probably 1 January 1922; ibid., p. 39.
25. Maurice Goudeket, *Près de Colette*, Paris, Flammarion, 1956, p. 166.
26. Undated letter; coll. Bertrand de Jouvenel.
27. Letter, 26 June 1912; *Lettres de la Vagabonde*, p. 70.
28. Letter to Léon Hamel, 10 July 1912; ibid., p. 71.
29. *L'Entrave*.
30. Letter to Léon Hamel, 17 August 1912; *Lettres de la Vagabonde*, p. 75.
31. *La Maison de Claudine*, Paris, Ferenczi, 1922, p. 156.
32. Letter, 27 September 1912; *Lettres de la Vagabonde*, p. 80.
33. Letter, 10 April 1923; *Lettres à Marguerite Moreno*, Paris, Flammarion, 1959, p. 63.
34. A famous restaurant and *salon de thé* in the boulevard Saint-Germain.
35. Letter, 26 July 1924; *Lettres à Marguerite Moreno*, pp. 84-5.
36. Letter, early April 1939; *Lettres à ses pairs*, p. 131.
37. Letter to Marguerite Moreno, 21 September 1943; *Lettres à Marguerite Moreno*, p. 255.
38. Colette, *L'Etoile Vesper*, Geneva, Editions du Milieu du Monde, 1946, p. 205.
39. Letter to Georges Wague, 15 July 1913; *Lettres de la Vagabonde*, p. 94.
40. Letter, 4 October 1913; ibid., p. 97.
41. Moreno, *Souvenirs de ma vie*, p. 231.
42. Unpublished letter; coll. Louis Guitard.
43. *Le Fanal bleu*, p. 177.
44. Letter to Léon Hamel, 16 October 1914; *Lettres de la Vagabonde*, p. 111.
45. *Les Heures longues*, Paris, Arthème Fayard, 1917.
46. My thanks are due to Monsieur J. L. Lécard, who inherited these letters.
47. Letter, 28 June 1915; *Lettres de la Vagabonde*, p. 119.
48. Postcards to Annie de Pène, 26 June and 3 July 1915; coll. J. L. Lécard.
49. Bertrand de Jouvenel, *Un Voyageur dans le Siècle, 1903-1945*, Paris, Laffont, 1963, p. 49.
50. Unpublished letter to Annie de Pène; coll. J. L. Lécard.
51. Ibid.
52. *Trois . . . six . . . neuf*, pp. 66-7.
53. Ibid., p. 71.
54. Morand, *Journal d'un attaché d'ambassade*, Paris, Gallimard, 1963, p. 119.
55. Unpublished letter to Annie de Pène, 3 December 1917; coll. J. L. Lécard.
56. Morand, *Journal d'un attaché*, pp. 129-30.
57. Unpublished letter, 3 December 1917; coll. J. L. Lécard.
58. Unpublished letter to Annie de Pène, 1917; coll. J. L. Lécard.
59. Ibid.
60. Unpublished letter to Annie de Pène, 5 January 1917; coll. J. L. Lécard.
61. Unpublished letter to Annie de Pène, 1917; coll. J. L. Lécard.
62. Unpublished letter to Annie de Pène, 6 March 1917; coll. J. L. Lécard.
63. Unpublished letter to Annie de Pène, 22 September 1916; coll. J. L. Lécard.
64. Unpublished letter to Annie de Pène, 30 April 1917; coll. J. L. Lécard.
65. Ibid.
66. Unpublished letter to Annie de Pène, summer or autumn 1917; coll. J. L. Lécard.
67. Ibid.
68. Ibid.
69. Ibid.
70. Ibid.
71. Ibid.
72. *Le Pur et l'Impur*, p. 191.
73. Ibid.
74. Ibid., p. 194.
75. *Lune de pluie*, in *Chambre d'hôtel*, Paris, Arthème Fayard, 1940.
76. *Le Pur et l'Impur*, p. 194.
77. Ibid. p. 195.
78. Letter, October 1923; *Lettres à Marguerite Moreno*, p. 73.
79. *Lettres de la Vagabonde*, p. 126.
80. Unpublished letter; coll. Bertrand de Jouvenel.
81. *Lune de pluie*, p. 179.
82. Letter to Georges Wague, late October 1918; *Lettres de la Vagabonde*, pp. 128-9.
83. Germaine Beaumont and André Parinaud, *Colette par elle-même*, Paris, Seuil, 1951, p. 8.
84. *Trait pour trait*, in *En Pays connu*, Paris, Ferenczi, 1950, p. 96.
85. Ibid., p. 97.
86. *L'Etoile Vesper*, p. 68.
87. Léautaud, *Journal littéraire*, III, p. 82 (entry dated 8 November 1912).
88. Unpublished letter, 6 August 1917; coll. J. L. Lécard.
89. Barney, *Souvenirs indiscrets*.

After her marriage Colette often stayed at Castel-Novel, the Jouvenel estate at Varetz, Corrèze (336). She found that her mother-in-law ('Mamita' – on the right in Ill. 335) and Henry's half-sister Edith ('Didi') rather got on her nerves, and she confected the little dialogue below in a letter to Annie de Pène.

335

Edith's Fiancés (A Play)

The action is set in a magnificent dining-room overlooking a little courtyard.

Mamita: Hein, non mais, croyez vous, dites, poor little Didi, she's had such bad luck, that's her third fiancé killed since the war began!

Colette: ??

Mamita: Mais houi, her third! The young De Lhomond boy, the Montroudenez boy and young Duke Honneau! My poor Didi! The third one was the nicest! And of course he was a Duke . . .

Colette: ??

Mamita: No, I hadn't met him. But it would have been just perfect.

Colette: ???

Mamita: No, I hadn't met the family either, but (*with a knowing air*) I think I can say that his parents were delighted. Me, *vous savez, non, mais,* when I have an intuition about something, I'm *straw*dinary. Only yesterday Madame Speyo was saying to me, '*Non, mais, vous savez, vous vrai,* you're just *straw*dinary!' My poor Didi, there there, you've had such bad luck!

Colette: ???

Mamita: No, Didi had never seen him. But she's upset, specially as it's the third time it's happened. She thinks 'There's a curse on me!'

Colette: ???

Mamita: No, she hadn't met the other two either. But she really went through it just the same. Didn't you, my Didi? We'll find you another one, there, my Didi. A fine girl like you, virtuous and rich, and intelligent! If you knew what that girl had achieved down at Castel-Novel! Henry should light a candle for her, she's a saint! She counted all the hens, then all the ducks, then she went to see the little pigs when they were born, and then she caught a chill from counting the trees down by the river with the estate-manager . . . *Non, vrai, vous savez, sans rire, dites,* Henry should be grateful! I don't know how we'd have managed without her! Isn't that right, my Didi? So, her future husband doesn't know how lucky he is . . . By the way, he's charming, her future husband. It's the De Franqueville boy. When they're married they're going to spend their honeymoon in Ceylon. And they're getting married the same day as the Franquevilles' daughter, and the four of them will set off together, my Didi's already chosen her going-away outfit, and the Franquevilles have a relative with a yacht and he's going to take them on it, all four, *oh! non, vrai, moi, vous savez, sans blague,* I think the only smart way to travel is on a yacht, and I'm sure the Franqueville boy will agree with us absolutely, isn't that right, my little Didi – when we meet him? (*A chorus of agreement. Curtain.*)

336

337 Caricature of Colette by Rouveyre.

338 Sidi and Colette went abroad together for the first time to Switzerland. On this postcard to her mother, from Ouchy, Colette tells Sido that Jouvenel says he cannot live without her.

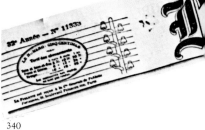

Colette the journalist. From the end of 1911 she contributed regularly to *Le Matin* (340), of which Jouvenel was one of the editors-in-chief.

339   Colette in Venice in 1915 on an assignment for the paper.

341, 342   For *Le Matin* Colette covered the celebrated case of Jules Joseph Bonnot, who led a notorious gang professing anarchy and practising robbery, until his capture in 1912 in a garage at Choisy-le-Roi.

343   Colette on the press bench during the trial of Landru.

339

Mardi 9 Mars 1915

342

341

343

Premier vol

344

345

346

347

The reporter takes to the air.

344, 345 Colette preparing for her first flight, in the Caudron airbus, and photographed with its pilots on 26 January 1912.

346 Colette making a balloon ascent for *Le Matin*, on 12 September 1912: 'in the gondola were the pilot, the intrepid novice, the celebrated lawyer, the seasoned lady balloonist and me.'

347 Preparations for the maiden flight of the dirigible 'Clément Bayard', June 1912.

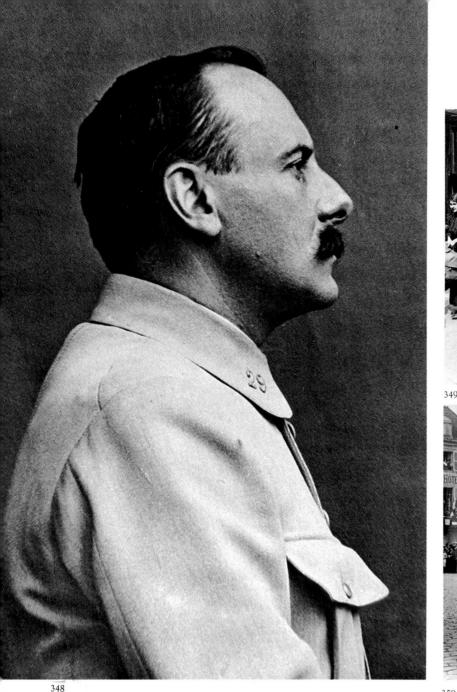

348

349

350

351

August 1914, and the men go off to war. Henry de Jouvenel became a second lieutenant in the Territorials (348). The 6th Territorials were photographed entraining at Dunkirk for the Front (349), and elsewhere a small town in Ile-de-France said goodbye to its sons (350). Jouvenel was eventually mentioned in divisional orders for bravery (351).

352 A front-line trench at Verdun. Colette joined her husband in the town in the winter of 1914. Behind the lines, people were dancing waltzes to the latest tunes.

353 Life in the trenches. 'Everything around us is peaceful. But then you suddenly hear that eight hundred wounded have just been brought in.'

354 Being in Verdun clandestinely, Colette would go out only at night, for a walk along the Meuse. In 1914 Jouvenel wrote, 'I have to admit that Verdun is the biggest flop of the war. They promised us that we would be at the centre of everything, but here we are in a forgotten corner.' By 1916, the area was shattered.

352

353

354

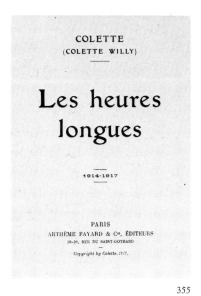

355

355   Colette's account of the wartime years, published in 1917.

Debout au lieutenant!

Members of the 1914 'phalanstère du XVIe arrondissement'.

356, 357 Colette and Annie de Pène, 'better than the best'. Annie came from Normandy and was a superb cook.

358 Marguerite Moreno, with her 'miraculous seed of laughter'.

359, 360 Jeanne Roques, known in films as Musidora and to her friends as Musi, was a hard-headed professional in the cinema but with a disastrous taste in men. She inscribed her photograph as a vamp, 'For Annie de Pène. In memory of the campaign of 1914, when I got to know her and learned to love her as a second Colette.'

357   358   359

360

361

362

363

364

361 Colette in 1912.

362 Colette pregnant, sketched by herself in a letter of April 1913 to Sacha Guitry.

363 Henry de Jouvenel with Colette and their daughter Colette – nicknamed 'Bel-Gazou' – at Castel-Novel.

364 Colette with her daughter and one of the dogs.

365, 366 Colette de Jouvenel (Bel-Gazou) 'looks like Sidi and like me too'; 'she is superb, golden brown as a pie-crust, with muscles like her mother's, happy . . . '

367

368

367 Colette and Sidi in Rome, 1917. Jouvenel was there to represent France at a conference of the Anglo-French Entente. 'I am seeing lots of people, but I will not let myself be invaded . . .'

368 Gabriele D'Annunzio, who occupied the room next to Colette's in the hotel where she stayed in Rome in 1915, and became her friend.

369 *La Chambre éclairee,* a collection of short stories written during the war years, published in 1920.

370 A portrait of Colette in Rome in 1917, by René Carrère. She was then forty-four.

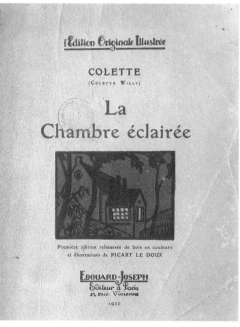

369

370

Souvenir de Rome
René Carrey

371

372

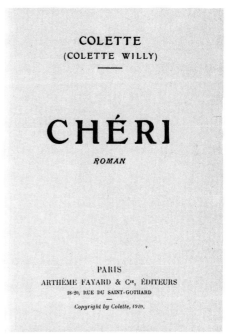

374

375

373

Chéri was finished in June 1919, at Castel-Novel. It was first published in serial form in *La Vie parisienne*, then in book form, in 1920 (**374**).

371 The actress Suzanne Derval, Colette's model for the character of Léa.

372, 373 Illustrations to *Chéri* by Vertès.

375 *La Fin de Chéri* (1926) was highly recommended by Drieu La Rochelle – although he disliked Colette – for its insights into the disaffection of young men after the war.

376-378 Colette with her pet serval, and in her Paris garden with her husband, two dogs and a cat. Henry de Jouvenel was beginning to tire of living in a menagerie.

376

377

379

379 Colette at work – 'l'angoisse de la page bleue . . .'

380-382 Jouvenel became even more committed to politics and diplomacy, and frequently travelled abroad. (He is seen in London, left, with his daughter.) More distressing to Colette, and in the end fatal to his marriage, was his passion for women. One of Colette's chief rivals was the novelist Princess Bibesco (**382**).

380

382

381

383 Colette by Henry Bataille.

384 Colette in a cloche hat (charcoal sketch, 1925).

385 The lecturer at her desk.

386 Cartoon by Julhès, in *Guignol* (1923); it was captioned, 'From the Moulin Rouge to the Institut [de France], what Academies, what Academies!'

387 The first colour photograph of Colette.

385

384

386

387

V The Ripening Seed

At the beginning of 1920, a new figure appeared on the scene: the son of Henry de Jouvenel and Claire Boas. His name was Bertrand, he was sixteen and he was to play an important role in Colette's life. Colette was forty-seven and had just published *Chéri*. The main character in that novel is based upon Auguste Hériot, but it is also a premonitory book in that it tells the story of a love affair between a mature woman and a young man.

The first Baronne de Jouvenel had retained custody of her son and had until now refused to let him have anything to do with his father's new household. In 1920, Henry suddenly expressed a desire to get to know his son, now an adolescent. He lost his temper and told his ex-wife that if she would not let Bertrand visit him – and Colette – he would forbid her to use his name.

Claire was no fool. She wanted to keep her married name and realized that she would have to be more flexible. She sent Bertrand to take a bunch of flowers to Colette in the boulevard Suchet. Trembling with fear, Bertrand obeyed. He was an awkward youth, tall for his age, thin but very handsome, and anything but bold.

Bertrand's parents had been divorced when he was four and he had been brought up by an Irish governess in his mother's spacious apartment. There he met Claudel, Bergson, D'Annunzio and Anatole France, who used to tell him stories when he was small. Apart from two short periods at a boarding school in Normandy and at a school in the boulevard Suchet, this spoiled only child had been educated at home by private tutors. In 1918, a the age of fourteen, he entered the Lycée Hoche in Versailles and went straight into the final year class. He was boarded with an old Protestant spinster. He was a brilliant pupil – he had learned to read before he was five – and was preparing for his *baccaulauréat* in mathematics and philosophy. In later life, he became a distinguished political commentator.

He knew nothing about women. He had romped in the haystacks at Castel-Novel with his aunt Edith, who was only four years older, and he did have a girlfriend – the sister of his best friend – but his relationship with her had always been purely platonic. His main interest was reading. He enjoyed sport, especially boxing, but his mother would have preferred him to play golf. He did not enjoy the elegant balls she made him attend. The problem was that Bertrand was very, very shy.

This, then, was the boy who was waiting for Colette in her drawing room in February 1920. His heart was in his boots at the thought of meeting his father's second wife. He had never even seen her, but he had heard a lot about her and one can easily imagine the tales he had heard. He was so intimidated that he hid behind a piano in the darkest part of the room. Suddenly, the door opened and a rather plump little woman dashed in. Seeing no one, she said, 'Where is he? Where is the child?' Finally she saw him and stared up at him with curiosity. Bertrand was struck by the curl tumbling over her forehead, the perfect triangular shape of her nostrils, her superb blue eyes outlined with kohl, her rouge, and her fine lips. 'My sole impression was one of strength, but its effect on me was gentle.'[1] Colette tamed him by showing him her gardens and her animals, and Bertrand was forced to admit that this stepmother was very unlike the woman he had dreaded meeting.

He saw her again and met Colette de Jouvenel, his seven-year-old half-sister, during the Easter holidays at Castel-Novel. Colette wrote to Marguerite Moreno from the Corrèze: 'Claire Boas almost came with us, because after only twenty minutes together in Paris, we felt as though we were old friends. She entrusted her charming son to me, and Mamita agreed to join us.'[2]

It was at Henry de Jouvenel's insistence that Bertrand was allowed to spend his next summer holiday at Rozven.

For Colette, the villa with its large garden was a paradise. It was her own, as Missy had generously not asked for the return of her gift. (She may in fact have had little choice in the matter, as Baronne du Crest, the previous owner, had refused to sell the villa to Missy 'because the Marquise dressed as a man'.[3] Missy paid for it, but officially it was in Colette's name.) At Rozven, Colette had all the things she loved: the sea, which she adored and which always did her good, the house at the foot of a little valley running down to the beach of La Touesse, the scented privet, the terrace, the flowers and the trees. The villa was surrounded by woods and heathland where she would go for long walks with her dogs, gathering flowers as she went.

Rozven was no palace; in fact it was rather basic. It was lit by oil lamps and there was a stove for the evenings, which can be chilly in Brittany. Water had to be heated on a coal fire to do the washing, and there was no running water until 1921. But it was a happy house, and all Colette's friends liked staying with her there. Sacha and Charlotte Guitry bought a mill in the neighbourhood. Francis Carco and his wife Germaine, Léopold and Misz Marchand, Hélène Picard and Germaine Beaumont all came frequently to Rozven. Even Meg Villars came to stay; she had divorced Willy and she and Colette were now friends. They did not, however, all come at the same time as the house was not large and Colette could not provide rooms for everyone. With her friends, Colette shared all the joys of summer holidays by the sea: swimming, sunbathing, shrimping in the rock pools left behind by the tide, not to mention the simple but divine *gueulardises* of lobsters, fish and shellfish washed down with cider or Muscadet.

When she was at Rozven, Colette was beautiful and tireless. Walks on the beach, as yet unspoiled by holiday-makers, left her superbly tanned and fit. She would spend hours on the beach, either barefoot or in espadrilles, looking for rare shells, or simply romping in the waves and on the sand and staring in wonder at the rainbow-coloured jellyfish as they drifted along in the water. They reminded her of the glass paperweights she collected. At Rozven, there was no formality and no need to dress up. According to Colette, 'a canvas hat costing 14 francs 90' was the height of fashion.

Colette also spent a lot of time on the house and garden, which she dug, planted and tended. She did household repairs and painted what needed to be painted: 'for a long time I was proud of being a competent handyman and of being good with hammer and nails, rake and dibble.'[4] She mended furniture and brought in more, using her royalties to replace what Missy had taken away. Not even the most unpleasant tasks were beyond her. She told Germaine Beaumont, for instance, that 'disregarding the passive complaints of my entourage, I emptied the downstairs privies, alone, suitably armed, serene and proud.'[5]

Colette was good with her hands. She liked tools, especially knives with one or more blades, and was very good at choosing them ('not everything with a blade is a real knife,' she used to say). She could pick out a good knife – the kind that never lets you down – at a glance. In Paris, walking home from *Le Matin* in the evening, she used to buy knives from particular street-vendors near the Hôtel des Ventes, who called her 'la petite dame râleuse qu'ajète des lingues' (the haggling little lady who buys knives).[6] She often consulted Roret's craft handbooks, which provide the do-it-yourself enthusiast with all kinds of useful hints. Like all women of her generation, Colette had been given a solid grounding in domestic science and her bedside books included the bible of every good housewife of the Second Empire period, Madame Millet-Robinet's *La Maison rustique des dames*. From it she learned how to knead bread correctly, to serve drinks at the right temperature, how to arrange her cupboards and cellars and when fruit and vegetables were at their best.

Colette was never bored at Rozven. When she was alone there with Germaine Beaumont, their favourite pastime was walking to Saint-Coulomb (about 1.5 kilometres away) to buy remnants of cotton batiste and silk crepe from Mahé-Guilbert, the draper's on the corner by the church. Colette and Germaine loved the draper, as she proudly told them that the material had come 'all the way from Saint-Malo' and spread it out in a jumble of rainbow colours on a big table.

They would then go home and make simple nightdresses to a pattern of their own invention: four metres of material, folded in two, with seams down the sides, a hem at the bottom and a hole for the head. Crocheted scallops in a contrasting colour, stitched directly into the fabric of the square neckline and also forming loose sleeves, completed the garment. As they were not particularly skilled dressmakers, their nightdresses were sometimes rather lop-sided, with one side shorter or longer than the other. 'That doesn't matter,' said Colette, 'we will stay in bed. Only the tops will be visible.'[7] What they really enjoyed was the feminine pleasure of handling the material and the coloured thread.

Germaine was, on the other hand, very good at tapestry, and Colette acquired a taste for it from her. Years later she talked about it in *L'Etoile Vesper* and, like George Sand, she found that the act of pushing 'the needle with its woollen tail' through the canvas helped to relax her mind.

During their sewing-bees at Rozven, the two women giggled, chattered and gossiped. They could both be catty and both had a good sense of humour. They had no compunction about demolishing the reputation of anyone they did not like.

Germaine was ten years younger than Colette and admired her enormously. Colette taught her to write and told her the names of flowers and insects. She also taught her how to look for things in junk shops:

'Beware of anything misshapen,' she told me, objects which have about them 'something crooked or skew or difficult to handle, that makes them unpleasant to look at and dangerous to use.' [. . .]

Colette also taught me to avoid anything – be it a radish or a speech – that sounds hollow, anything that is superficial, skimped or hurried – cooking food too quickly, rushing out for a walk without taking time to digest a meal properly, overindulgence in stupid sports. She was naturally very vigorous, but she taught me to save my strength; she claimed to be lazy, but she taught me that business comes before pleasure.[8]

Colette never failed to amaze her. Germaine describes how they were once invited to Paramé to hear a lady sing Fauré, Duparc and Debussy. They found her distraught: her accompanist was ill and the recital could not take place. To Germaine's astonishment, Colette immediately sat down at the piano and sight-read the accompanist's part. She could play perfectly well, but had never mentioned the fact to Germaine. 'Remember this,' she told her: 'there are always some things in life that you have to keep for yourself.'

She also taught Germaine about life. She was her adviser in matters of the heart, as we can see from Colette's wonderful letters. In 1921, when Germaine was hesitating whether to marry the political columnist Henry Barde, although she was in love with him, Colette told her: 'We can hesitate a thousand times over the colour of a dress, but for heaven's sake we ought to be able to get married without thinking about it. On the day, you should be so carefree that you can go before the mayor without even noticing.'[9]

226

On another occasion, when Germaine had been telling her how difficult she was finding it to live with a man, Colette replied:

I have long been convinced that the active presence of a man – the man you love, a man you might love, or a man who wants to be loved – can at certain times, and there are many such times, be harmful. When we are in the presence of a man, our faces, our postures, and our way of thinking or not thinking are no longer the same. When we are tired or depressed, as you are at the moment, the presence of a man can act like a drug, as a stimulant or a depressant. If a stimulant, we don't see the harmful side-effects; if a depressant, we can all to clearly see the damage he is doing.[10]

She also gave Germaine a terrible warning:

You know how much I persist in believing in chance, in unexpected meetings, in the man who may at this very moment be about to turn the corner to meet us. You will meet him. And when you have him opposite you, at a restaurant table or in the office, you will remember past mistakes and begin to play the great game of betrayal, spying and hypocrisy – a game whose rules you have probably broken more than once. He may be the man you will love more than any other, the man to whom you will tell the most lies, to whom you will lie most assiduously, with a zeal that borders on devotion – because you want to keep him.[11]

Bertrand de Jouvenel, who is now over eighty but still a handsome man with a beard and thick white hair, still becomes emotional when he thinks of the summer of 1920. It was an important stage in his life. 'Yes,' he told me, 'now that everyone is dead, I can tell you what happened.' It is difficult to tell whether his eyes are blue, grey or green. 'Look into my eyes. Colette had the same eyes, and we were going to form a club for people with sea-green eyes.' Images of the sea at Rozven haunt his memory. It was Colette who really revealed the sea to

him for the first time. She taught him to swim, and within two days he was at home in the water. He sees the beach at low tide and the rocks where Colette taught him to part the seaweed with a shrimping net; his half-sister Bel-Gazou was already good at catching shrimps. He sees himself running along the long, empty beach in his swimming costume. Bathed in perspiration, he goes back to the house where Colette is waiting for him. She strokes his hip with the instinctive gesture that makes her touch anything that is beautiful: a fine head of lettuce, the supple back of a cat or a well-built man. Bertrand shivers at a thrill he has never experienced before.

That year, both Germaine Beaumont and Hélène Picard were staying at Rozven. The Carcos had yet to arrive and Henry de Jouvenel had been called away, either by politics or by one of his love affairs. Bertrand was alone with the three women. He was filled with wonder. Accustomed to the luxury in which his mother lived, he had never had such a simple, happy holiday. He discovered books not to be found in Claire Boas's library. Colette introduced him to Marcel Schwob, Jean de Tinan and, which was more important, to A l'Ombre des jeunes filles en fleurs. Colette loved Proust, who was not at the time very well known, and compared him to Balzac.

She gave Bertrand a copy of her latest novel, Chéri, and worked the title into her dedication: 'A mon fils chéri, Bertranslle Jouvenel'. That may have contributed to a misconception that still makes Bertrand angry. No, he was not Chéri. If he did inspire any of Colette's books, it is more likely to have been Le Blé en herbe or possibly La Fin de Chéri.

One evening, he went to say goodnight to Colette before going to bed. He was carrying an oil lamp. Colette kissed him on the lips and not on the cheek, and Bertrand was so surprised that he almost dropped the lamp. 'She simply said, "Hold the lamp steady".'[12]

It is well known that the sea puts all kinds of strange ideas into women's heads. Hélène, Germaine and Colette held mysterious confabulations which left them choking with laughter. Bertrand, a complete innocent, did not realize what was going on, even when Colette told him 'It is time you became a man.'

One day she asked him which of them he found most attractive: Germaine, Hélène, or her. Bertrand did not know what to say. He loved listening to Hélène reciting poetry, Germaine made him laugh, and he found Colette fascinating. But he still did not realize what they wanted from him. One night Germaine took him to her bedroom. He emerged depressed and unhappy in the middle of the night. But Colette had waited up for him. She used all her skills, and Bertrand not only 'became a man' but fell in love.

What began as an eighteenth-century tale of libertinage was to become a love story featuring a novelist of forty-seven and a boy not yet seventeen.

Colette's biographers have unanimously accepted Natalie Barney's facile explanation that Colette seduced her stepson in order to be revenged on her unfaithful husband. It is of course possible that this was her thought at first. But if vengeance was all she wanted, matters would have gone no further than that. It seems more likely that she gave in to a sudden impulse and then found herself caught. The facts are there: Bertrand was in love with a woman old enough to be his mother, and Colette was in love with a boy she treated as a son. And their love for one another was to last for five years. They were probably the happiest five years of Colette's life.

Bertrand was the object of her last real passion, and he gave her a tenderness and fidelity she had never known. 'Until 1925, I was completely, absolutely and effortlessly faithful to her.' When they did break up, it was on Colette's initiative. She was too clear-headed to prolong an affair she knew to be doomed. She loathed sadness. The author of *Chéri* shared Oscar Wilde's view that what we write comes true, and she had no intention of sharing Léa's fate.

The summer of 1920 passed happily at Rozven, and Bertrand became more and more attached to a stepmother who meant more to him than any girl possibly could. She taught him that 'bread has a savour, privet has a scent, and poppies have colour.'[13] She introduced him to beauty and to gastronomic self-indulgence – to every form of indulgence.

In September, Bertrand had to leave to spend the rest of the holidays with his parents. They scarcely recognized him. He had grown, he had colour in his cheeks and he was more lively, if not more cheerful. Colette wrote to Francis Carco: 'Bertrand was reduced to despair as soon as he left us. He had never had a carefree holiday like that, and he can't get over it. Things will sort themselves out.'[14]

Things did not sort themselves out. Bertrand sent a long, passionate letter to Colette at *Le Matin* (where she had become literary editor and theatre critic the previous year). She was alarmed, and gave him a terrible scolding: what if Henry had seen the letter? Bertrand never did it again.

Fortunately, Henry was too busy to notice what was going on. Claire, however, was a mother – and a Jewish mother at that – and with a mother's perspicacity she soon guessed the truth. She later did everything she could to fling Bertrand into the arms of another woman so as to distract him from Colette, but to no avail.

In September 1920, Colette was in excellent form. *Chéri* was selling like hot cakes. Once again, the success of the novel was largely due to the scandal it caused. Men were very shocked by this story about a mature woman and a young man. They found it improbable that Chéri, with his beautiful young wife, could be seriously devoted to his middle-aged mistress. Women took a different view. Gide was very enthusiastic about the novel and wrote to Colette to tell her so.

Joys never come singly, and Colette had just received something that meant a great deal to her: she was made a *Chevalier* of the Legion of Honour. That may sound somewhat out of character, but contradictions were always part of Colette's charm. She was the daughter of an old Zouave, and perhaps it was only to be expected that, as she grew older, she would want a red ribbon of her own. To Natalie Barney she wrote, 'With my red ribbon, by lamplight I look no more than forty.'[15]

Although Colette and Claire Boas were supposed to be friends, they soon fell out. After Bertrand's visit to Rozven, Claire made certain that he saw as little of Colette as possible. For a while he visited her only once a week, and that only because Sidi insisted that he come to Sunday lunch at their house in the boulevard Suchet. On these occasions Bertrand found his stepmother disappointingly cold and reserved. Colette was in fact trying to keep her distance; realizing that her relationship with Bertrand was madness, she tried to drive him away by behaving coldly towards him. But her efforts did not have the intended effect and when Bertrand went to Rozven with his half-brother Renaud the following summer the relationship became stronger than ever.

Colette was now doing a lot of work for *Le Matin*, where she read manuscripts submitted by young writers for a regular feature entitled 'Les Contes des mille et un matins' (Tales of the Thousand and One Mornings). One of the young writers she introduced to the public was Georges Simenon.

Irène Le Cornec, now an astonishingly lively eighty-year-old, was one of the other young writers. Colette published twelve short stories by the shy young woman

and a friendship developed between the two. They began to exchange letters when Irène left Paris with her husband to edit a local newspaper at Vire, and went on corresponding until Colette's death.[16]

Colette appreciated Irène's sense of humour, but she did not approve of her docility – she was doing all the housework on top of her journalism. 'One day,' said Irène, 'she cut off my hair. She did not like long hair. "It makes you look like a slave," she said.' On hearing that Irène had hurt her thumb on the feed mechanism of a linotype press, Colette wrote to her immediately:

Because you are by nature a charmingly romantic little goat, I am tempted to classify you as one of those creatures who should never be left alone for five minutes, firstly because they like solitude, and secondly because they take advantage of being alone to hurt themselves . . . When do you do your own work? I cannot imagine how you can work properly surrounded by so many men [Irène's husband and sons], or preoccupied by your concern for them.[17]

Early in 1921, Henry de Jouvenel was elected Senator for the Corrèze, and Colette often went to Castel-Novel to perform her duties as the wife of a parliamentarian. The lavish official dinners for sixty guests that she was required to give did nothing to improve her figure.

But it was soon time to go back to the delights of Rozven. The Panther's son Renaud was there too. The boys, who were fourteen and seventeen respectively, got on very well with the eight-year-old Bel-Gazou, and Colette must often have repeated Sido's old cry, 'Children, where are you?' Bel-Gazou and Renaud, who was nicknamed (in English) 'The Kid', were particularly close. They were so boisterous that they were often scolded by Colette. For Bel-Gazou, Colette was 'maman'; for Renaud she was 'Madame' or 'Tante Colette'; for Bertrand she was 'ma mère chérie' ('darling mother').

Colette was simply happy, as she told Léopold Marchand when she wrote to invite him to Rozven for 'the sea, bathing in the sand, in the water and in the sunlight, the ceaseless breathing of the waves, the cider, the warm nights, the cool days, the striped cats, three delightful children – and me. The coast is baked and scented; in the evening a necklace of lighthouses sparkles around the bays.'[18]

Léopold Marchand was a strapping young man of about thirty, one of the young writers Colette had met through Le Matin. He was working with Colette on a stage adaptation of Chéri, which was due to open at the Théâtre Michel in December. They became close friends, but whereas Colette called him tu, Léo always addressed her as vous and called her 'Madame'.

The children adored Léo, who was always in a good mood and inventing games. One of these consisted of slipping unexpected adjectives into a sentence and always produced hilarious results: 'When we arrived at a jocular presbytery, the maid-servant, who was mouldy, gave us gothic blackberries washed down with a glass of well camphorated water.'[19] Another game consisted of finding definitions for the absurd characters he drew: 'Khong' was 'a Canaanite tribe with pear-shaped heads, now dying out as a result of massacres'; 'Gondin' was 'a funny little woman who is a slave to fashion'. Bertrand was particularly fond of Léo, who liked sport and was a boxing fan.

The great clandestine love affair between Bertrand and his 'darling mother' lasted until 1925, and she often speaks of him in her letters with the tenderness of a mother and of a lover. He was 'the leopard', 'my great greyhound of a boy' who 'follows me like a dog', 'a sweet little canary', 'my big little boy'. She worried about his health – he was not very strong – his weight – he was always very thin – and his happiness. When he left her to go back to Paris she entrusted him to Germaine Patat. In August 1921, she wrote to Marguerite Moreno:

Not only have I become gaga, living only through my body, but I am also surrounded by a terrible horde. Once they have been let loose, these Jouvenel's brothers [English in the original] play with the dogs, roll about on the ground, shout and bound about. [. . .] Then there is Bertrand de Jouvenel, entrusted to me by his mother for his health and his misfortune. I give him a rubdown, stuff him with food, rub him with sand and let him go brown in the sun.[20]

In September, Bertrand went with her to Castel-Novel, along with the other two children and Sidi, who had to attend to his constituency. Colette's affection for her daughter was beginning to turn to annoyance. The girl looked more and more like Sidi, and had inherited not only his looks but his 'extremely Jouvenel' imperious manners. And as Colette liked Jouvenel less and less, she had less and less patience with her daughter. With Bertrand, on the other hand, she was happy, even though she knew that her happiness could not last forever. In a letter to Marguerite Moreno, who appears to have been having doubts about embarking on an affair, possibly with another woman, Colette wrote: 'Content yourself, I beg you, with a passing temptation and give in to it. What can we be certain of, except what we hold in our arms, while we hold it in our arms? We have so few opportunities to own things.'[21]

For the one hundredth performance of Chéri, on 28 February 1922, Colette returned to the stage to play Léa. Bertrand was now a student in Paris, reading at first science and then, in preparation for a diplomatic career, law. He was beginning to escape Claire Boas's vigilance, but she still kept an eye on him and was still jealous of Colette.

With the collusion of Hélène Picard, Colette rented a second-floor studio in the rue d'Alleray (Hélène lived on the fourth floor of the same building), furnished it and had it papered with a flowered wallpaper which even covered the ceiling, as she always hated white ceilings. It was there that she had her secret meetings with Bertrand.

All lovers tell their partners about the earlier chapters in their lives, and Colette told Bertrand about her childhood in Saint-Sauveur. The following autumn, she took him there, just as she had once taken Willy. It was at Bertrand's suggestion that she wrote the delightful *La Maison de Claudine*, which was published in 1922.

'We even went to Algeria together,' says Bertrand, adding in a dreamy voice, 'Strange, no one ever found out about that.' Although Colette does describe Algeria in *Prisons et Paradis*, she never mentions the fact that she took Bertrand there at the end of April 1922. They took the boat from Marseilles. In Algiers, they gazed with wonder at the strelitzia in the gardens of the Hôtel St Georges. Years later, Colette would say that it looked like the hand of a Siamese dancer, with thumb and index finger straight and the other fingers bent backwards.[22] Bertrand recalls how 'when she published *Pour un herbier* in 1948, she reminded me of *our* strelitzia in the dedication.' They visited Bou-Saada and Ouled-Naïl, sinking up to their ankles into the warm, silky sand, and saw the beautiful Yamina dance naked. 'Colette offered me the young dancer,' says Bertrand, 'presumably as a challenge. I could have had her. But I didn't want her.'

Colette must have given some excuse at home for running off like this. Perhaps she claimed that she was going to write an article on Algeria and wanted to gather material. No one knew about her trip with Bertrand; no one, that is, except Germaine Beaumont (and probably Marguerite Moreno). Colette wrote to Germaine from Castel-Novel to describe their eventful return to France:

We embarked, and the boat pitched and tossed for two nights and a day. When we reached Marseilles, we found that there was not a room or even a bed available because of the Exposition Coloniale. Nothing at either the Bristol or the Louvre. Finally, an unexpected departure from the Splendid meant that we could have a twin-bedded room with a bath. We took advantage of both.

There were no trains for a week. Three hours before we sailed, an Arab had stolen my remaining 1,300 francs, and I could not afford to stay on in Marseilles. The porter from the Splendid performed a miracle (at a price) and found two berths on the 7 o'clock sleeper. We took them. When we got back to the boulevard Suchet, we found Sidi packing his bags. 'I am going to Castel-Novel. Are you coming?' Weakly, I said yes. [...] Bertrand is here, paying for his heroic struggle against seasickness by suffering intestinal agonies.[23]

To say that things did not go well for Colette in the spring of 1922 would be an understatement. In May, a lorry ran into her convertible in the avenue de Breteuil: miraculously she escaped unhurt, but the car was a complete write-off. Colette was feeling ill. She weighed 81 kilos (178 pounds, or nearly 13 stone) – 'She never let me see her naked', said Bertrand – and thought she was pregnant. She went to see Dr Trognon, who told her that she was in fact beginning the menopause.

At the beginning of July, Bertrand came to Rozven, but only for four days. He returned in August. Colette claimed that she looked like a 'fat Triton' in the bath, and said that she had gone on a diet, though she probably did not stick to it. Her relationship with Sidi was getting worse by the day. Fortunately, he, as usual, did not stay long at Rozven. The days when Colette used to wait anxiously for him to arrive and weep when he went away were long gone. That summer, Bel-Gazou irritated her more and more. The decision was finally taken, and in the autumn Colette sent her to a boarding school in

Saint-Germain-en-Laye. Bel-Gazou was only nine years old. She spent a year in Saint-Germain and then, in 1925, was sent to England. She spent her holidays with Germaine Patat in the Loiret. In later years, she spent more time with the Jouvenels than at her mother's.

Life was far from easy for Colette between 1922 and 1925. The final break with Jouvenel was obviously coming. Colette was in love with Bertrand but she did not want to impose her love on him, or to be crushed by grief herself. Maintaining some kind of emotional equilibrium required such an effort that she had no energy left for conventional maternal feelings. Colette, who was in fact extremely well-balanced, attended to first things first. She refused to go under.

1923 was a year of upheavals for Colette. She had reached the age of fifty and *Le Matin* had begun to serialize *Le Blé en herbe* – the first of her works to be signed 'Colette' – before its publication by Flammarion in June; but some of *Le Matin's* readers were shocked by the novel, and the serialization was stopped.

Colette spent a peaceful summer at Rozven. It was very hot, and the fishing was good. As usual, Colette ate too much. 'I recover my strength as soon as I reach the sea', she wrote to Marguerite Moreno.[24] Sidi, who had recently returned from the Balkans, where he had been attending the Petite Entente conference, stayed with her for a week. Bertrand too arrived from Saint-Moritz, where he had been on holiday with his mother. 'There is nothing new here,' Colette wrote a few weeks later, 'except a child who has been brought back to me ruined by excessive altitude, too much tennis and too many dances and costume balls – all that a harmful maternal presence could think of to encourage. Compared with her, all the Mamitas in the world [an illusion to her own mother-in-law] are like sugar beets.'[25] Claire was evidently trying everything to make Bertrand forget Colette.

In October, Sidi was spinning out love's sweet dreams with Princess Bibesco. Colette was still in Castel-Novel, where the autumn roses were more beautiful than ever. The situation was becoming acrimonious, and reached a climax at the end of the month.

'We were at table,' Bertrand told me, 'when my father announced that he was sending me to Prague for a training course. "No" said Colette. "What do you mean, 'No'?" said my father. "Bertrand will say with me. I do not want him to go away."'

On the spur of the moment she gave away the very thing she had been hiding for months: her affair with Bertrand. As a father, Sidi was stupefied; as a husband he was furious, then shattered. Had he really suspected nothing?

The atmosphere in the house in the boulevard Suchet was becoming unbearable. In December, Colette went off on a lecture tour that was to take her to Marseilles, Nantes and Bordeaux. She changed her lecture, which was originally to have been on 'The Problems of Living as a Couple' (now rather inappropriate), to 'My Life in the Theatre'.

Colette was relieved at having come into the open about Bertrand, but she was shaken by the inevitable results of her confession and was worried about what might happen when she got back to Paris. It had certainly been a difficult pill for Jouvenel to swallow, but after all, he himself had been carrying on for a long time. A letter to Anatole de Monzie, the lawyer and mutual friend who was now Minister for Education, shows just how distraught Colette was:

I am trying not to let it show, and I can get through the day, but I still have to get through the evenings and the nights. Try to make Sidi understand that I am not being hostile when I refuse to open hostilities. But I simply refuse to become the type of woman who takes legal action against her husband. If he thinks he has enough grounds to turn the separation into a divorce, he can do so.[26]

He did so.

Colette, as usual, sought refuge from her worries in food. She invited Léopold Marchand to come with her to sample some 'andouillette [sausage] and tripe'. And she wrote to her friend Marguerite Moreno from Marseilles: 'I am preparing to fight it all by developing a methodical appetite that is directed mainly towards seafood.'[27]

In the event, things worked out very simply. While Colette was lecturing in the provinces, Henry de Jouvenel moved out of the boulevard Suchet house without a word.

But Bertrand stayed, and in January 1924 Colette, who needed to relax, took him to Gstaad and then to Montreux in Switzerland. She had never been on a winter sports holiday. In Gstaad, they stayed at the Royal Hôtel et Winter Garden, and Colette wrote to Germaine Beaumont:

It is only 8.30 in the morning. I have already breakfasted and given the child his breakfast. That great ruffian of a boy [ce grand galapiat], as you call him, with your flair for the precise technical term, gave me trouble at first with the snobbish idea, picked up in Mégève, that he had to spend all his time skiing. But God is watching over him: He arranged for a sensible doctor to be on hand in Gstaad. He told the boy, 'Drink milk, eat, sleep and take some exercise. Taking exercise does not mean that you have to squander your reserves of strength in sports as demanding as skiing.' I won. Bertrand is sulking; everything is fine.[28]

She told Marguerite about her first ventures out on to the slopes:

As soon as I got here, I realized that I would not be able to stop myself plunging into everything to the physical limit. I had my first ski lesson the first day we were here. Then I went skating and tobogganing. I won't miss a single opportunity to fall! They find me on the piste, flat on my back like a beetle, waving my front legs clad in wool, my back legs tangled up in my skis. [. . .] When Bertrand comes with me – he skis well and goes out with the guides – he looks after me. I come off my toboggan on the bends, and I love it all. [. . .] I shall come home ruined and in a good mood. My nose has caught the sun.[29]

She also wrote to Germaine Beaumont from Montreux:

I arrived here with colic in my soul and with neurotic intestines, and forty-eight hour later, I was bob-sleighing with Galiffet (two fs? one f?).[30]

'Ruined and in a good mood' . . . But Colette was going to have to face some complicated financial problems when she got back. As she had suspected, she could no longer write for Le Matin now that she had separated from Jouvenel. On 17 February 1924, she wrote to Monzie:

Do I stay on Le Matin or do I go over to Le Journal [Le Matin's rival]? I think Le Journal will have me, but professional ethics being what they are, they won't take me on for another three months and in the meantime I'll have no regular work and will have to live like a woman of independent means. I don't mind having no regular work, but I do not have any independent means. I saved nothing while I was married. By 11 May I will be very short of money.[31]

Did Colette really have so many financial problems? In another letter to Monzie written at the end of February, she gives details of her outgoings and explains why she will have to start looking for money again after 15 April. Bel-Gazou's school fees were costing her 6,000 francs a year and by June she had to find 5,500 francs, the balance due for the household linen at Castel-Novel. Her adventures with Bertrand in Switzerland had cost her 75 francs a day. She added that she had sold 'a charming sketch by Toulouse-Lautrec which belonged to me' to raise money. Flammarion gave her only 21,000 francs as an advance against her royalties. 'You see how my *phynances* [an illusion to Jarry's *Ubu roi*] are always in a bad way . . .'

Colette had certainly not often been rich, and her peasant mentality tended to make her always extremely worried about money. But she was not mean with money. Occasionally, for instance, she helped Hélène Picard, who was poor and whose books were selling badly, by asking their joint publisher secretly to transfer some of her royalties to Hélène's account. She could spend money like water, and at the same time worry about being short of it. In 1940, when she was extremely famous and had absolutely no reason to fear for the future, she asked Lucie Delarue-Mardrus, 'Tell me about pensions from the Société des Gens de Lettres. Would they award me one?'[32]

Colette stopped writing for *Le Matin* in February 1924. Robert de Flers, *Le Figaro's* editor, commissioned her to write a regular Sunday column. The first appeared in May, but the arrangement lasted only until September. Because of 'the high cost of living', *Le Figaro* wanted two articles for the price of one. Colette was not convinced by Flers' arguments and resigned.

In April 1924 Bertrand finally decided to go on the course in Czechoslovakia, and Colette did not hold him back.

Bertrand has left for Prague, and I think he will be away for a long time. But he is right to go. It is the beginning of his career; and on the way from Strasbourg to Nuremberg he experienced the joy of his first triumphs, receptions, and ovations, and made speeches (with the strange freedom and self-confidence that comes out when this parliamentarian's son has an audience), waved to the crowd from a car, and was invited to call on the Queen of Roumania. It really has worked out well and he was right to choose his own time to go; if he had gone a few months ago, it would have meant going into forced exile. I have not, thank God, been a bad adviser to the boy.[33]

The veiled irony of these lines sounds like the beginning of a farewell. Colette had realized that, like his father, he was destined to live in a world that was alien to her.

In July, Bertrand came home for the funeral of his uncle Robert de Jouvenel. Colette was annoyed to hear that one of the guests invited to stay at the château for the funeral was the daughter of Senator Lémery (they were still trying to find a match for Bertrand), 'a gorgeous, tawny girl who was married for three months [. . .] I think they brought her along just in case [. . .] she is a little sparrowhawk with a sharp beak.'[34]

That year, Colette spent the summer alone at Rozven with Germaine Beaumont, and then with the Marchands. 'Bertrand has been in Paris for a week, the idiot. He is organizing a *jeunesse démocratique* or something equally stupid. I think he should be back on the fifteenth.'[35]

At the end of August Colette set off alone in her car for Mont-Saint-Michel, where she had arranged to meet Bertrand. They ate omelettes at Mère Poulard's and watched the sea 'racing in around that weird conical thing.'[36]

In December she took *Chéri* on tour to Monte-Carlo and Marseilles, with Pierre Fresnay playing young Peloux. She spent the next year on tour, visiting Paris and various spas, with Marguerite Moreno playing Charlotte Peloux. It must be said that Colette was much better suited for mime than for acting, where her accent was a considerable handicap. She drew an audience but, as some critics were quick to point out, people came to see her out of curiosity rather than anything else. Two years later she finally gave up the theatre.

The Boas-Jouvenel conspiracy at last paid dividends, and before the end of 1924 Bertrand gave in and agreed to become engaged to a certain Mademoiselle de Ricqulès, a very rich heiress. In accordance with the rules, Henry de Jouvenel, dressed in yellow kid gloves and morning coat, went to ask her parents for her hand in marriage.

On the day of his formal engagement, Bertrand turned up on Colette's doorstep in the boulevard Suchet, appalled at the thought of the lunch that had been arranged to mark the occasion. 'I can't face this reception', he said. Colette said nothing, but she had a glint in her eye. Then she said, 'If you really can't face it, don't go.' As he left, Bertrand dragged his feet, as though he were marching to his execution. In the garden, he turned to look back. Colette was watching from the window. She threw a small piece of paper into the air and it drifted down towards Bertrand. He picked it up. Colette had written three words on it: 'I love you.' 'It was the first time that she had ever told me that,' said Bertrand. 'And I did not go to the lunch.'

The scandal was dreadful. The families quarrelled. The Ricqulès took the view that they had been mortally insulted. Claire Boas and Henry de Jouvenel were furious. Once again, Colette had won.

She had got Bertrand back, but she knew that he was being subjected to pressures against which she was powerless and that, sooner or later, she would lose him. She was clear-sighted enough to realize that, family pressures aside, the age difference between them was the greatest threat to their love. Bertrand had his whole life in front of him, but most of her life was already behind her. Colette was about to write La Fin de Chéri. For her, pain was the worst thing imaginable, and she forestalled the inevitable.

1. Bertrand de Jouvenel, *Un Voyageur . . .*, p. 55.
2. Letter, 4 April 1920; *Lettres à Marguerite Moreno*, p. 47.
3. Abbé J. Auffret, *Saint-Coulomb des origines à nos jours*, Saint-Brieuc, Les Presses bretonnes, 1982.
4. *L'Etoile Vesper.*
5. Unpublished letter; coll. J. L. Lécard.
6. Colette, 'Gîte d'écrivain', *Le Figaro littéraire*, 24 January 1953.
7. Beaumont and Parinaud, *Colette par elle-même*, p. 20.
8. Ibid., pp. 12-13.
9. Unpublished letter, 21 February 1921; coll. J. L. Lécard.
10. Unpublished letter, July 1921; coll. J. L. Lécard.
11. Unpublished letter, 23 September 1921; coll. J. L. Lécard.
12. Bertrand de Jouvenel, 'La Vérité sur *Chéri*', unpublished manuscript.
13. Bertrand de Jouvenel, *Un Voyageur . . .*, p. 56.
14. Letter, September 1920; *Lettres à ses pairs*, p. 218.
15. Unpublished letter; coll. Richard Anacréon.
16. Most of the letters they exchanged were unfortunately destroyed when Vire was bombed during the Second World War.
17. Unpublished letter.
18. Letter, July 1921; *Lettres de la Vagabonde*, pp. 138-9.
19. Beaumont and Parinaud, *Colette par elle-même*, pp. 20-21.
20. *Lettres à Marguerite Moreno*, p. 53.
21. Letter, 21 August 1921; ibid., p. 58.
22. *Pour un herbier*, Lausanne, Mermod, 1948, p. 114.
23. Unpublished letter; coll. J. L. Lécard.
24. Letter, 31 July 1923; *Lettres à Marguerite Moreno*, p. 70.
25. Letter to Marguerite Moreno, 18 August 1923; ibid., p. 71.
26. Unpublished letter; coll. Richard Anacréon.
27. Letter, 23 November 1923; *Lettres à Marguerite Moreno*, p. 77.
28. Unpublished letter; coll. J. L. Lécard.
29. Letter, 22 January 1924; *Lettres à Marguerite Moreno*, p. 78.
30. Unpublished letter; coll. J. L. Lécard. The reference is to the grandson of General Galliffet, whom Colette had once known.
31. Unpublished letter; coll. Richard Anacréon.
32. Letter, 10 April 1940; *Lettres à ses pairs*, p. 176.
33. Letter to Léopold Marchand, 12 April 1924; *Lettres de la Vagabonde*, p. 175.
34. Letter to Marguerite Moreno, 10 July 1924; *Lettres à Marguerite Moreno*, p. 82.
35. Letter to Marguerite Moreno, 12 August 1924; ibid., p. 85.
36. Letter to Marguerite Moreno, 30 August 1924; ibid., p. 87.

la mer est ici

388

389

390

391

392

Between 1910 and 1924, Colette spent many happy summers at Rozven ('rose of the winds'), a house bought for her by Missy, near Saint-Coulomb in northern Brittany, in a small valley leading down to the beach of La Touesse. It was the setting of *Le Blé en herbe*, which gave its name to the path linking the house to the sea.

388 The house, from the seashore.

389 Renaud de Jouvenel, his half sister Colette ('Bel-Gazou') and her nurse Miss Draper.

390, 391 Germaine Beaumont and Colette.

392 Standing, Bertrand de Jouvenel and Hélène Picard; seated in the chair, Germaine Carco; on the ground, Germaine Beaumont, Colette and her daughter.

393 Bertrand and Colette.

394 In front, Hélène Picard, Colette and Francis Carco; behind, Germaine Carco and Bertrand.

393   394

395 *Le Blé en herbe,* about a young man in love with an older woman, shocked its readers when it was published in 1923. Colette was concerned with niceties of typography on its title page.

396 Bertrand de Jouvenel. 'That great ruffian, as you call him, with your flair for the precise technical term.'

397 Gstaad, where Colette and Bertrand escaped for a holiday together, in January 1924.

398 Colette tobogganing: 'I won't miss a single opportunity to fall!'

396

397

238

La Vagabonde was adapted for the stage and given its first performance in February 1923, with Cora Laparcerie and Harry Baur. In a subsequent production, at Monte Carlo in December 1926, the leads were played by Colette herself and the famous couturier Paul Poiret.

399   A poster for the original production.

400   A rehearsal for the 1926 revival. With Colette are Paul Poiret (seated in the chair) and Léopold Marchand (standing at the foot of the stage), who had worked with her on the adaptation.

401   Paul Poiret and Colette.

402   Vertès's view of Colette acting Léa in a revival of *Chéri*, on tour in 1923. The caption advises her to stick to writing.

399

400

401

Voici qu'après Tristan Bernard, jouant dans son " Prince Charmant ", Colette a repris dans " Chéri " le rôle de Léa de Lonval si bien
créé par Jeanne Rolly. Colette a bien tort. Elle écrit des livres remarquables, pour lesquels aucune artiste ne saurait la remplacer
Qu'elle continue et laisse jouer les comédiennes. Le personnage de Léa a besoin d'être réalisé par une femme élégante et belle, sans que
Chéri devient tout à fait ignoble, inexcusable, et tourne au greluchon très indélicat.

Dessin de VERTÈ

402

403 Watercolour drawing of Colette in 1926 by Texcier.

404 Maurice Ravel. *L'Enfant et les sortilèges,* the opera which he wrote with Colette, was first performed in 1925, after the composer had 'worked in secrecy for four years, under the blue, nyctalopic gaze of his Siamese cats'.

405 Colette riding in a barouche in Nice, where she was appearing in the stage version of *Chéri,* in 1923. With her are Marguerite Moreno and Léopold Marchand.

403

404

405

406 Colette in 1930, by Andrée Sikorska.

407, 408 *Sido*, published in 1930, marked a triumphal return to the theme of her childhood. Among the memories it evoked was that of the big iron gate of the château of Saint-Sauveur; Sido's children loved to hear the four musical notes it emitted as it squeaked open or shut.

407

ANDREE SIKORSKA

406

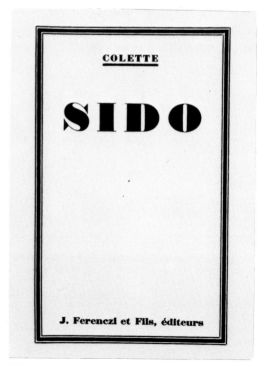

COLETTE

SIDO

J. Ferenczi et Fils, éditeurs

408

409 Colette's brother Léo, playing the piano. 'Léo won't be able to get away from music', his mother was fond of predicting.

« REGARDE… »
PAR
COLETTE ET MÉHEUT.

412   A famous photograph of Colette by Edward Steichen.

413 A very '1930s' portrait of Colette.

VI A Fine Autumn

414 Maurice Goudeket

Marguerite Moreno was a charming, witty woman who moved in many different circles, and in the winter of 1924-5 she introduced Colette to a man called Maurice Goudeket.

Maurice Goudeket was born in Paris into a modest middle-class Jewish family; his father was Dutch and his mother French. He was a dealer in precious stones, an astute businessman and certainly no fool. He was reserved and interested in the arts. At thirty-five, he was sixteen years younger than Colette.

When they first met, they were rather wary of each other. They then met again at Easter at Cap d'Ail on the Côte d'Azur. The company included Goudeket, Colette, Marguerite Moreno and her young lover, the actor Pierre Moreno. Pierre was also her nephew; Colette had obviously started a trend! Another couple were there too; the woman was Goudeket's mistress. Colette nicknamed her 'the Gracious Chihuahua'. The atmosphere was very cheerful.

Bertrand de Jouvenel was in Cannes, having been sent there by his mother after the scandal of the broken engagement. He had been very ill and was convalescing in the sunshine of the Midi. Maeterlinck's niece Marcelle Prat was also in Cannes. She was intelligent, good company, and in love with Bertrand. It was no coincidence that she should be there; Claire Boas thought that she would make a perfect daughter-in-law and had seen to it that the two young people would be near one another.

Was Colette aware of this new plot? One morning she telephoned Bertrand to invite him to Cap d'Ail for lunch. Bertrand left Mademoiselle Prat and came running. He found the lunch very difficult. For some reason, Goudeket irritated him. The ease of the older man made him shyer than ever. Colette sat beside Goudeket, and looked like a sly cat. All this looked very ominous to Bertrand. It was, however, Bertrand that Colette summoned to her bedroom that night. It was to be the last night they would spend together. Bertrand and Colette talked until dawn. ('I was ready to spend my life with her', says Bertrand.) But in the morning they decided to separate.

Colette returned to Paris in Goudeket's car.

The morning after their last night together, Colette wrote Bertrand a long letter. He never had the opportunity to reply to it, as Marcelle Prat, who was jealous of Colette, stole it and destroyed it. (Not until much later did she admit this to Bertrand.) In December 1925 they were married, much to the relief of his family.

After this, Colette and Bertrand rarely saw one another. But Bertrand never lost touch with her, and years later he still referred to her as his 'darling mother'. In 1931, Colette received several letters from him; he was in love with a woman who did not love him. In one letter he reminded her of their trip to Algeria and of how they had sunk up to their ankles into the sand. The letters were charming and nostalgic. Bertrand was feeling lost and was asking for help from the woman who had taught him to recognize the delicate scent of paeonies and who had showed him such tenderness. He concluded, 'I will always be the worst of your books.'

In Paris, Colette and Maurice Goudeket saw more and more of one another. On 7 May 1925, Colette wrote to Marguerite Moreno: 'Last night, I had a very long conversation with that fellow. I find that he is at his best when he lets himself go a little.'[1] He was soon to let go completely, much to the distress of the Chihuahua. Colette took her place, just as she had taken that of the Panther, and made short work of her rival.

On 21 June, Marguerite Moreno received a very revealing letter:

Oh dear. Dear, oh dear, oh dear! Your friend is in a fine mess, in it up to her neck, in it up to here. Oh! calm people can be so satanic! I say that for the benefit of that bloke Maurice. Do you want to know what that bloke is?

He is a bastard, a so-and-so, a good kid [chic type], and a satin skin. You see what a state I am in.[2]

Marguerite replied: 'Well, well, what a mess! What a lovely mess. So you've had another bout of it, have you, you wretched woman? Will you never calm down? I give you a slave, and presto! you make him into a master.'[3]

Colette's letters to Marguerite show that even though she was now over fifty, she had lost none of her exceptional physical vigour. At roughly the same time, Paul Léautaud noted in his journal: 'She is still very pretty – no, pretty is not the word. It would be truer to say that she radiates voluptuousness, love, and passion, though the underlying melancholy is very obvious too.'[4]

Colette's vigorous sensuality meant that she enjoyed physical pleasure even at an advanced age, and some people found that shocking. Duhamel, by then a grand old man, once heard her say, 'I cannot stand people who confuse orgasm with sensual pleasure', and added rather bitterly, 'she said it with conviction and as though she were an expert.'[5]

After she met Goudeket, Colette's life did however begin to slow down and to change. After a final season in La Vagabonde with Paul Poiret in Monte Carlo late in 1926, she said farewell to the theatre. She also said farewell to her mad, passionate affairs with young men. It was not that Goudeket was an old man: he entered her life in 1925 and when they at last married, ten years later, he was only in his mid-forties. Paul Valéry, who always liked smutty jokes, referred to him as 'Goudkéket' or 'Monsieur Bonnequeue' (puns on quequette and queue) – 'Mr Goodprick'. Colette spoke lovingly of his 'satin skin', but above all he was her 'best friend'. His reward for the tireless devotion he showed her was the privilege of sharing her last years.

Colette said farewell to her beloved Brittany and to Rozven's sea-breezes and mists, and exchanged them for the heat of the Midi, which until then she had not liked (she called it 'le bas de la France', the bottom of France).

It is worth noting that, despite the strength of her personality, Colette always followed her husbands, even if she did end up by becoming the dominant partner. Just as she had gone to the Jura with Willy and to the Corrèze with Jouvenel, she now went to the Côte d'Azur with Goudeket who, like all Dutchmen, adored the warmth of the south. In 1926 she bought a villa called La Treille Muscate at Saint-Tropez.

She also said farewell to some of her old friends, not all of whom liked Maurice Goudeket. Germaine Beaumont, for instance, began to drift away from her.

From 1925 onwards, she travelled for pleasure or to give lectures, but she also concentrated more and more on her writing.

In 1925, her poem *L'Enfant et les sortilèges*, with music by Ravel, was performed in Monte Carlo.

Colette's health declined in the course of the twenty-nine years that remained to her. She was subject to bronchitis and her feet gave her trouble, which is why she wore open sandals like those affected by Isadora Duncan for the rest of her life. (Chanel said that Colette had 'feet like an apostle'.) Over-eating gave her digestive problems, and she suffered from rheumatism. In 1931 she broke her fibula, which slowed her down considerably, and between 1946 and her death in 1954 arthritis of the hip immobilized her completely.

Writing became a refuge and a means of escape. That in itself is something of a paradox because, although she was prolific, Colette always claimed to find writing very difficult and to loathe it.

When I was young, I never, never wanted to write. No, I did not get up secretly in the middle of the night to write poetry in pencil on the lid of shoe boxes. No, I did not cast my inspired words to the west wind and to the moonlight. No, I did not get nineteen out of twenty for a composition when I was twelve or fifteen. Day by day, I realized more clearly that I was cut out *not* to be a writer.[6]

In 1921, she described her reluctance to get down to work and the difficulties she had with writing in a letter to Natalie Barney from Fontainebleau: 'I came here because I was so tired with doing nothing but work. Work is very bad for me. I like tiring myself out with pleasant things, not unpleasant things.'[7] She said the same thing to Francis Carco: 'I am working like a navvy, dragging a collection of short stories out of my memory and my imagination. It's disgusting work.'[8] She also told him: 'I am working like a madwoman, and it may well be the death of me. Work is not the right climate for me.'[9] And she told Marguerite Moreno: 'Scratching away at a piece of paper is such a gloomy task. No witness, and no one to take care of you. And no passion.'[10] Or again, 'I will have to leave you now. With great reluctance, I have to go and sweat out an article for a de luxe publication on Digitalin . . . I loathe writing. I would like to go on living the life of unbridled luxury I am living here [at La Treille Muscate]: bare feet, a faded bathing costume, an old jacket, lots of garlic and going swimming whenever I feel like it.'[11] She also told Natalie Barney, 'I am working, with horror in my soul, on a novel [*La Fin de Chéri*] which has to be completed by 5 December [. . .] so I am like a bear with a sore head.'[12]

Although Colette claimed to be lazy, when she did work she worked hard and she was totally dedicated to her vocation as a writer. She worked slowly – in January 1928 she claimed to have written only thirty-five pages in nineteen days – tearing up her work and starting again, and renouncing all pleasures until the task was completed.

Colette polished her words and sentences with the patience of a conscientious artisan, armed with her Rouaix thesaurus, which went everywhere with her.[13] 'I work with a rigour which may not produce a lot, but it does preserve my self-respect. This is the *eighth* time I have started the scene with the man [in *La Naissance du jour*].'[14] She said something very similar to Irène Le

Cornec: 'I rewrote the last four or five pages of *La Dame du photographe* eight times.'

Colette's lively, spontaneous style, her extraordinary ability to evoke a great deal in very few words, and the clarity of her writing did not, then, come about by accident. They are the result of unremitting work and pitiless self-criticism. It was presumably Willy who first taught her to avoid overloading her style and to cut out any padding. Colette said that whenever she revised a page she had written, she cut out half the adjectives. In early summer 1923, when she was completing *Le Blé en herbe*, she wrote to Marguerite Moreno: 'The final page alone cost me the whole of my first day at Castel-Novel – and I defy you to doubt my word when you read it. What? Those twenty lines, with no jewels and no ornamentation? Alas, that is how it is. It was the *proportions* that gave me so much trouble. I loathe bombastic endings.'[15] Over the years, her taste for sobriety became more pronounced. In 1949, she rewrote her stage adaptation of *Chéri*, cutting out what she called the 'unnecessary ornamentation'.

When Marguerite Moreno was writing her memoirs, Colette gave her some invaluable advice:

You've not yet got the hang of it: you haven't got the effect of spontaneity that would make it read like a diary. You give the impression of writing up your men one after the other like a school exercise [. . .] I'm being as tough on you as I am on myself [. . .] you are magic itself when you talk, but most of the effect gets lost when you write. Either you don't work at it enough, or it all becomes washed out [. . .] Don't *narrate*, for God's sake! Use separate brushstrokes and colours, and don't feel you have to compose an *ending* [. . .] Give me a setting, guests, even the names of a few dishes, otherwise it won't work. [. . .] And try, my dearest, not to let us guess what a sweat it is to write.[16]

When Renée Hamon, a great traveller whom Colette called her 'little corsair', admitted that she wanted to write a book but had no idea how to go about it, Colette replied:

Never having had much idea myself, I can at least tell you how not to go about it. Do not depict anything you have not seen. Ignore things that don't appeal to you; but contemplate things that hurt you at great length. Be faithful to your first impressions. Alter them only if doing so produces a more truthful picture. Do not wear yourself out searching for rare words; a word only becomes rare when it has the good fortune to meet another word that gives it a new meaning. Do not lie: lies develop the imagination, and imagination is the reporter's curse.

Take notes
Do not take notes } strike out where not applicable

Do not write your book while you are on the spot. You will not recognize it when you get back here. You cannot write a book about passion when you are making love. But think about it just enough for it to nag at you.[17]

Colette also advised her to be careful about how she used the ellipsis:

You put ellipses everywhere. You're ruining the effect, don't you see? An ellipsis has to make an impact; and it should only be used once in a while.[18]

Colette's distrust of lyricism, ornamentation and super-fluities kept her away from ideology and poetry: 'There are three accessories that don't suit me at all: hats with feathers, generalizations and earrings.'[19] She rejected the idea that she was a poet, telling Germaine Beaumont: 'I am not fanciful, and my eyes are not clouded by that magical substance, "poetry".'[20] She was capable of appreciating the poetry of others, but studiously avoided writing poetry of her own:

You have before you an example of an extremely rare species, almost a freak: a writer of prose who has never written poetry. [. . .] I appeal to you all, men and women alike, to all of you who bear in your memory that secret, that faded rose, that old wound, that shameful thing – a poem in verse.[21]

Just as she could repress her emotions in her day-to-day life, she could discipline her style so as not to lapse into classical poetry and or those lines of verse that sometimes creep unnoticed into prose.

If I did not keep my prose under strict control, I know that I would be a bad undisciplined poet rather than an anxious and disciplined writer of prose. I keep my eye on it and I am vigilant. But even so, the delinquents do sometimes get past me. In some of the novels I wrote when I was young, there are unintended lines of verse that are not even camouflaged. As many as three, one after another. I will not tell you where.[22]

Although Colette refused to write formal verse, she was in a way like Molière's Bourgeois gentilhomme in reverse: she wrote poetry without realizing it – or wanting to realize it. But she never lost control, and when she felt she was straying into lyricism, she deliberately used very down-to-earth words to undercut an emotion of which she disapproved.

While she avoided any suggestion of metrical structure, Colette's prose constantly uses imagery which is unforgettably evocative and which is in a more fundamental sense poetic. She perceives the world in terms of senses. She sees it, touches it, listens to it and, above all, she smells it. Her books are full of scents, fragrances, odours and even stenches, from the most delicate to the most overpowering. She breathed in the scent not only of flowers, grass, the sea and truffles, but of houses, streets and the passing seasons, and she makes us smell them too. In *Claudine à Paris* she describes the odours of a department store:

I made a special study of the various smells in the Grands Magasins du Louvre and Bon Marché. The fabric department is intoxicating [. . .] Does the sugary scent of new blue cotton delight me or does it make me feel sick? Shame upon the flannel and the woollen blankets: they smell much the same as rotten eggs. The smell of new shoes has its charms, as does that of purses. But they cannot equal the divine fragrance of the thick blue paper used for tracing embroidery patterns; that compensates for the sickening stink of the perfumes and soaps.[23]

What, too, could be more poetic than her evocation of sounds? In a letter to a friend she writes:

The sound of a horse trotting along an empty road in the distance always makes me catch my breath, especially when I hear it at night. That goes back to my childhood, to the black mare and the memory of riding the forty kilometres from Auxerre to Saint-Sauveur at night.[24]

Colette's style is inimitably light, elegant and relaxed. She once said 'I write on air'.[25] André Billy in 1953 remembered how

her first books seemed to us to be a refreshing breath of cool air. The generation who came after us can scarcely imagine the surprise and enchantment we felt when we first read them, because by their day Colette's genius was already part of the general literary climate. You need to have grown up in the rarified atmosphere of Symbolism to appreciate the value of Colette's contribution. She opened up the world of scent and touch and the thousand sensations that make up our daily lives. [. . .] One of the reasons why we are so loyal to Colette is that ideology and rhetoric are so alien to her. Ideological and rhetorical books date so quickly.[26]

Then there is the note of humour that always creeps in when one least expects it.

But it all took tremendously hard work. Sometimes she worked for seven, eight or even eleven hours at a sitting. 'I work like an ant. I drag things home, store them away down below and then I start again.'[27]

When it was time to work, Colette was blind and deaf to the outside world. But she always found it difficult to settle down to work and tried to put off the fatal moment.

She would go through a whole ritual, a kind of insect dance. She would sit down, then get up again . . . I've forgotten my rug . . . I haven't got the right pen . . . not enough paper . . . What time is it?[28]

On the other hand, Germaine Beaumont observed,

I have seen her deny herself a fishing trip or a walk on the salt marshes [...] She would stay at home with the windows closed and settle down to the task in hand. She would doodle in the margins, touch the things that she kept on her desk to stroke and admire, as though touching them would bring her luck, and then she would plunge into her work, losing herself in it completely. Hours later, she would emerge, as though she had been delivered of a great burden.[29]

Like all writers, she had her working habits. They were not simply fads: she needed to be absolutely comfortable. She would only write on the smooth blue paper she bought by the ream from Toury-Méles in the rue du Four (she took Pierre Laval there to choose paper) because it hurt her eyes less than white paper. For the same reason, the lamp in her apartment in the rue de Beaujolais was always shaded with a sheet of blue paper. She called it her 'fanal bleu', or blue lantern.

Colette had her own recipes for finding the isolation and peace she needed to write. 'What love would like, chaste work demands. Lock the door, turn on the light at midday, draw the curtains and see that everything is quiet.'[30] She needed artificial light to concentrate. 'I have to have the light on, otherwise my attention wanders. I cannot write in natural light.' In order to spare her eyes, she bought blue-tinted 'daylight' bulbs, which artists use because they do not distort colours (they can still be bought). When she was writing she always wore a particular dressing-gown, and worked in her bare feet. She taught Germaine Beaumont the benefits of having a rug on her knees in winter: 'don't let your feet dangle, stretch out your legs, and try to be slightly too warm when you are working. There comes a moment when loss of heat can cost you a page – or at least it costs me a page.'[31] She was very fussy about the way her table was balanced and about the height of her chair. She insisted on having her books to hand in a bookcase. And she always had a whole battery of pens – Watermans bought in Paris from Hardmuth in the rue de Hanovre, American fountain pens acquired in New York in 1935 – of which she sometimes preferred to use one and sometimes another.

As a writer, Colette was a complete perfectionist, and she was extremely annoyed if she found cuts or misprints in the final text. In 1929, Pierre Brisson wanted to publish La Seconde in Les Annales, the magazine edited by his mother, Yvonne Sarcey. Colette did not trust him: the magazine was intended for girls, and she was afraid that her novel might be cut by its puritanical editor. She was assured that nothing of the sort would happen, that things had changed. Colette gave in and was then respectfully requested to alter certain passages. After an argument, a compromise was finally reached. When the first instalment appeared, Colette noticed a printing error: an extra s had crept into the text. She immediately rang Pierre Brisson and attacked him for introducing an obscenity into her work; the intrusive s had transformed 'Jane coupa son fil avec ses dents' (Jane cut her thread with her teeth) into 'Jane coupa son fils. . .' (her son). She added, 'I told you it would end up with something being cut.'[32] When La Chambre éclairée was published in a de luxe edition with illustrations by Picart-Ledoux, Colette noticed that the publisher had shortened one chapter. In the copy she sent to Germaine Beaumont she wrote on the offending page: 'The publisher has dropped the end of the chapter. I will drop the publisher.'[33]

In the fifties, when Hélène Lazareff wanted to publish a piece by Colette in Elle, it took her a long time to persuade her to cut a sentence referring to a man with 'clear semen'.[34]

When she was twenty-seven Colette had told Rachilde, 'If people annoy you, hit back. That's my solution.'[35] In later life she did not let anyone tread on her toes, nor did she mince her words: 'All the people at

Flammarion are tremulous, colourless old grubs, who know nothing of what goes on in their own firm.'[36]

She also drove a hard bargain in terms of contracts and freelance rates. When Arthème Fayard asked her for an article for *Les Nouvelles littéraires*, he magnanimously told her, 'You can name your own fee.' When he heard how much she wanted, he stammered, 'But Gide asks a quarter of that for an article.' Colette replied sharply: 'Gide is wrong. If that is the way famous writers behave, what happens to the ones who are hungry?'[37]

From 1926 onwards, Colette concentrated on arranging the house in Saint-Tropez to her liking. It was smaller than Rozven (which she had recently sold), with only four plain rooms and a north-facing terrace covered with wistaria outside the kitchen. But it also had two acres of land, with vines, a small pine wood, fig trees, and a well surrounded by the muscat grapes which gave the villa its name, 'La Treille Muscate'. Over the years, Colette transformed the house, adding on more rooms, a patio and a garage down by the road. She had green fingers, and before long the garden was a mass of flowers: mimosa, oleander, turpentine-tree and volubilis. She was also very proud of the results of the autumn grape harvest.

For the next twelve years, La Treille Muscate was to be her favourite home. She often went there to write, both in winter and in summer. *La Naissance du jour* is full of its scents.

Colette would get up with the sun and go for a walk, always with a cat or a dog at her heels. She went swimming – she could now swim better than ever, even underwater – gardened or worked on the house. Breakfast was always eaten beneath the wistaria.

Colette was very hospitable and entertained a great deal at La Treille Muscate. Her guests included old and new friends: the painters Dunoyer de Segonzac and Luc-Albert Moreau, with his mistress Moune, the violinist Hélène Jourdan-Morhange, the critic Gignoux, Thérèse Dorny and Nora Auric all visited her there.

Bel-Gazou, who was growing up to be a pretty girl, was often there.

Lunch was washed down with wine from Colette's vines, and was always a cheerful meal. Many people must remember the green melons, the anchovies, the stuffed scorpionfish, the *bouillabaisse* and the *aïoli* (garlic mayonnaise) they enjoyed at Colette's home in the south. Héléna Bossis, who used to go to La Treille Muscate with her mother Simone Berriau, remembers seeing Colette turning a salad with her fingers, her hands dripping with olive oil. There was always an aroma of garlic in the house, which mingled with the scent of the pink lilies, the petunias and the tuberoses in the garden. Throughout the day, Colette crunched cloves of garlic as though they were sweets. As night fell, as the cicadas began to chirp and the scent of petunias filled the air, Colette went back to the terrace, where she liked to sleep out under the stars.

Although she was now leading a more settled life, Colette had not finished moving about. In 1927 she left the house in the boulevard Suchet, which she had never really liked and which contained too many reminders of the past, and took one of the small apartments of the Palais Royal in the rue de Beaujolais, which was on the mezzanine floor and looked out beneath the arcades. It was dark and had a low ceiling; Colette called it 'my tunnel', 'my drainpipe', 'my muff', or 'my drawer'. Goudeket was still living in his bachelor establishment, a ground-floor apartment in the avenue du President Wilson.

Colette was now truly famous. Two biographies had appeared and translations of her books had been published in England, Italy, Germany and the United States. What more could she want? The one thing she wanted was to be promoted to the rank of *Officier* of the Legion of Honour. In order to get what she wanted, she brought out the big guns, including Anna de Noailles, who was a close friend of Edouard Herriot, mayor and *député* for

Lyons and at the time Minister for Education, and Marguerite Moreno. In the summer of 1928, Anna de Noailles wrote to Goudeket to assure him that all was going according to plan: 'I keep watch and then, like a bull, I charge at the red ribbon which the thrilling genius of our glorious friend demands. Herriot has been wonderful, and I think that only a few jealous individuals will try to prevent justice being done to her supreme gifts.'[38] On 5 November Colette's wish came true and she was promoted from *Chevalier* to *Officier*. She was still not satisfied; in 1936 she was promoted to the rank of *Commandeur*, and in 1953 she finally achieved the supreme rank of *Grand Officier*. Her promotion caused a lot of talk. Even Léautaud, who admired Colette's talent, thought that 'it really is going too far to give a woman the cravate [of *Commandeur*], or even to make them *Officier*. Make them *Chevalier* by all means. But that should be enough. It's typical of the way everything is falling apart nowadays.'[39]

Until 1932, Colette wrote and travelled a great deal, with Goudeket at her side. He was the ideal husband for a woman writer; silent, docile and obliging. In 1929, as Colette was returning with him from a country house hotel in Belgium where she had gone to finish her novel *La Seconde*, she wrote to Anna de Noailles: 'Maurice? I made him live a dreadful Belgian life. All the time I was working – up to nine hours at a sitting – I was sullen and silent. He was stoical.'[40] In 1930, she published *Sido* and five new *Dialogues de bêtes*.

In the summer she went to Saint-Tropez, with its cicadas and flowers, but she was already beginning to find it less pleasant. In August 1930 she had to take legal action against someone who was selling postcards of 'Colette's House' without her permission. In the same month she wrote to Marguerite Moreno: 'I make a point of staying away from the harbour, which is swarming with *le tout Paris* and *le tout Montparnasse*.'[41] In 1933 she told Hélène Picard,

Whenever I go into 'town', I am stopped by all the people I avoid in Paris, dressed up as Mexican planters, clowns, cabin boys from flower boats, and negresses. No, no, and no. I prefer the coastal path at six in the morning, when everything is wet with dew. The path is at sea-level and is lined with trees heavy with black figs that bleed white juice when you pluck them.[42]

She loathed the crowds that were invading the coast and noisy events like the 'Bal des Nouilles' which were beginning to drown out the sound of the cicadas.

Colette always hated snobbery, crowds and society life. She liked to choose her own company and avoided what she called 'clowns who waste your time'. Journalists who came to see her were often surprised to discover that she was not what they had expected at all. 'I had to break off to be interviewed by an American journalist. She was even more American than you could possibly imagine. Her preconceptions about Colette would have delighted you. She thought I was a fashionable socialite.'[43]

In 1930, Colette and Goudeket bought La Gerbière, an estate near Paris above Montfort-l'Amaury (where Germaine Beaumont lived) – a comfortable, pretty house with a lawn, a garden and a small woods. Before the year was out, they had sold it to Chanel. Colette claimed that the house was haunted, but the truth was that the economic crisis of the thirties had resulted in a lot of bankruptcies, and had had a bad effect on Goudeket's business. They could not afford to keep up two houses and two apartments in Paris.

Colette's travels at this time were almost always for work, or as someone else's guest. In 1929 she and Goudeket went to Spain and Morocco, where Simone Berriau's friend the Glaoui placed a house in Tangiers at her disposal. In the summer of 1930, Henri de Rothschild invited them on a cruise to Norway on his yacht, the *Eros*. Colette's trips to Belgium, Austria, Roumania and North Africa were paid for by the lectures she gave there.

257

In September 1931 – the year of Willy's death – she tripped in a rut in a road near Saint-Tropez and broke her fibula. She had to stay in plaster for three weeks; the fracture was very painful, and, because of her age (she was fifty-eight), slow to heal. The resultant spell of limping may have been the origin of the arthritis of the hip which was to cause her so much pain eight years later and which finally immobilized her. Bel-Gazou was very upset by the accident, but when she tried to say so, Colette treated her very coldly. 'My daughter rushed to my side. She was very emotional, but I soon put an end to her outbursts. [. . .] I have not been mithridatized against every emotion – I mean against every manifestation of emotion – and I am less afraid of catching the itch than of showing how dreadfully weak I am.'[44]

André Maginot, notorious for his ill-fated 'Line', was an unfailing source of doomed ideas. One day around 1925 he had lunch with Colette in her house in the boulevard Suchet and suggested that she should open a beauty salon selling products under her own name. The idea surfaced again in 1931. The economy was still in crisis, Goudeket's business was going badly and Colette's royalties were not enough to cover all their expenses. Why not go into business? She had Goudeket to look after the commercial side of things. The rest would be fun: playing shops, trying out perfumes, stirring little pots of make-up, looking for colours and, best of all, transform- ing women's faces. 'The human face has always been my landscape . . .' Ever since she had become Colette, she had felt an urge to alter the hairstyle of every woman who came near her. It was as though she wanted to leave her mark on them. Annie de Pène, Germaine Beaumont, Hélène Picard, Claude Chauvière and others had all cut their hair on Colette's advice – or at her orders.

The singer Mireille, the wife of Emmanuel Berl, still wears her hair in the style Colette advised her to adopt when they first met. Colette had very definite ideas about hairstyles. Long hair was out. Anyone who had a broad forehead – she hated her own 'monstrous forehead' – had to hide it. 'A woman's face needs foliage', she would say. And she did not like it when her advice was ignored. She once told a mother that her daughter should wear her hair in a fringe. 'That would be a waste. She has such a pretty forehead, why hide it?' 'True,' said Colette, 'but I'm sure she also has a pretty arse, and you hide that.'

As for make-up, she was an expert. She had spent hours putting on her own make-up in theatre dressing rooms. She knew how to heighten the blue of her eyes by outlining them with kohl (grey antimony) and how to make her teeth look whiter by painting her tongue and her gums with madder. She knew how to turn defects to advantage, and to enhance her best features. Once she had reached a certain age, she would have only head-and- shoulder photographs taken, because she knew that the rest of her body was not fit to be seen. She also knew what colours make you look healthy, that pastel tones highlight a suntan and pink tulle cheers up a pasty complexion. When it came to perfume, she had all the expertise of the Queen of Sheba, and her acute sense of smell meant that she could use sultry perfumes like chypre, patchouli and jasmine. She was an expert in the 'entertaining alchemy' that brings out a woman's charm and beauty.

For aeons, I faithfully bought my kohl from Bichara, a 'Syrian parfumier' [. . .] He sold hot perfumes, a sort of clay for washing the hair, soap moulded into little cylinders which looked good enough to eat [. . .] It was from a woman from Oran that I learned to use antimony every day and picked up a few good customs from the harem, including the habit – indeed, the necessity – of using kohl.[45]

Her fame guaranteed success, so why shouldn't she use her knowledge to set up a profitable business? 'I would boil up quince pulp and the mucilaginous flesh around the stones, beat cold cream and squeeze the liquid out of cucumbers for myself and my friends.'[46] So why not for customers? She looked for 'sleeping partners' and found them: Princesse Winnie de Polignac, the Glaoui (Pasha of Marrakesh), Simone Berriau and all her other wealthy friends were pressed into service.

While *Ces Plaisirs* (which was republished as *Le Pur et l'Impur* in 1941) was being serialized in the extreme right-wing *Gringoire*, Colette went around the laboratories and factories to perfect her beauty products. She even asked Marguerite Moreno to steal her 'some Max Factor' so that she could copy the formula. At the beginning of 1932, Colette wrote: 'We are working hard, and are often at the factory [. . .] Our products are wonderful – I am not joking.'[47] 'There is so much curiosity that I cannot curb the enthusiasm of the journalists. Whether I like it or not, they have already given me 50,000 francs worth of publicity.'[48]

By now Colette had moved into a small apartment with a south-facing terrace on the top floor of Claridge's Hotel. She spent her days running around the laboratories and went back there at night, dead tired and dragging her leg, which had still not healed properly.

Finally, in June 1932, she opened her beauty salon at 6 rue de Miromesnil, near the place Beauvau. Every elegant woman in Paris was invited to the opening by a card, printed in a facsimile of Colette's handwriting, which read: 'From Wednesday 1 June onwards my shop will be open for the sale of beauty products. I would be happy, Madame, to welcome you in person to 6 rue de Miromesnil and to advise you as to the most suitable make-up for stage and town. Colette.'

Everyone wanted to be made up by the great novelist. When the doors opened, there was a stampede and customers fought over the rouge, the little paintbrushes 'like cats' paws' that Colette had invented to put it on with, the creams and the perfumes. Madame de Comminges, the Panther, was one of the first to arrive. The days when, madly jealous, she had tried to kill Colette were long gone and the two women were now friends. As

the customers left, they were given a little red folder containing beauty tips from Colette: 'If you have blue eyes, do not use too much blue eye make-up. Your irises must be bluer than the artificial halo which surrounds them.' 'If you live in the sun by day and by artificial light at night, use kohl, even *at night*.' 'Laugh if you have reason to laugh. But do not weep if you do not wish to see your beauty fade too soon.'

Colette spent the next year travelling across France to promote her beauty products and gave lectures and demonstrations in more than thirty provincial towns. A branch was opened in Nantes, and then a second on the waterfront in Saint-Tropez.

But no one can become a beautician at the drop of a hat, and Colette was definitely better at writing novels than at applying make-up. The results of her experiments were far from brilliant. In her memoirs, Natalie Barney describes Cécile Sorel leaving the rue de Miromesnil after being made up by Colette; she looked twice her real age. Natalie Barney also had difficulty in recognizing the fresh-complexioned Bel-Gazou, who had been atrociously made up by her mother. Colette gradually lost her customers.

One afternoon in May 1933, Colette went back to see Fraya the clairvoyant, who was now living in the rue Chardin. (Shortly afterwards, Colette was to take Simone Berriau to see her.) Colette told Fraya about her new venture, which she was already finding 'futile, demanding and certainly not very profitable'. Fraya told her, 'If you had consulted me earlier, I would have advised you not to try to do so many things at once. . . . Give up the world of business; it will only bring you heartbreak.'[49]

Before long, Colette did in fact abandon an experiment that had been both costly and disastrous. Fortunately, the success of *La Chatte*, which had just been published, compensated to some extent for the money she had spent on her beauty salon.

Colette went back to her writing and produced the screenplay for *Lac aux dames,* a film by Marc Allégret based on a novel by Vicky Baum. Maurice Goudeket turned to what he hoped would be a more profitable line of business and went into hardware. Among other things, he sold 'a flexible tube for unblocking toilets which should bring him luck, a little masterpiece of taste and ingenuity. I chose its name myself: "The Ferret".'[50] Before long, he too began to try his hand at journalism and writing for the stage. He had a good teacher.

In 1933, Anna de Noailles, who had been claiming for years that she was dying, finally did die, and that brought Colette closer to their mutual friend, the Princesse de Polignac. Winnie de Polignac, widow of Edouard, was an American, the daughter of Singer, inventor of the sewing machine. She was a patroness of painters and musicians, and a high priestess of the religion of Lesbos. According to Jean Cocteau, she looked like Giotto's portrait of Dante. Colette had first met her in 1893, at one of the Saint-Marceaux musical *soirées,* and they had never lost touch. Now they drank mulled wine and talked about the good old days at Natalie Barney's 'Temple of Friendship' in the rue Jacob. Colette also re-established contact with Winnie's friend Violet Trefusis and with Misia – now the wife of her old friend the painter José Maria Sert – whom she had known since the days when she was Misia Natanson. Although she was suspicious of newcomers, Colette was always loyal to her old friends. It was through Misia that she met Coco Chanel.

In 1934 *Duo* was published, and Colette wrote a scenario and screenplay for *Divine,* filmed by Max Ophüls.

In 1935, Claridge's went bankrupt. The hotel, where Colette had once met Alexandre Stavisky in the corridor, was in chaos and she was forced to leave her refuge in the sky. 'I tied up my furniture in a bundle and jumped across the Champs-Elysées'[51] – to Goudeket's apartment at No. 33, on the eighth floor of the Marignan building. There she lived with him for two years.

In fact she did rather more than that. At the age of over sixty she married a man sixteen years her junior, with whom she had been living for ten years. The excuse for this surprising development was an invitation to go on the *Normandie*'s maiden voyage to New York. New York was still very puritanical, and an unmarried couple would not have been allowed to share a room. It is not quite certain who was more in favour of the marriage. The idea seems originally to have come from Goudeket, who had every reason to want to become Colette's husband. On the other hand, Colette was becoming more frail as she got older. She did not like living alone and enjoyed being fussed over by her 'best friend'.

Whatever the explanation, Colette announced the news to Hélène Picard in telegraphic style: 'By the way, Maurice and I have been married for about ten days. Ceremony lasted seventeen minutes in all. Two witnesses formed the wedding procession [Luc-Albert Moreau and his wife]. In the ten years we've been together, we've never had a morning free to "regularize" our situation.'[52] She was rather more expansive in *L'Etoile Vesper,* where she describes their wedding lunch: 'It consisted of gammon joints that melted in the mouth, cooked as a *pot-au-feu,* dressed in their pink fat and their rind and moistened with a broth that smelled of celery, nutmeg, horseradish, and all the wholesome vegetables that are the aromatic servants of Mistress Meat. We also had *crêpes.*'[53]

A few months later, in October, the man she had called Sidi, whom she had loved and then hated so much, died of thrombosis as he was leaving an exhibition in the Grand-Palais. The day before he died, Pierre Laval had offered him the post of Minister for Foreign Affairs.

During a brief stay of less than three days in New York in June, Colette discovered 'a city more beautiful than we expected' from the twenty-fourth floor of the Waldorf

Astoria. Needless to say, she went round all the shops to buy pens. When her husband pointed out that she could buy the same pens in Paris, she replied, 'Of course, but they're fresher here.' One evening she found a kitten mewing in a New York street. 'At last,' she said, 'someone who speaks French!'[54]

In 1936 she published *Mes Apprentissages*, an autobiographical account of her early years. Her harsh treatment of poor Willy shocked those who had known them when they were together.

As she grew older, Colette dwelled more and more on her childhood. In March she gave a talk at the ABC on her early days in the music hall and began to sing on stage, saying, 'I can't sing, that's why I dare to.' To the delight of her audience, she sang the old songs her father had taught her, in her deep but tuneful voice: *Les Filles de Marseille, Les Deux Petits Boeufs, Le Meunier, Il est pourtant temps* . . .

The year 1936 was one of triumph. In January Colette received the *cravate* of a *Commandeur* of the Legion of Honour, and on 4 April, she was installed as a member of the Académie Royale de Langue et de Littérature Françaises de Belgique. She was elected in succession to Anna de Noailles (and was, in her turn, succeeded by Cocteau).

She was both pleased and frightened at the idea of the reception that awaited her in Brussels. 'I need scarcely tell you that I am all misanthropy, anxiety, stomach pains, stammering and general debility. [. . .] I turned pale writing my speech. [. . .] This is not the kind of work I was born to do.'[55] The speech she had to deliver was in fact far from easy to write, as it had to be a eulogy of her predecessor. Colette found Anna de Noailles extremely irritating with her caprices and her insistence on acting the part of a fragile woman who might be carried off by a puff of wind. Her theatrical fear of life and her constant talk of the fascination of death often made the sturdy Burgundian grumble, 'I am not interested in death, not even in my own death.' Nor was she a great admirer of Anna's poetry.

Colette's arrival in Belgium, accompanied by Goudeket and Winnie de Polignac, was eventful. They were stopped at the border by a customs officer, who noticed that Colette's passport had expired and refused to let her set foot in the country. It made no difference to him that she was expected at the Académie Royale. Winnie had to throw a real Polignac tantrum before Colette was finally allowed entry.

Maurice Martin du Gard, who attended the reception, describes the amazement of the venerable gentlemen who had elected Colette when they saw her enter the palace of the Prince of Orange in a shiny black silk suit and a black and white satin shirt. She was wearing sandals (as always) and had bright red varnish on her toenails.

The poet Valère Gilles made a speech of welcome and Colette began to speak. The charm of her unusual voice immediately won over the audience. She accomplished the remarkable feat of evoking Anna de Noailles so vividly that she seemed to be present in the room, without ever saying a word about her poetry. Ovations and compliments. The next day, Colette was invited to the French Embassy for one of those formal dinners that bored her so much. Before sitting down at the noble table, she whispered to Martin du Gard, 'Places where I cannot say *merde* make me ill.'[56]

In the winter of 1937-8 Colette moved house for the last time. She returned to 9 rue de Beaujolais, but this time she moved into the *piano nobile* above her 'dark tunnel', and took a small apartment overlooking the gardens of the Palais Royal. There she wrote her last books, in the end confined by her arthritis to the divan she called her 'raft', and there she died seventeen years later.

Colette loved the Palais Royal, which is virtually a village in the centre of Paris. She knew all her neighbours, and that reminded her of her childhood.

The apartments on the square are never very comfortable, but what a self-contained little province! Madame Masse [a weaver who owned a restaurant in the passage Choiseul] sends me stewed pears, the woman who owns the bistro over the road dispatches a couple of filled *crêpes*, the antique dealer comes up to say hello and gives me joss sticks, and when the groundsman sees me walking my dog without a lead, he shouts, 'Are you quite incorrigible?'[57]

In 1938 she spent her last summer in Saint-Tropez. Paid holidays had been introduced in 1936, and the beaches of France were being invaded by holiday-makers. Saint-Tropez was not spared. Colette had to say farewell to the little beach where she used to swim naked. The little harbour was no better, as it had been invaded by *le tout Montparnasse*, just as, twenty years later, it would be invaded by *le tout Saint-Germain*. The invaders provoked a fine piece of Colette satire, in a letter to Goudeket:

It was a fine Saturday. A dense crowd, a warm evening. The Almanac de Gotha in dungarees. A very aristocratic old queer in a khaki cotton shirt and a navvy's belt. 'Society' women in cheap men's shirts. Fernande C. in evening dress, with her jewels and lacquered hair, and a face like a fat butcher . . .

From a table around which were sitting women with cropped hair and men wearing long scarves a bony old hag in blue canvas trousers costing nineteen francs got up and said, 'I am so pleased to see you.' As you can imagine, I said nothing. 'We've not met since that evening at Madame de . . .' I looked blank and as welcoming as a hedgehog, and she finally told me her name [. . .] The ladies then began to dance, with cigarettes hanging from their lips, and the said princess whistled at table. No one in the rue Blomet would dare to dance like that. The negresses in the rue Blomet have at least a little self-respect.[58]

Colette's fame also brought her unwanted visitors who thought they had every right to go into her garden. Twenty years later, Brigitte Bardot's privacy was similarly invaded. And so, in 1938, Colette sold her beloved

Treille Muscate to the actor Charles Vanel. 'People think that I gave it up out of frivolity or boredom. And it is true that I do the impossible to make them think that.'[59] In its place, she bought a house in Méré, near Montfort-l'Amaury, the home of Germaine Beaumont, with whom she still kept in touch.

Although her hip was giving her a lot of pain, Colette was still working hard. *Paris-Soir* sent her to Morocco to cover the trial of a man who had killed a number of prostitutes. She did some work for *Marie-Claire*, *Candide* and *Le Petit Parisien*. She also wrote advertising copy and 'other bits and pieces to keep the home fires burning', made radio broadcasts, and wrote *Le Toutounier*, the sequel to *Duo*.

In 1940 Claude Farrère, who admired both these books, and who had been in love with Colette since the early days when he was one of Willy's ghostwriters, wrote to her: 'You are the glass of water I never drank, my mad, unquenchable thirst, I have worshipped you for thirty years without ever saying a word.'[60]

Colette was in Dieppe with the Marchands when war broke out in August 1939, and returned to Paris. Goudeket was too old to be called up.

Denise Tual, who was Colette's neighbour in the Palais Royal at the time and who knew her well, recalls the advice she gave her: 'The first thing to do is to lay in a supply of coal. And don't forget the potatoes.'[61] Only once did she go down to the cellar during an air raid.

During the June exodus, Colette left Méré by car with her husband and Pauline, and fled to the old Château de Curemonte, which her daughter had inherited. The château, 38 kilometres from Castel-Novel, was in fact little more than a ruin and it was only partly habitable:

We are in a lush green tomb where absolutely nothing reaches us. Not a friendly word, not a newspaper, not a telegram, nothing. [. . .] We never see *Paris-Soir*. The letters we sent, addressed to Prouvost at the propaganda bureau, do not seem to have reached their destination

262

[. . .] A hundred years have gone by in a fortnight. [. . .] We would so much like to have a living soul to talk to. [. . .] We are short of a lot of essentials like butter, milk, oil, etc.[62]

. . . We heat the copper for the washing (just as at Rozven) with the remains of Louis XV alcoves.[63]

As the summer came to an end, Colette began to chaff at the bit. She was bored and missed the Palais Royal ('I usually spend my wars in Paris') but had no petrol for the return journey. She watched her daughter making English-style pickles: 'She puts nasturtium seeds, strands of fennel, gherkins, garlic, carrots, puny little tomatoes, woody radishes, basil and vinegar into a preserving jar and begins to "enjoy" it nine days later.'[64] Colette finally returned to Paris on 11 September, taking two short stories with her: *Lune de pluie* and *Chambre d'hôtel*. They were both published in October.

On 12 December 1941, Maurice Goudeket, who was Jewish, was arrested at dawn and taken to a camp in Compiègne. Colette was in a terrible state. Like any lioness, she would do anything to defend her cubs. She sprang into action, and when Colette sprang into action, things got done. She appealed to everyone she knew who had contacts with the occupation forces and who might be able to spare Goudeket the worst. Not all of them were wholehearted supporters of the Resistance by any means. She appealed for help to Sacha Guitry, Hélène Morand – who was a friend of the wife of the German Ambassador – Coco Chanel, and Drieu La Rochelle, a close friend of Bertrand de Jouvenel who later got Jean Paulhan out of a German prison and who prevented his ex-wife (who had become Madame Tchernia) and her two young children from being deported. She also appealed to Misia's husband José Maria Sert, who was neutral Spain's ambassador to the Vatican. Sert was openly pro-German and used his credit with the Germans to save his Jewish friends. He failed to save Max Jacob, but he did save Goudeket,[65] who was released after two months, having

lost a few kilos and gained a few lice. He had narrowly escaped death.

During the agonizing weeks of waiting that she describes in *L'Etoile Vesper*, Colette experienced the warmth and solidarity that women can display in times of danger.

Councils were held; her friends organized themselves in relays to be with her. There are lots of bicycles in the entrance hall. The 'lady cyclists', as we call them, see to it that she is never alone. Hélène Jourdan-Morhange, Antonia Lichwitz and Geneviève Leibovici are all there, also Simone Berriau, who has a car. Dr Marthe Lamy, who watches tenderly over Colette's health, comes every day.[66]

Marthe Lamy was a friend of Willy's niece Paulette Gauthier-Villars, who was also a doctor, had known Colette for a long time. She was to remain her friend and doctor until the end.[67]

These were difficult years for Colette. Goudeket had been saved, but he was still in danger as more and more Jews were being rounded up in Paris, and he went into hiding with friends in the Midi. Colette's arthritis was giving her more and more pain. On the advice of her doctor, she went cycling in the Bois de Boulogne – on a superb 'Alcyon' which she had persuaded the manufacturer to give her – but that brought her little relief. 'I can just see the obituary: "At the age of almost seventy she took up cycling, and her exploits will long be remembered, especially the Paris-Les Mesnuls run which she covered in under forty-eight hours."'[68] (Les Mesnuls was Luc-Albert Moreau's house near Montfort-l'Amaury.)

She was now sixty-nine, and the rest of her life was to be one long martyrdom. In between sessions of radiation treatment which burned her stomach, painful intravenous injections, and acupuncture, she wrote *Gigi*, which was published in the autumn of 1942. In years to come, French, Swiss, English and American doctors all tried in vain to alleviate her pain.

She also had to contend with emotional blows. In the summer of 1942, Léo Marchand's charming wife Misz, who had been so happy at Rozven, committed suicide in a fit of depression. She was Jewish and did not want to cause trouble for her husband. In 1943, Colette lost her protegée Renée Hamon, the 'little corsair', who died from cancer at the age of forty-four.

In the midst of her own sufferings, Colette never lost her sense of humour. She had always had problems with her teeth, and in 1921 she wrote to Germaine Beaumont: 'Why don't we have all our teeth out and replace them with green jade?'[69] Despite all the treatment she underwent in an attempt to overcome what she called her 'legs attacks', she kept on joking. 'Today, they fed me male hormones. But why did they tell me that I would grow a beard? And likewise something I cannot mention?'[70]

She called the wheelchair she used to get around her 'electric wheelbarrow'. 'I have ordered a superb vehicle like the ones disabled veterans use,' she told Luc-Albert Moreau in 1942. 'Electric motor: 12 kilometres per hour! Expected range: 30 kilometres a day! When you see me coming in that, the whole neighbourhood will go wild with excitement.'[71]

Even so, she went on writing and produced *Julie de Carneilhan* (1941), *De ma fenêtre* (1942), *Le Képi* (1943) and *Trois . . . six . . . neuf* (1944).

She wrote short stories and articles for the newspapers. She also contributed to a de luxe anthology edited by Sacha Guitry, dedicated to the glory of France, under the unfortunate title *De 1429 à 1942, de Jeanne d'Arc à Philippe Pétain*. (He wouldn't be allowed to forget that title three years later!) Colette was in good company: the other contributors included Paul Valéry (on Descartes), Pierre Benoit (on Victor Hugo), Rosny *jeune* (on Rousseau), Duhamel, the Duc de Broglie, La Varende and Cocteau. The frontispiece was by Maillol and represented 'France revealing herself, aided by the Genius of the Arts'. Colette contributed an essay on Balzac. She also made radio broadcasts, advising her listeners on how to deal with food rationing, what to use in place of real coffee, and so on.

Arthritis or no arthritis, war or no war, Colette had lost none of her interest in food. On the contrary, the shortages stimulated her appetite. The shortages she experienced were relative, in any case, as a chain of friends made sure that she got supplies. She also had her faithful Pauline, who called at some mysterious addresses when she went shopping. Colette received gifts from all over France. Her old friend Curnonski took her out to eat the oysters she loved so much, and sent her bacon from a pig he had had raised in the country. She was also supplied from Brittany by Thérèse Sourisse and Yvonne Blanchard, whom she called 'my little farmers'. She had met the two young women, who were both school teachers, in Nantes in 1933. They had set up one of the first poultry farms in France and were raising a young she-wolf they had tamed. They both admired Colette greatly, and Yvonne still speaks of her with respect. Throughout the war, they sent her sizeable food parcels.

They were not the only ones to help her. Someone would bring her a rabbit, someone else fresh eggs. A third friend would bring her the muscat grapes she liked, or perhaps a pot of jam. Colette admitted in the middle of the war that everyone had lost twenty kilos except her.

There are lots of good restaurants in the Palais Royal area. Colette was at home in the 'Louis XIV' and the 'Roi Gourmet' in the place des Victoires, and above all in the 'Grand Véfour', on her doorstep, whose owner, Raymond Oliver, became a friend. One day she went to feast on garlic mayonnaise in the restaurant on the top floor of the Grands Magasins du Louvre. Even in time of famine, Colette could be counted upon to find foie gras, cassoulet, a leg of lamb, some pâté or a quiche. She was quite prepared to put up with the consequences. 'Intestinal trouble . . . Horror of horrors, I've lost a kilo in nine days. My clothes will soon be flapping around me like a flag in the wind.'[72] Reluctantly, she went on a starvation diet, but it did not last for long.

Her friend Richard Anacréon, from Granville, kept her supplied with butter that he brought back from Normandy. He also kept her amused: 'Anacréon came yesterday and told us more of his crazy stories.' Anacréon owned a bookshop in the rue de Seine and was a great collector.[73] His friends included Paul Valéry, Farrère, Jouhandeau and Cocteau. He had a sense of humour that equalled his enjoyment of life, and it was natural that he and Colette should like each other enormously. He would take her to Tonton's at 'Liberty's' in the place Blanche for lunch, and if she could not go out, he came to her. He had a caustic sense of humour and the way he introduced Parisian slang into his cultivated speech amused her. He brought her snippets of gossip about the social and literary world she could no longer frequent.

When he was over seventy, Anacréon still remembered the jokes he shared with Cocteau and Colette in the rue de Beaujolais. 'We invented the word *pédale* [slang for a homosexual] in about 1935. I had a Swiss friend who wrote pornographic books and had a liking for boys, especially telegraph delivery boys. He got them to his house by sending himself *pneumatiques* [express letters]. Colette thought that was very funny and kept asking me, "How is your *pédale*?" (alluding to the telegraph boys' bicycles). Cocteau found the expression amusing and spread it around the town.'

In 1945, Colette's health deteriorated. Now, she could hardly move at all.

My seventy-second birthday finds me resigned to many reasonable things. But I am fighting every inch of the way. I haven't been out for over a month. As long as my general health is respectable, I consent to official impotence on my converted bed. When you see my small, regular handwriting, just remember that it conceals the long, stubborn arguments I have with myself in silence.[74]

The settling of scores that followed the Liberation disgusted her: the trials of collaborators 'are *dégueulasse* [make you want to puke]. *Dégueulasse* is an ugly word, and I use it deliberately.'[75] She had a number of arguments with her daughter over this. Colette de Jouvenel had been in the Resistance and was now the joint editor of a new political weekly, in which she argued the opposite view to her mother's. 'Have you seen my daughter's article in *Fraternité*?', Colette wrote to Charles Saglio. 'Just look at the tone that *jouvenelle* adopts.'[76]

Colette was now internationally famous. On 2 May 1945, she was elected to the Académie Goncourt. She was only the second woman to have been elected since the establishment of the Prix Goncourt; the first, in 1920, was Judith Gauthier. It was initially Sacha Guitry's idea that she should replace Jean de La Varende, who had recently resigned. In 1949 she became president of the jury by reason of seniority. This was not in fact the first time she had been a member of a literary jury: she had had the pleasure of being one of the Prix de la Renaissance judges – 'if', she wrote to her daughter, 'you can call those moments of acrimony and affectation that we call a meeting of the selection committee pleasure . . .'[77] The arrival of the new *goncourte* (as she called herself) brought new blood into the selection committee, even though she was seventy-two.

Her first action was to fight with all her usual obstinacy to have the prize awarded to an unknown young school teacher named Jean-Louis Bory. He was twenty-four and his novel, *Mon Village à l'heure allemande*,[78] describes the attitudes of ordinary French people towards the occupation. It was very different from the long-winded heroic epics about the Resistance, and also from the other fashionable genre of the time: it had none of the 'messages' of 'committed literature'. Colette liked the fresh feel to his story of village life. It also made her laugh. Besides, in their will, the Goncourt brothers stated that they wanted to give material help to young writers who were just starting their careers. Colette was so persuasive that Bory was finally awarded the prize, despite the protests of his elders. Years later, Bory told me how he went to thank Colette in her apartment:

I was frightened to death. The great Colette, can you imagine? Everyone said she was a terrible man-eater, [. . .] and I was terribly shy. [Bory also preferred boys.] My publisher insisted that I go. So I went. Trembling with fear, I rang the doorbell in the rue de Beaujolais. Pauline showed me into Colette's room, where I found her reclining on her bed. I heard a deep voice saying, 'Come closerrr, come closerrr, young man. I *adorrre* young *fleshshsh*.' She was doing it on purpose; I couldn't believe my ears. [. . .] You see, I was the same age as Chéri. Well, I went closer [. . .] she told me to sit down beside her. I stayed for an hour. [. . .] She was very good. She didn't touch me.

Colette was a very conscientious judge. In November 1947, she wrote to Marguerite Moreno:

I spend the best part of my time reading the Prix Goncourt submissions. Last year we had a terrifying number of books, but I think there are even more this year. The fashion for *romans-fleuve* means that we have books of seven or eight hundred pages, all in small print. Tomorrow I am going to the penultimate Drouant lunch, and I will tell them what I think of *romans-fleuve*. I am reading all day and all night. The strange thing is that some of these monsters (*Le Temps des rencontres* [by Michel Zerrafa], *Planète sans visa* [by Jean Malaquais]) have a lot of good qualities. So much the better. It keeps us on our toes.[79]

Just as she could divine the presence of water (an ability she called *sourcellerie* – a play on *source* (spring) and *sorcellerie*), Colette was quick to recognize young writers with talent. The choice of Prix Goncourt novels reflected her presence on the selection committee; after her death in 1954, the quality declined considerably.

In 1948 the last great tragedy in Colette's life occurred when Marguerite Moreno, *her* Marguerite, her oldest friend, her accomplice and confidante, died on 14 July, carried off by congestion of the lungs in the middle of summer. This time, Colette may well have wept in secret. Her grief inspired her to write a very fine article on Marguerite Moreno which appeared in *Le Figaro littéraire* in the autumn.[80]

Colette no longer had a house of her own in the country or by the sea, and she rarely left the rue de Beaujolais except to stay with friends, usually in the Midi – at Simone Berriau's estate at Mauvannes, at Les Salins d'Hyères, and with Charles de Polignac and his wife in Grasse.

To her friends she passed on the secrets of a lifetime's experience of looking after animals and making gardens. She taught Luc-Albert Moreau's wife that you should never plant a poplar near a house because it has shallow roots and may fall in a storm. Yews, on the other hand, are eminently suitable. She had sent Marguerite Moreno one of Sido's remedies for chilblains: 'Marinade red rose petals in very good wine vinegar for a month. Put a well-soaked compress on the chilblain at night. Apart from anything else, it smells wonderful. When I was little I never had chilblains. But I said that I did so that I could suck the compress. Even at that age, I loved vinegar.'[81]

When she was not working on her last book, *Le Fanal bleu*, Colette did tapestry work, and in the evenings played belote with Goudeket. On Sundays they would go to the country, to lunch with Luc-Albert Moreau and his wife Moune. Before setting out for Montfort-l'Amaury, Colette insisted on going to the best shops in Paris to buy cheese and meat to take with them.

Colette had her couch, which was covered with a rug of squirrel fur, moved to the window overlooking the Palais Royal gardens. She wrote on her lap, using a table given to her by Winnie de Polignac. A low red lacquer table at her bedside was littered with pens, pencils, scissors, a watch, a portable inkwell, her spectacles, a phial of salts and her make-up.

Her room, which she rarely left now, became a refuge, a *salon*, and a museum. It was filled with her favourite furniture and ornaments, her books, and all the paper-weights and other objects made of glass that she had collected over the years. (She had even gone so far – she confessed in a letter to Germaine Beaumont – as to steal an electrical insulator made of green glass from a construction site in Saint-Tropez: it was worth nothing, but she found it fascinating because it was so like her beloved glass marbles and paperweights.)

It was here that she received her visitors, who were all screened by Pauline. Admirers and journalists came from all over to interview and film her. Here she chatted with her friends – Francis Carco, Dignimont, Paul Géraldy, and old Marcel Boulestin, who had once worked with Willy and who had now opened a very good restaurant in London. Her friends and neighbours from the Palais Royal often went up to see her. Emmanuel Berl, to whom she had often given refuge at Saint-Tropez during his stormy love life, was a frequent visitor. He was now more settled and lived nearby in the rue de Montpensier, with his wife, the singer Mireille. He once told Colette: 'In my opinion, you are the greatest living French writer. Then,' Berl says, 'without showing the slightest surprise or changing her tranquil expression, she replied "Quite so."'[82] Jean Cocteau, 'caring, charming, tormented by lack of money', was another frequent visitor. He would sit at the foot of her bed, and no doubt they reminisced about the good old days when the twenty-year-old Cocteau used to dance on the tables at Larue's. He was often accompanied by Jean Marais and his dog Moulouk. Colette liked Marais, who was attentive and gentle with her. She told him, 'You're the only one who can hug me without hurting me.'

The devoted Maurice Goudeket had alienated some of Colette's friends, but they arranged to visit her when he was out. Among them was Bertrand de Jouvenel, who had loved her better than anyone. Bertrand had married, been left a widower, and then remarried, but love of Colette always remained deep in his heart. One day, she wrote him a sad, sweet letter:

So you have surfaced again, my boy. It is indeed true that I have had a lot of letters, and still get them. How I will manage to answer them is another matter. My daughter is not stupid enough to offer to help me, and I have been swallowed up by arthritis (legs) for months and months.

You have a pretty house. And children you are proud of? I feel somewhat responsible for all these things, and would like to see them, even on a scrap of postcard. I can't walk at all. Five days from now, Maurice will be taking me to Monte-Carlo, as he did last year. When I get back, the mirror will tell me whether or not I can call you. But will you still be young enough? With all my love, my boy, Colette.[83]

The bonds of affection were never broken.

Germaine Beaumont later described how, when Marguerite Moreno was still alive, she, Lili de Clermont-Tonnerre and Natalie Barney would telephone Pauline from a nearby café in the rue de Beaujolais to make certain that 'madame was alone'. If their accomplice told them that Goudeket had gone out and that the coast was clear, they would hurry to Colette's side, giggling and chattering like schoolgirls.

Colette's neighbour Denise Tual also visited her:

Whenever I went to see Colette, Pauline would make me wait for a while before showing me in to give her time to titivate herself. Standing in the dark doorway I could see her silhouetted against the window, quickly back-combing the front of her hair to make it curl, filling the air with a pearly cloud of the rice-powder she used on her face. Pauline would tie a mauve tulle scarf around her neck, which she fluffed up with a flick of the hand; she would examine herself in the mirror she held on her knees; and then she would indicate that I could come in. She would be propped up on a pile of snow-white pillows, frothy with hemstitching and embroidery, and she would push her desk away a little and look at me with her penetrating periwinkle blue eyes, as though to ask me a thousand questions about life in the outside world. One rebellious toe peeped out from beneath the rug that covered her legs and punctuated the conversation with twitches of amusement or annoyance.[84]

In 1951, *La Seconde* was adapted for the stage. André Luguet, Hélène Perdrière and Maria Casarès came to the Palais Royal to act out a few scenes for Colette. Yannick Bellon also came to film her at home.

In 1952, Colette wrote to Germaine Beaumont: 'It's strange – I cannot walk at all now. So I live in bed. How simple. I am quite blasé about aeroplanes. And today I am entering my eightieth year. Would you think so to look at me? Perhaps not.'[85] Colette's eightieth birthday was greeted with all the celebrations that had greeted Victor Hugo's. Tributes poured in and her photograph was in all the newspapers.

Towards the end of her life, Colette often travelled by air, as she found cars tiring and as it was impossible for her to travel by train. In the spring of 1950, she went to Monte-Carlo to consult Dr Gibson, who was said to be able to cure arthritis. He did not cure her, but she went back to Monte-Carlo every year, with Goudeket and Pauline, as the mild climate suited her. Whenever she arrived at Nice airport, she was met by a delegation bearing flowers: 'I feel like a *sous-préfet*.'

At the luxurious Hôtel de Paris, every effort was made to surround her with comfort and friendship. Prince Pierre of Monaco, the father of Rainier III, worshipped Colette and inundated her with flowers and sweets. Knowing how much she loved plants, he also took her to see his exotic garden. The hotel staff waited on her hand and foot, and the barley water and radishes she loved so much were always available in the bar. Colette moved around the hotel in her little wheelchair. One day in 1951, she found the foyer in turmoil: a scene for a film was being shot. Colette's attention was caught by an unfamiliar young actress called Audrey Hepburn. In a flash, Colette decided that she was the very person to play Gigi on Broadway. The play was due to open in the autumn and the director was looking for a young actress to play the role. At Colette's request, Audrey Hepburn was given the part.

Early in 1952, Colette spent almost three months in Monte-Carlo. Cocteau was still there. He was worried and depressed about his old friend's state of health.

I find her very ill, cut off from the world by her hearing and her fatigue. Very pale and very far away. I have seen such blue-black eyes before, on my green grasshopper when it was approaching death. [. . .] Maurice pushes Colette's wheelchair into the bar [. . .] A gypsy plays *Gigi* at Colette's shoulder [. . .] Maurice disturbs the wall of cotton wool round Colette as little as possible. He only passes on what really matters [. . .] Maurice seems to look after his wife's affairs admirably. She thinks there are a few banknotes in her drawer. The drawer was always her savings bank; she would fill it by writing articles and empty it to pay Pauline. Judging by the size of the interim tax payments Maurice admitted to me, she must have made a great deal of money. Colette is both a peasant and a child. She takes life as it comes. She is almost happy living in the cloud that protects her from a cruel world she cannot understand and which is no longer that of her flowers and animals.[86]

Colette was certainly more and more cut off from the world, but on occasion she was still capable of being strikingly seductive. In August 1952 she was invited to Deauville. The young writer Jacques Laurent (alias Cecil Saint-Laurent) found himself standing next to her wheelchair at a ball at the casino. Colette was watching the dancers and suddenly noticed a very pretty girl in a pink dress. 'I want her', she murmured. She asked Jacques Laurent to go and bring the girl to her. Somewhat embarrassed, very surprised, but curious as to what would happen, he went to tell her that Colette would like to speak to her. 'I wondered what would happen. The girl was English and didn't speak a word of French (Colette could not speak English), and, to make matters worse, she did not even know who Colette was. Even so, a quarter of an hour later, I noticed that they were not only still chatting, but that the girl was going off with Colette, as though fascinated.'

Colette was now in pain both night and day, and withdrew further and further into her cloud. The only thing that brought her back to earth occasionally was her love of food.

One of Colette's greatest pleasures was talking to her friend Raymond Oliver of the 'Grand Véfour', who did all he could to make her happy. He would send a sedan chair for her, so that she could dine in his restaurant, and made all her favourite dishes for her: cassoulet, *blanquette à l'ancienne*, pâtés made with sparrows, larks or ortolans, and his delicious *coulibiac de saumon*, of which he had devised a special, light version which she could eat even though she had no teeth. Sometimes he would have one or two portions of a dish he knew she would enjoy sent up to her. She constantly asked him for a special type of apricot jam that Sido used to make. 'If you forget the jam, I will have harsh words to say to you.'

Occasionally, she would telephone Oliver in the middle of the afternoon: 'I am pining for you. Come up and eat chocolates with me. We have lots to talk about.' Oliver would go to her, and they would drink champagne and gossip together. 'I made two meals for her eightieth birthday – one in her apartment, a lark pie; the other in the "Grand Véfour", hare *à la royale*, which she insisted on having cooked *à la poitevine*, with forty cloves of garlic and forty shallots.'[87]

On the morning of 3 August 1954, Raymond Oliver brought her a vegetable broth she had asked for. It was to be her last meal.

By the afternoon, Colette was fading fast. Dr Lamy, Colette de Jouvenel and Maurice Goudeket were at her side. Dr Lamy was a devout Catholic, and when she judged that Colette, who was barely conscious, had not long to live, she said that it was time to send for a priest. Goudeket objected. By eight in the evening, Colette was with Sido.

Two years before her death, Colette had been made a *Grand Officier* of the Legion of Honour, and she was therefore given a state funeral. But the Church, in the person of Cardinal Feltin, Archbishop of Paris, staunchly refused to add its blessing, despite a protest to the Cardinal from Graham Greene. This severity was not due only to the fact that Colette had been divorced. Willy was the only man she had married in a religious ceremony, and he had died; her civil marriages had no validity in the eyes of the Church. No. The Church's objections were the same as those put to Vincent Auriol in 1952 as reasons why she should not become a *Grand Officier*: her past career in the music hall and the air of scandal that had clung to her ever since. In his journal, Jean Cocteau describes a lunch at the Elysée Palace in December 1952 when President Auriol told him about 'his fight to get Colette her cross [of *Grand Officier*]'. 'One wonders why', Cocteau continues, 'they gave her the *cravate* [of *Commandeur*] and then refused to go any higher. Nothing could be more ridiculous than these fine distinctions. But "she appeared naked on the music hall stage".'[88]

Colette's immoral past weighed heavily upon her – and still does. For a long time her books were on the Index, and I myself was expelled from a church school for reading *Claudine à l'école* and lending it to someone else.

For once, the State proved less cowardly than the Church and awarded the old lady the one thing that could still give her any pleasure: the cross of a *Grand Officier*. The churchmen acted like bureaucrats and rejected a sheep who may well have gone astray according to a strict interpretation of the rules, but whom Christ would surely have welcomed back into the fold.

Obviously, neither Colette's books nor her life were models of piety, but she had been baptized, had learnt her catechism, had taken her first communion and had been married in church. No note of anticlericalism ever crept into her writings. On the contrary, as we have seen, she publicly defended the church schools when they came under attack.

The woman to whom Mauriac had read the Bible and who had agreed to be her friend Claude Chauvière's godmother spent one of the last Christmas Eves of her life listening to midnight mass on the radio. Colette's beliefs were never expressed in orthodox fashion, but in times of difficulty she fell back on her childhood faith. Her faith was based upon superstition, but that may be as valid as any faith. When Marguerite Moreno's nephew was a prisoner during the war, Colette wrote to tell her, 'I am going round to my neighbour, Notre-Dame-des-Victoires, to light a candle for your absent boy.'[89] Speaking of a holy medallion that had been sent to someone in distress, she also said: 'There are times when one does not hesitate to mingle gris-gris, fetishes and rosaries, and when one feels that they can be reconciled without any contradiction.'[90] One wonders what would have happened if Dr Lamy had succeeded in calling a priest to her friend's deathbed.

There is no cross on the stone that marks Colette's grave in the Père Lachaise cemetery. But in any case that is not where we would find her. Colette is to be found wherever a colour, a scent or a harmonious form gives birth to love. We can still find Colette in the sea breezes of a beach in Brittany as the tide goes out, in the sumptuous melancholy of a September rose, in the joyous appetite stimulated by fresh oysters or by the springy step of a young man in the street. All that was best in her lives on in her writings. That will never die and will remain with us to the end of our days.

1. *Lettres à Marguerite Moreno*, p. 101.
2. Ibid., p. 108.
3. Letter, 23 June 1925; ibid.
4. Léautaud, *Journal Littéraire*, V, p. 56 (entry dated 16 June 1925).
5. Georges Duhamel, *Le Livre de l'amertume*, Paris, Mercure de France, 1983, pp. 107-8.
6. *Journal à rebours*, Paris, Arthème Fayard, 1941.
7. Unpublished letter, 3 November 1921; coll. Richard Anacréon.
8. Letter, summer 1921; *Lettres à ses pairs*, pp. 221-2.
9. Letter, 1922; ibid., p. 223.
10. *Lettres à ses pairs*.
11. Letter, 5 August 1933; *Lettres à Marguerite Moreno*, p. 234.
12. Unpublished letter; coll. Richard Anacréon.
13. Paul Rouaix's *Dictionnaire des idées suggérées par les mots* – the French Roget – is an indispensable tool for any writer. First published by Armand-Colin in 1921, it has been reprinted many times.
14. Letter to Marguerite Moreno, 15 June 1928; *Lettres à Marguerite Moreno*, p. 156.
15. Letter, May or June 1923; ibid., p. 64.
16. Letter, mid September 1924; ibid., pp. 89-90.
17. 'Project de Lettre-Préface, *Lettres au Petit Corsaire*, Paris, Flammarion, 1963, pp. 68-9.
18. Ibid., p. 47 (*Journal de Renée Hamon*, entry for 6 April 1938).
19. *Paysages et Portraits*, p. 211.
20. Unpublished letter; coll. J. L. Lécard.
21. 'La Poésie que j'aime' (lecture to L'Université des Annales, 10 December 1937), *Paysages et Portraits*, p. 214.
22. Ibid., pp. 221-2.
23. *Oeuvres*, I, p. 240.
24. Letter to Marguerite Moreno, 23 January 1932; *Lettres à Marguerite Moreno*, p. 225.
25. Letter to Marguerite Moreno, 30 October 1943; ibid., p. 257. She is alluding to *Ecrit sur de l'eau* ('Written on Water'), an insipid novel by Francis de Miomandre which won the Prix Goncourt in 1908.
26. André Billy, 'Une Sorte de dandysme féminin', *Le Figaro littéraire*, 24 January 1953.
27. Letter to Marguerite Moreno, 1 September 1931; *Lettres à Marguerite Moreno*, p. 220.
28. Transcript of a radio broadcast by Germaine Beaumont; coll. J. L. Lécard.
29. Beaumont and Parinaud, *Colette par elle-même*, pp. 13-14.
30. *Trois . . . six . . . neuf*, p. 33.
31. Unpublished letter; coll. J. L. Lécard.
32. Goudeket, *Près de Colette*, p. 77.
33. This copy is now in the collection of J. L. Lécard.
34. D. Dubois-Jallais, *La Tzarine*, Paris, Laffont, 1984.
35. *Lettres à ses pairs*, p. 45.
36. Letter to Marguerite Moreno, 11 September 1926; *Lettres à Marguerite Moreno*, p. 135.
37. Claude Chauvière, *Colette*, Paris, Firmin-Didot, 1931, pp. 87-8.
38. *Lettres à ses pairs*, pp. 88-89.
39. Léautaud, *Journal littéraire*, XI, p. 91 (entry dated 24 October 1935).
40. Letter, 10 January 1929; *Lettres à ses pairs*, p. 93.
41. Letter, 31 August 1930; *Lettres à Marguerite Moreno*, p. 210.
42. Letter, August 1933; *Lettres à Hélène Picard*, p. 165.
43. Undated letter to Hélène Picard (probably late 1931 or early 1932); ibid., p. 170.
44. Unpublished letter to Hélène Morhange, 28 September 1931.
45. *Le Fanal bleu*, pp. 200-201.
46. *L'Etoile Vesper*.
47. Letter to Marguerite Moreno, 19 February 1932; *Lettres à Marguerite Moreno*, p. 226.
48. Letter to Léopold Marchand, 1932; *Lettres de la Vagabonde*, p. 227.
49. Tervagne, *Une Voyante à L'Elysee*.
50. Letter to Hélène Picard, August 1933; *Lettres à Hélène Picard*, p. 165.
51. *Trois . . . six . . . neuf*, p. 97.
52. Letter to Hélène Picard, 13 April 1935; *Lettres à Hélène Picard*, p. 174.
53. *L'Etoile Vesper*, p. 13.
54. Goudeket, *Près de Colette*, p. 105.
55. Letter to Hélène Picard, 1 April 1936; *Lettres à Hélène Picard*, pp. 181-2.
56. Maurice Martin du Gard, *Les Mémorables*, Paris, Grasset, 1978, III, p. 206.
57. Letter to Charles and Lucie Saglio, January 1938; *Lettres à ses pairs*, p. 130.
58. Maurice Goudeket, *La Douceur de vieillir*, Paris, Flammarion, 1965.
59. Letter to Renée Hamon, 9 June 1938; *Lettres au Petit Corsaire*, p. 74.
60. Unpublished letter; coll. Bertrand de Jouvenel.
61. Tual, *Le Temps Dévoré*.
62. Letter to Léopold Marchand, late June 1940; *Lettres de la Vagabonde*, p. 276.
63. Unpublished letter to Germaine Beaumont; coll. J. L. Lécard.
64. Ibid.
65. Arthur Gold and Robert Fizdale, *Misia – The Life of Misia*, New York, Alfred A. Knopf, 1980.
66. Tual, *Le Temps dévoré*.
67. Dr Lamy continued to practise as a gynaecologist until shortly before her death in 1978. She was kind enough to discuss Colette with me.
68. Unpublished letter to Moune Moreau.
69. Unpublished letter; coll. J. L. Lécard.
70. Unpublished letter to Germaine Beaumont; coll. J. L. Lécard.
71. Unpublished letter, 6 June 1942.
72. Letter to Marguerite Moreno, 28 July 1943; *Lettres à Marguerite Moreno*, p. 252.
73. He bequeathed his collections to his native Granville, to establish a museum named after himself. Colette's comment is taken from a letter to Moune Moreau, 7 April 1942.
74. Letter to Lucie Saglio, early 1945; *Lettres à ses pairs*, p. 137.
75. Ibid., p. 138.
76. Letter, 6 May 1945; ibid., p. 139.
77. Unpublished letter; coll. Michel Remy-Bieth.
78. Paris, Flammarion, 1945.
79. Letter, 4 November 1947; *Lettres à Marguerite Moreno*, p. 332.
80. 'Marguerite Moreno', *Le Figaro littéraire*, 11 September 1948; reprinted in *Le Fanal bleu* and *Lettres à Marguerite Moreno*.
81. Letter, February 1947 (?); *Lettres à Marguerite Moreno*, p. 316.
82. Berl, in Patrick Modiano, *Interrogatoire*, Paris, Gallimard, Collection Témoins.
83. Unpublished letter; coll. Bertrand de Jouvenel.
84. Tual, *Le Temps dévoré*.
85. Unpublished letter; coll. J. L. Lécard.
86. Cocteau, *Le Passé défini I : 1951-1952*, Paris, Gallimard, 1983, pp. 166-7.
87. Oliver, *Cuisine pour mes amis*, Paris, Albin Michel, 1976.
88. Cocteau, *Le Passé défini*, p. 401.
89. Letter, 12 March 1944; *Lettres à Marguerite Moreno*, p. 273.
90. Letter to Marguerite Moreno, 18 March 1944; ibid., p. 275.

415

417

Colette's third husband came into her life in 1925.

415 Léon Barthou, Maurice Goudeket and Colette in southern France.

416 Colette returned to Paris in Goudeket's car, and in thanks sent him a signed copy of *La Vagabonde*.

417 A self-portrait sketch.

418 A photograph of Colette in contemplative mood, by Germaine Krull.

418

416

à Maurice Goudeket
en souvenir de mille
kilomètres de vagabondage
Colette

LA VAGABONDE

419

VILLA DE MADAME COLETTE
La Treille muscate

9948 — SAINT-TROPEZ (Var).

420

421

In 1926 Colette bought La Treille Muscate at Saint-Tropez (**419**),
and spent twelve happy years there until she was finally driven away
by the resort's growing popularity. As early as 1930 postcard sellers
were capitalizing on her fame – and misspelling her name (**420**).

Among the many friends who came to stay with her was
Luc-Albert Moreau, who made this painting of the house in its lush
setting (**421**).

Colette's painter friends left a
rich record of life at La Treille
Muscate.

422 Colette at table by Luc-
Albert Moreau.

423

423-425 Dunoyer de Segonzac,
a frequent visitor, sketched
Colette with her pets sunbathing
in 1928, and also captured her
fierce concentration when she
cut herself off to write.

424

425

426-430 Colette at Saint-Tropez, with Maurice Goudeket (**429**), photographed on the beach by Lartigue (**428**), and painted at her desk by Luc-Albert Moreau.

426

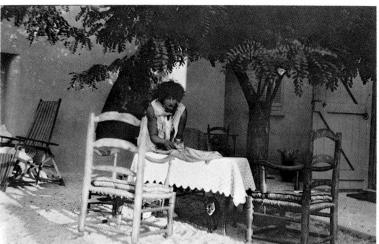

427

428

429

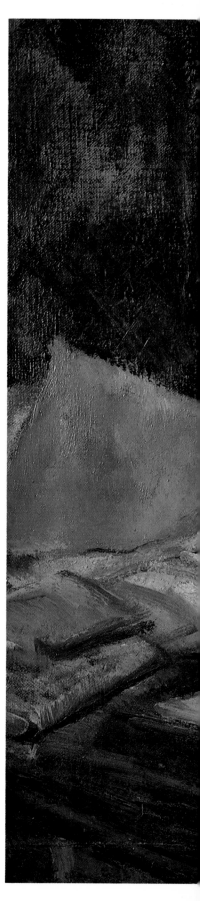

430

431 Colette in 1930, her feline
quality stressed by André
Kertesz.

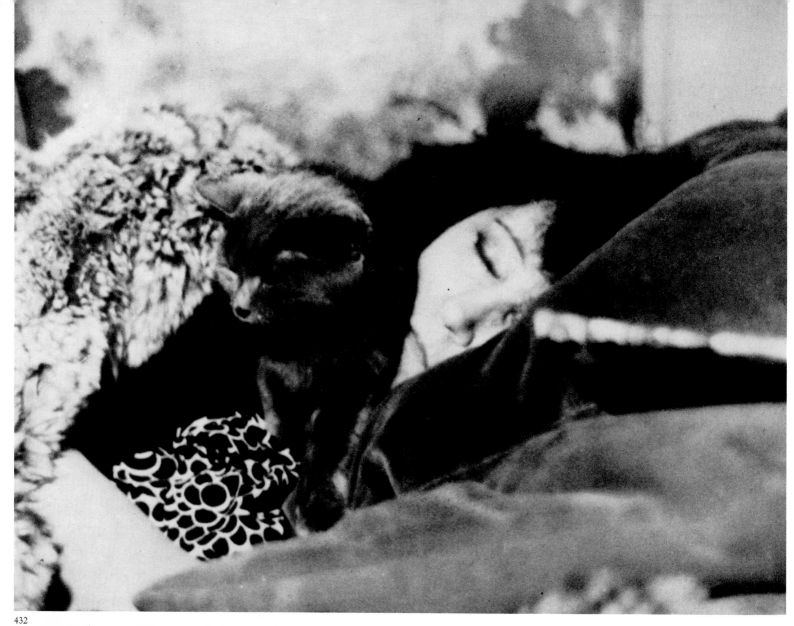

432

432, 434, 435 Colette with her cats. Of all her stories about cats, the finest and most sensuous is undoubtedly the novella 'Nonoche', in *Les Vrilles de la vigne*.

433 Colette on the terrace of her apartment on the top floor of Claridge's, where she moved in 1931. 'Come and see my captain's bridge, my gale-force wind, my roost, my look-out post, the amazing isolation and the view' (letter to Georges Wague, early 1931).

433

434

435

437

436

436 Colette and Maurice Goudeket on holiday.

437, 438 In June 1935 they sailed to New York and back on the maiden voyage of the *Normandie*. 'We will never see it again, and we will never forget it.' Sight-seeing included a visit to the top of the Empire State Building. They had used New York's puritanical hotel regulations as an excuse for getting married before the trip, in April.

438

quarante-
deux kilos, le
chapeau et le sac à
main compris — ne suf-
foque-t-elle pas d'indigestion
rien qu'à me lire ? Elle va quitter,
offensée, je le sens, mon goûter rus-
taud pour des agapes dignes d'elle, de sa
sveltesse d'anguille, de sa robe du soir à
laquelle il ne manque, ma foi, que d'être
une robe et non un pagne constellé... S'il
vous plaît, Madame et lectrice élégante, je vous suivrai, d'un peu loin,
et d'un peu loin je vous contemplerai, vous, la table, et les convives.

Là, j'admire. Une belle table française, apprêtée pour un « grand dîner » mérite
presque autant de considération qu'un bon tableau. Sa blancheur traditionnelle,
que frappent les feux d'un lustre indiscret, rebondit jusqu'aux visages qui la ceignent.
La lumière réverbérée atteint l'arcade sourcilière, la saillie de la lèvre supérieure, le rebord
du menton, et plus d'une beauté féminine s'en trouve fardée d'un éclat théâtral.
Rivières, pendants, bracelets, le diamant échange avec les cristaux taillés, des bluettes
multipliées. Longue, pavoisée de fleurs, la table du dîner ressemble à une île fortunée,
enfantée par un rouge, décevante comme lui, car le flux, le reflux réguliers de sombres
serviteurs qui touchent ses bords ne la pourvoient, trop souvent, que d'un clair potage,
d'un pâle poisson translucide et d'une cotonneuse volaille, avant que le plus aqueux
des entremets glacés n'affaisse et ne dissolve au creux des
jattes, sa chimique vanille et sa framboise rosâtre...

Colette

LA GRANDE MAISON DE BLANC

440

By using famous authors to endorse products, advertising agencies effectively became patrons of the arts in the 1930s.

439 Colette's face and writing promoted Corcellet coffee.

440 Advertisement for La Grande Maison de Blanc, signed by Colette.

441 Colette's draft of advertising copy for Hermès.

439

ANNONCE HERMES   Texte de COLETTE

Un gant violet, vide, se tient debout sur la petite jupe brodée de sa manchette; un autre gant, rose, l'index malicieusement levé, nous fait signe; une ceinture luit comme une anguille à tête de joyaux: autant de petits personnages magiques qui semblent jaillis de Cocteau ... A l'arrière plan de la vitrine une minuscule commode ancienne entr'ouvre ses tiroirs, verse un flot de perles, une cordelière d'or, un ruban d'Arles, un bracelet en pomponne, une Malines un peu rousse,... Sur le tapis gisent un miroir en châsse d'argent, un carnet de bal aux feuillets d'ivoire, et l'éventail de Clara d'Ellébeuse, déployé comme un cygne en plein vol... Une jeune fille d'autrefois, lasse d'avoir dansé jusqu'au jour, vient-elle de jeter là ses parures? une amoureuse a manié des reliques, relu des lettres, brûlé des roses séchées? L'intimité d'un tel spectacle, derrière la vitre d'un magasin, à un carrefour de Paris, est d'un humour ensemble si poétique et si piquant que les passants s'y arrêtent: vous

avez reconnu la vitrine d'Hermès, et son art d'attirer l'attention en composant une vitrine avec une science picturale. Chaque tableau d'Hermès nous appelle à constater qu'après la longue incertitude où le commerce de luxe, en France, se débattait, c'est un solide que la femme élégante donne à présent sa faveur. Le

solide, digne d'une pareille confiance, s'est épuré, a gouverné ses lignes vers une sobriété, une nudité qui lui interdit toute erreur. Le cuir a montré ses belles surfaces lisses ou grenues, ses piqûres dont on peut compter les points; les bois polis ont poncé leurs veines, et le cristal s'est fait sévère. En même temps le goût féminin devenait sensible à ce qui dure. La beauté de la matière veut la perfection du travail, celui-ci fût-il caché. A présent il faut que le dessous vaille le dessus, et le dedans le dehors. Adieu, fioritures! Un fermoir d'argent, une boucle de cuir, une barette d'onyx: c'est assez.

441

286

une
LUCKY STRIKE
avec
COLETTE

Après le déjeuner, l'heure délicieuse où COLETTE nous offre le café et une cigarette ; l'appartement dont les fenêtres donnent sur le jardin du Palais-Royal est chaud d'une poétique intimité ; souriante et grave à la fois, l'auteur de *La Vagabonde* nous dit : Oui, il faut fumer en buvant son café.... rien de meilleur n'a été inventé dans ce domaine.... et puis, la fumée d'une LUCKY STRIKE et l'arome du café prennent dans mes rêves la même couleur....

Texte de Blaise Allan

"It's toasted"

N'irritent pas la gorge, ne font pas tousser

442 Colette and the artist Paul Colin joined forces to endorse Lucky Strike cigarettes.

442

443, 444 The penalties of being famous: Colette signs autographs for a flock of admirers at the Librairie Girardot, and poses with the other judges of the Prix de la Renaissance – one of 'those moments of acrimony and affectation that we call a meeting of the selection committee'.

443

445 An advertisement for Colette's beauty salon, opened in June 1932.

444

Êtes-vous pour, ou contre
le "second métier" de l'écrivain?
Colette

7, rue de
Miromesnil

445

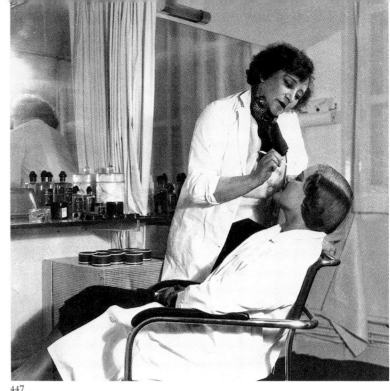

447

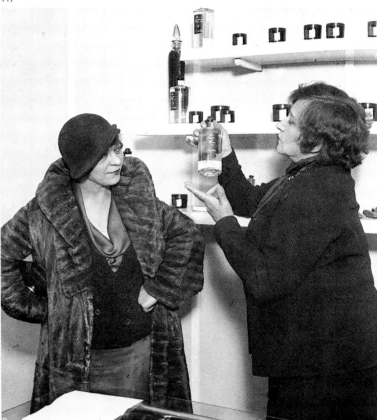

448

The ill-fated beauty salon in the rue de Miromesnil.

446 The trademark of Colette's beauty products.

447 Her daughter acts as a guinea-pig. Quince water, sold as 'Peau d'ange', smelt of quince jelly and rose-water.

448 Colette with her friend Hélène Jourdan-Morhange.

449 Colette the make-up artist was not in the same class as Colette the writer, and Cécile Sorel, whom she made up for the revue *Vive Paris!*, did not repeat the experiment.

449

450 Vertès's drawing for
Fantasio was captioned 'Colette
de l'Institut' – Institut de beauté,
not Institut de France.

451

452

453

454

Past and present friends.

451 The poetess Hélène Picard, who adopted Colette's hairstyle.

452 Colette agreed to serve as godmother to her friend Claude Chauvière. They were photographed for the occasion with the priest.

453 The brilliant Coco Chanel. She met Colette through their friend Misia, and in 1930 took over Colette's house, La Gerbière.

454 Germaine Beaumont.

455 Misia Natanson, later Edwards, later Sert. 'Misia,' wrote Colette, 'you who know the many faces of solitude . . .'

456 Renée Hamon, the 'petit corsaire', in the Marquesas Islands in 1937.

455

456

457

457, 458   In the winter of 1937-8 Colette moved to a flat in the
Palais Royal – 9 rue de Beaujolais – where she lived until her death.
It looked out over the formal gardens (photographed from her
window by Robert Doisneau). Who but she knew the name of the
flower in the beds, penstemon?

459

460

459 Colette by Vertès.

460 Colette at her desk, seated on a chair whose tapestry cover she herself embroidered. It now belongs to Bertrand de Jouvenel.

461 Colette by Gisèle Freund. By now bedfast through arthritis, she writes on a lap-table propped over her squirrel-fur coverlet.

461

462

463

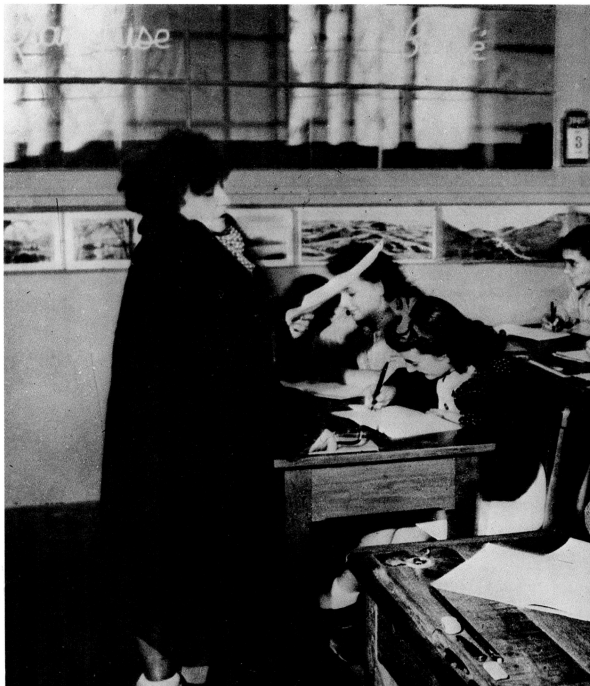

465

The Second World War.

462 Colette had lived through one war already, and knew the need for stocking her cupboards.

463 Once again men were called up; but this time they would not be away long.

464 In 1939 the evacuation of Paris was planned, and departure schedules were posted – here in the place de l'Opéra.

465 Colette, the distinguished visitor, reading a dictation to a class of children during the war.

466 From June to September 1940 Colette and Maurice Goudeket took refuge with her daughter in a decrepit Jouvenel castle at Curemonte, in the Corrèze.

464

466

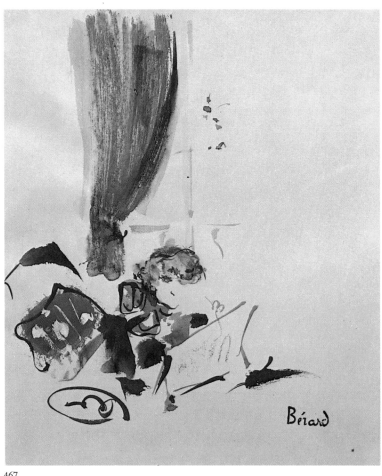

467

468

467 Colette by Christian Bérard.

468 Colette with Paul Géraldy, author of *Toi et moi.*

469 In the gardens of the Palais Royal with her neighbour, Jean Cocteau. Their friendship was founded on laughter and shared secrets.

470 Colette by Jean Cocteau.

469

471, 472   Colette loved what she called the 'self-contained little
province' of the Palais Royal, with its enclosing arcades. From her
window looking out over the gardens, which were in the end all the
world she could see, she watched the changing seasons, the gusting
wind, children trampling the flowers and robbing birds' nests. 'The
destructiveness of children is instinctive, and frighteningly cunning.'

302

473

473 Reading on her 'divan-raft' by the light of the blue-shaded lamp made famous in *Le Fanal bleu*.

474, 475 'For half a century I wrote in black on white, and now for nearly ten years I have been writing in colour on canvas.'

474

475

476 Colette with her collection of paperweights and glass ornaments, photographed by Robert Doisneau. They were presented to the museum at Colette's birthplace, Saint-Sauveur-en-Puisaye.

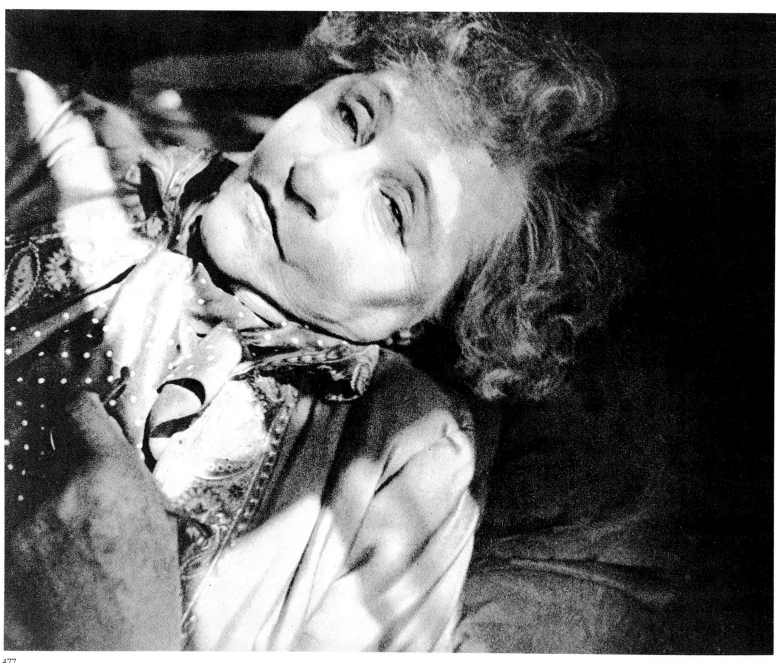

477

477 Colette, photographed by Cecil Beaton in the last years of her life – 'very pale and very far away' (Jean Cocteau).

478 Colette in her wheelchair with Edith Piaf and Edouard Herriot, at an awards ceremony for the Prix du Disque.

479 The only woman at a meeting of the Prix Goncourt judges. Sitting next to her is her old friend Francis Carco.

480 Colette at Simone Berriau's, with Jean-Paul Sartre and Christian Bérard.

481 Jean Marais, who was going to play Chéri at the Théâtre de la Madeleine, came to Colette's flat in 1949 to run through the text. 'You're the only one who can hug me without hurting me', she told him.

478

480

479

481

482

483

484

482-484 Maurice Goudeket was attentive to Colette's every need, flying with her (483) and sharing her enthusiasm for food (484). The uncharacteristic smile that Gisèle Freund captured at Deauville in 1953 was probably provoked by the shrimps, which Colette adored.

485 Colette and the birds of the Palais Royal.

On the following pages:

486 Colette photographed by Ora. 'She is almost happy living in the cloud that protects her from a cruel world . . . ' (Jean Cocteau).

487 With her faithful Pauline, by Henri Cartier-Bresson.

485

488 'And try, my dearest, not to let us guess what a sweat it is to write' (Colette to Marguerite Moreno).

Chronology

Colette's works are listed under the year of first publication in French. Titles of English-language translations are given in square brackets, with the date of first publication, whether in Britain or the United States. Different dates indicate different translations.

1873 28 January: birth of Sidonie Gabrielle Colette in Saint-Sauveur-en-Puisaye, Yonne.

1885 Marriage of C.'s half-sister Juliette Robineau-Duclos to Dr Roché.

1889 1-2 July: C. passes her *brevêt élémentaire* at Auxerre, and leaves school.

1890 The Colette family move to Châtillon-sur-Loing (now Châtillon-Coligny), Loiret, to the house of Sido's eldest son, Achille Robineau-Duclos.

1893 15 May: marriage of C. and Henry Gauthier-Villars ('Willy'). The couple live in Willy's bachelor rooms, then in a flat at 28 rue Jacob. C. is initiated into the world of literary and musical *salons*.

1894 Following a serious illness, C. convalesces at Belle-Ile, accompanied by Willy and Paul Masson.

1895 C. and Willy visit Saint-Sauveur-en-Puisaye, staying at the school. September: C. makes the first of several visits with Willy to the Bayreuth Festival.

1896 The Gauthier-Villars move to 93 rue de Courcelles.

1900 *Claudine à l'école* published under Willy's name (Paris, Ollendorf) [*Claudine at School* 1930 / 1956].

1901 *Claudine à Paris* published under Willy's name (Paris, Ollendorf) *Claudine in Paris* (UK), *Young Lady of Paris* (USA) 1931 / [*Claudine in Paris* 1958].
The Gauthier-Villars move to 177bis rue de Courcelles.

1902 *Claudine en ménage* published under Willy's name (Paris, Mercure de France) [*The Indulgent Husband* 1935 / *Claudine Married* 1960].
22 January: premiere of *Claudine à Paris* at the Théâtre des Bouffes-Parisiens, with Polaire playing Claudine.

1903 *Claudine s'en va* published under Willy's name (Paris, Ollendorf) [*The Innocent Wife* 1934 / *Claudine and Annie* 1962].

1904 *Minne* published under Willy's name (Paris, Ollendorf) [see below, 1909, *L'Ingénue libertine*].
Dialogues de bêtes, first book 'by Colette Willy' (Paris, Mercure de France).
From now until 1913 she uses the name 'Colette Willy'.

1905 *Les Egarements de Minne* published under Willy's name (Paris, Ollendorf) [see below, 1909, *L'Ingénue libertine*].
Sept Dialogues de bêtes published under the name Collette Willy, with a preface by Francis Jammes (Paris, Mercure de France) [*Barks and Purrs* 1931 / in *Creatures Great and Small* 1951].
17 September: death of C.'s father, Jules Colette.
Les Monts-Boucons sold.

1906 C. moves to 44 rue de Villejust, on her own.
6 February: C. makes her debut in *Le Désir, l'Amour et la Chimère* at the Théâtre des Mathurins.
March: C. appears in *Aux Innocents les mains pleines* at the Théâtre Royal.
1 October: premiere of *La Romanichelle* at the Olympia, with C. and Paul Franck.
28 November: premiere of *Pan* at the Théâtre Marigny, with C. as Paniska.

1907 *La Retraite sentimentale* published under the name Colette Willy (Paris, Mercure de France).
3 January: *Rêve d'Egypte* creates a scandal at the Moulin Rouge.
13 February: legal separation of C. and Willy.
1 November: premiere of *La Chair* at the Apollo, with C., Georges Wague and Marcel Vallée (replaced by Christine Kerf in May 1908).

1908 *Les Vrilles de la vigne* published under the name Colette Willy (Paris, Editions de la Vie parisienne).
29 August: premiere of *Son Premier Voyage* in Geneva, with C. and Saint-Mars.
18-29 November: *Claudine à Paris* presented at the Alcazar in Brussels, with C. as Claudine.

1909 *L'Ingénue libertine* published under the name Colette Willy (Paris, Ollendorf) [*The Gentle Libertine* 1931 / *The Innocent Libertine* 1968].
January-February: C. appears in her own play, *En camarades*, at the Théâtre des Arts and later at the Comédie Royale.

1910 21 May-1 October: *La Vagabonde* serialized in *La Vie parisienne*.
21 June: divorce of C. and Willy.
14 November: premiere of *Claudine* (an operetta in three acts by Willy, Henri Cain, Edouard Adenis and Henri Moreau) at the Moulin Rouge.
2 December: C. begins to write for *Le Matin*, where she meets Henry de Jouvenel.
The villa Rozven in Brittany is bought for C. by Mathilde de Morny ('Missy').

1911 *La Vagabonde* published under the name Colette Willy (Paris, Ollendorf) [*Renée, la vagabonde* 1931 / *The Vagabond* 1954].
August: premiere of *Bat' d'Af* at the Bataclan.
October: C. becomes a regular weekly contributor to *Le Matin*.
Autumn: C. moves to 57 rue Cortambert, with Henry de Jouvenel.
December: premiere of *L'Oiseau de nuit* at the Gaîté-Rochechouart.

1912 4 April: C. performs *La Chatte amoureuse* in the revue *Ça grise* at the Bataclan.
25 September: death of Sido.
19 December: marriage of C. and Henry de Jouvenel.

1913 *L'Entrave* (Paris, Librairie des Lettres) [*Recaptured* 1931 / *The Shackle* 1964 / *The Captive* 1970].
L'Envers du music-hall (Paris, Flammarion) [*Music-Hall Sidelights* 1957].
Prrou, Poucette et quelques autres (Paris, Librairè des Lettres).
From now until 1923 C. publishes under the name 'Colette (Colette Willy)'.
3 July: birth of C.'s daughter, Colette de Jouvenel.
31 December: death of C.'s half-brother, Achille Robineau-Duclos.

1914 2 August: Henry de Jouvenel is called up.
C. takes a job as a night nurse at the Lycée Janson de Sailly (converted into a hospital).
December: C. goes to Verdun and spends New Year with Jouvenel in the Argonne.

1915 From June, C. is in Italy.

1916 *La Paix chez les bêtes* (Paris, Arthème Fayard) in [*Creatures Great and Small* 1951].
C. spends the year chiefly in Rome.
Winter: return visit to Paris to move to 62 boulevard Suchet.

1917 *Les Heures longues* (Paris, Arthème Fayard).
Les Enfants dans les ruines (Paris, Editions de la Maison du Livre).
C. in Rome, where *La Vagabonde* is filmed starring Musidora.

1918 *Dans la foule* (Paris, Georges Grès et Cie).

1919 *Mitsou; ou Comment l'esprit vient aux filles*, with *En camarades* (Paris, Arthème Fayard) [*Mitsou; or, How Girls Grow Wise* 1930 / *Mitsou; or, The Education of Young Women* 1957].
C. becomes literary editor of Le Matin.

1920 3 January-5 June: *Chéri* serialized in *La Vie parisienne*, then published in book form (Paris, Arthème Fayard) [*Chéri* 1929/1951].
La Chambre éclairée (Paris, Edouard Joseph).
25 September: C. is made a *Chevalier* of the Legion of Honour.

1921 13 December: premiere of *Chéri* at the Théâtre Michel.

1922 *La Maison de Claudine* (Paris, Ferenczi) [*The Mother of Claudine* 1937 / *My Mother's House* 1953].
Le Voyage égoïste (Paris, Edouard Pelletan, Helleu et Sergent) [*Journey for Myself* 1971].
28 February: to celebrate the hundredth performance of *Chéri*, C. herself plays the part of Léa.

1923 *Le Blé en herbe* (Paris, Flammarion) [*The Ripening Corn* 1931 / *The Ripening* 1932 / *The Ripening Seed* 1955].
Rêverie de Nouvel An (Paris, Stock).
Beginning with these books, C. publishes under the name 'Colette'.
February: premiere of *La Vagabonde* at the Théâtre de la Renaissance.
March: C. goes on tour with *Chéri*.
November-December: C. goes on a lecture tour in the south of France.
December: separation of C. and Henry de Jouvenel.

1924 *La Femme cachée* (Paris, Flammarion) [*The Other Woman* 1971].
Aventures quotidiennes (Paris, Flammarion) [in *Journey for Myself* 1970].
January: in Switzerland with Bertrand de Jouvenel.
February: C. stops writing for *Le Matin* and from May onward contributes to *Le Figaro*, *Le Quotidien*, *L'Eclair*, etc.
Winter 1924-5: C. meets Maurice Goudeket.

1925 *Quatre saisons* (Paris, Philippe Ortiz) [in *Journey for Myself* 1970].
21 March: premiere of *L'Enfant et les sortilèges* in Monte Carlo, with music by Ravel and libretto by Colette (Paris, Durand) [*The Boy and the Magic* 1964].
6 April: divorce of C. and Henry de Jouvenel.
Easter: in Provence at Cap d'Ail with Marguerite Moreno, Goudeket and others.
June: holiday in Provence at Beauvallon.

1926 *La Fin de Chéri* (Paris, Flammarion) [*The Last of Chéri* 1932/1951].
February: C. is invited by the Glaoui to visit Morocco.
Purchase of La Treille Muscate at Saint-Tropez.
End of December: C. appears with Paul Poiret in *La Vagabonde* in Monte Carlo.

1927 C. moves to mezzanine flat in the Palais Royal, 9 rue de Beaujolais where she will live until February 1930.

1928 *La Naissance du jour* (Paris, Flammarion) [*A Lesson in Love* (USA), *Morning Glory* (UK) 1932 / *Break of Day* 1961].
Renée Vivien (Abbeville, Paillart).
5 November: C. becomes an *Officier* of the Legion of Honour.

1929 *La Seconde* (Paris, Ferenczi) [*Fanny and Jane* (UK), *The Other One* (USA) 1931 / *The Other One* 1960].
Regarde (Paris, Deschamps).
September: C. becomes drama critic of *La Revue de Paris*.

1930 *Sido* (Paris, Krâ) [*Sido* 1953].
Histoires pour Bel-Gazou (Paris, Stock).
C. and Goudeket buy La Gerbière, near Montfort-l'Amury, then sell it later in the same year.

1931 *Ces Plaisirs* serialized in *Gringoire*.
C. moves to Claridge's Hotel in the Champs-Elysées.
12 January: death of Willy.

1932 *Paradis terrestres* (Lausanne, Gonin) [*Earthly Paradise* 1966].
La Treille Muscate (Paris, Aimé Jourde).
Ces Plaisirs (Paris, Ferenczi) [*The Pure and the Impure* 1933 / *These Pleasures* 1934].
Prisons et Paradis (Paris, Ferenczi) [in *Places* 1970].
1 June: C. opens a beauty salon at 6 rue de Miromesnil.
Summer: lectures and demonstrations to promote her beauty products.

1933 *La Chatte* (Paris, Bernard Grasset) [*The Cat* (USA), *Saha, the Cat* (UK) 1936 / *The Cat*, with *Gigi* 1953].
June-July: C. writes the screenplay for Marc Allégret's film *Lac aux dames*.
8 October: C. starts to write a weekly column of theatre criticism for *Le Journal*.

1934 *Duo* (Paris, Ferenczi) [*The Married Lover* 1935 / *Duo* 1976].
La Jumelle noire, vol . I (Paris, Ferenczi).
September: C. writes the screenplay for Max Ophüls's film *Divine*.

1935 *Premier / Deuxième / Troisième Cahier de Colette* (all Paris, Aux Armes de France).
La Jumelle noire, vol. II (Paris, Ferenczi).
3 April: marriage of C. and Maurice Goudeket.
June: trip to New York on the maiden voyage of the *Normandie*.
10 August: marriage of Colette de Jouvenel.
October: death of Henry de Jouvenel.

1936 *Quatrième Cahier de Colette* (Paris, Aux Armes de France).
Mes Apprentissages (Paris, Ferenczi) [*My Apprenticeships* 1957].
Chats (Paris, Ferenczi).
26 February: C. is made a *Commandeur* of the Legion of Honour.
4 April: C. makes her inaugural speech to the Académie Royale de Langue et de Littérature Françaises de Belgique.
C. now living in Goudeket's flat at 33 Avenue des Champs-Elysées.

1937 *Bella Vista* (Paris, Ferenczi).
Splendeur des papillons (Paris, Plon).
Claudine et les contes de fées (Paris, Ferenczi).
La Jumelle noire, vol. III (Paris, Ferenczi)
Winter 1937-8: C. and Goudeket move to a first-floor (second-storey) flat in the Palais Royal, 9 rue de Beaujolais, where she will live for the rest of her life.

1938 *Paris. La Jumelle noire*, vol. IV (Paris, Ferenczi).
Trip to Fez for *Paris-Soir*.
Sale of La Treille Muscate.

1939 *Le Toutounier* (Paris, Ferenczi) [*Le Toutounier*, with *Duo* 1976].

1940 *Chambre d'hôtel*, with *La Lune de pluie* (Paris, Arthème Fayard).
C. gives a series of talks for American radio.
7 March: death of her brother Leo.
12 June: C. and Goudeket leave Paris to stay with her daughter at Curemonte, in Corrèze.
11 September: C. returns to Paris.

1941 *Journal à rebours* (Paris, Arthème Fayard).
Julie de Carneilhan (Paris, Arthème Fayard) [*Julie de Carneilhan* 1952].
Le Pur et l'Impur (Paris, Aux Armes de France) [*The Pure and the Impure* 1967 / and see above, 1932, *Ces Plaisirs*].
12 December: Goudeket is arrested by the Germans.

1942 *De ma fenêtre* (Paris, Aux Armes de France).
Gigi appears in *Présent* (see also 1944).
6 February: Goudeket is released.

1943 *Le Képi* (Paris, Arthème Fayard).
De la patte à l'aile (Paris, Corréâ).
Flore et Pomone (Paris, Editions de la Galerie Charpentier).
Nudité (Brussels, Editions de la Mappemonde).

1944 *Gigi* (Lausanne, Guilde du Livre) [*Gigi* 1952].
Trois . . . six . . . neuf (Paris, Corréâ) [extracts in *Places* 1970].
Broderie ancienne (Monaco, Editions du Rocher).
Paris de ma fenêtre (Geneva, Editions du Milieu du Monde).

1945 *Belles saisons* (Paris, Editions de la Galerie Charpentier).
2 May: C. is unanimously elected to the Académie Goncourt.

1946 *L'Etoile Vesper* (Geneva, editions du Milieu du Monde).

1948 *Pour un herbier* (Lausanne, Mermod) [*For a Flower Album* 1959].
Publication of the first volume of the *Oeuvres complètes* (Paris, Le Fleuron-Flammarion).
14 July: death of Marguerite Moreno.

1949 *Le Fanal bleu* (Paris, Ferenczi) [*The Blue Lantern* 1963].
C. publishes collected reminiscences and articles in *Trait pour trait*, *Journal intermittent* [in *Places* 1970], and *La Fleur de l'âge* (all Paris, Le Fleuron), and *En Pays connu* (Paris, Editions Manuel Brüker) [in *Places* 1970].
October: C. is elected President of the Académie Goncourt.

1950 First stay in Monte-Carlo, where she returns annually thereafter.

1951 Premiere of Yannick Bellon's film *Colette*.

1953 January: C. is awarded the *Grande Médaille* of the City of Paris.
20 April: C. becomes a *Grand Officier* of the Legion of Honour.

1954 3 August: death of C.
7 August: state funeral, followed by burial in Père Lachaise cemetery.

(In establishing this chronology and list of works, use has been made of the catalogue of the exhibition *Colette*, held at the Bibliothèque Nationale, Paris, in 1973.)

Picture Credits

Abbreviations

Anacréon = Musée Richard Anacréon, Granville
B. de J. = Fonds Colette, with the kind permission of Monsieur Bertrand de Jouvenel
BN = Bibliothèque Nationale, Paris
F.J. Gould = by permission of the Florence J. Gould Foundation

I Her Mother's House (pages 6-35)

1-3 B. de J.; 4, 5 priv. coll.; 6 B. de J.; 7 priv. coll.; 8-13 B. de J.; 14 Anacréon; 15, 16 B. de J.; 17 priv. coll.; 18 Roger-Viollet; 19 Flammarion; 20 B. de J.; 21 Flammarion; 22-28 B. de J.; 29 Luc-Albert Moreau—s.p.a.d.e.m.; 30 BN; 31 priv. coll.; 32, 33 coll. M. Boivin; 34 B. de J.; 35 priv. coll.; 36 F.J. Gould; 37 Anacréon; 38 Flammarion; 39 B. de J.; 40 Roger-Viollet; 41 coll. M. Remy-Bieth; 42 priv. coll.; 43 B. de J.; 44-46 priv. coll.; 47 B. de J.; 48, 49 Flammarion; 50 priv. coll.; 51 B. de J.; 52 Flammarion; 53 priv. coll.; 54 F.J. Gould; 55 priv. coll.

II Apprenticeships (page 36-121)

56 B. de J.; 57 Anacréon; 58 priv. coll.; 59 B. de J.; 60, 61 priv. coll.; 62-64 B. de J.; 65 priv. coll.; 66 B. de J.; 67 priv. coll.; 68 B. de J.; 69 Flammarion; 70 Anacréon; 71 B. de J.; 72, 73 Anacréon; 74 Jacques-Emile Blanche—s.p.a.d.e.m./photo B. de J.; 75 coll. M. Remy-Bieth; 76 Sem—s.p.a.d.e.m./photo BN; 77 Roger-Viollet; 78 F.J. Gould; 79 Sacha Guitry, copyright reserved; 80 coll. Sirot-Angel; 81-84 B. de J.; 85 Flammarion; 86 B. de J.; 87 Fix Masseau—s.p.a.d.e.m./photo F. J. Gould; 88 B. de J.; 89 Ferdinand Humbert, copyright reseved/photo priv. coll.; 90 B. de J.; 91 Bibliothèque de l'Opéra/photo BN; 92 Roger-Viollet; 93 Flammarion; 94, 95 B. de J.; 96 coll. M. Remy-Bieth; 97, 98 F.J. Gould 99 Anacréon; 100 photo Reutlinger—s.p.a.d.e.m./coll. B. de J.; 101 F.J. Gould; 102 B. de J.; 103 F.J. Gould; 104 Anacréon; 105 B. de J.; 106 Beraud—s.p.a.d.e.m./photo Giraudon; 107, 108 priv. coll.; 109-111 B. de J.; 112-114 F.J. Gould; 115 B. de J.; 116 F.J. Gould; 117 Flammarion; 118 B. de J.; 119, 120 Flammarion; 121 priv. coll.; 122, 123 phot Reutlinger—s.p.a.d.e.m./coll. B. de J.; 124 B. de J.; 125 Roger-Viollet; 126 photo BN; 127-130 B. de J.; 131 Jacques-Emile Blanche—s.p.a.d.e.m./photo BN; 132 Cappiello—s.p.a.d.e.m./photo BN; 133 Georges Lepape—s.p.a.d.e.m./coll. Claude Lepape; 134 Flammarion; 135 photo BN; 136 Forain, copyright reserved/photo Bulloz; 137, 138 B. de J.; 139 priv. coll.; 140-142 B. de J.; 143 Flammarion; 144, 145 photo BN; 146, 147 priv. coll.; 148 Roger-Viollet; 149 Jacques-Emile Blanche—s.p.a.d.e.m./Barcelona Museum; 150 B. de J; 151 Flammarion; 152 F.J. Gould; 153, 154

Flammarion; 155 Anacréon; 156, 157 Flammarion; 158, 159 F.J. Gould; 160 Pascau, copyright reserved/photo BN; 161 Roger-Viollet; 162 coll. M. Remy-Bieth; 163 B. de J.; 164, 165 F.J. Gould; 166 B. de J.; 167 photo BN; 168, 169 F.J. Gould; 170 B. de J.; 171 Flammarion; 172 B. de J.; 173 Flammarion; 174 coll. Sirot-Angel; 175 Flammarion; 176 B. de J.; 177, 178 photo BN; 179-181 priv. coll.; 182 Rip, copyright reserved/Anacréon; 183 Rip, copyright reserved/Flammarion; 184 Bac, copyright reserved/Anacréon; 185, 186 coll. Sirot-Angel; 187-193 B. de J.; 194 priv. coll.; 195 F.J. Gould; 196 B. de J.; 197 Musée de la Publicité; 198 F.J. Gould; 199 Cappiello—S.P.A.D.E.M./priv. coll.; 200 photo Reutlinger—S.P.A.D.E.M./B. de J.; 201 F.J. Gould; 202 coll. M. Remy-Bieth; 203 Flammarion; 204 Roger-Viollet; 205 priv. coll.; 206 coll. Sirot-Angel; 207 Jean Cocteau—S.P.A.D.E.M., from *Portraits-souvenir 1900-1914*, Paris, Grasset, 1935; 208 Georges Coudray, copyright reserved/photo BN; 209 Anacréon; 210 Sem—S.P.A.D.E.M./Anacréon; 211 Bibliothèque Forney, copyright reserved; 212-215 B. de J.; 216 Emilio della Sudda, copyright reserved/coll. Madame Maurice Boutterin, photo © Maria-Catherine Boutterin; 217 Flammarion; 218, 219 B. de J.; 220-222 priv. coll; 223 B. de J.; 224 Jacques Nam—A.D.A.G.P., from *Dialogues de bêtes*, Paris, Mercure de France; 225 B. de J.

III The Vagabond (pages 122-171)

226 B. de J.; 227 copyright reserved/photo BN; 228 B. de J.; 229 Roger-Viollet; 230 B. de J.; 231 F.J. Gould; 232-236 B. de J.; 237 Sem—S.P.A.D.E.M./photo Roger Viollet; 238 Roger-Viollet; 239 Sem—S.P.A.D.E.M./photo BN; 240, 241 B. de J.; 242 F.J. Gould; 243, 244 B. de J.; 245 F.J. Gould; 246 B. de J.; 247 priv. coll.; 248 B. de J.; 249 photo BN; 250 F.J. Gould; 251 priv. coll.; 252 B. de J.; 253-255 photo BN; 256 B. de J.; 257 coll. M. Remy-Bieth; 258 photo BN; 259 F.J. Gould; 260-262 B. de J.; 263 F.J. Gould; 264 coll. M. Remy-Bieth; 265 F.J. Gould; 266 Anacréon; 267 F.J. Gould; 268, 269 Flammarion; 270 B. de J.; 271 photo BN; 272-275 B. de J.; 276 Flammarion; 277 coll. Sirot-Angel; 278 F.J. Gould; 279 Matisse—S.P.A.D.E.M.; 280 Vertès—A.D.A.G.P./priv. coll.; 281 B. de J.; 282 Bibliothèque de l'Arsenal/photo BN; 283 Sacha Guitry, copyright reserved, from *Comoedia*; 284 B. de J.; 285-287 Bibliothèque de l'Opéra/photo BN; 288-294 B. de J.; 295 Bibliothèque de l'Opéra/photo BN; 296 B. de J.; 297 photo BN; 298, 299 B. de J.; 300 coll. René Dazy; 301-304 B. de J.; 305 priv. coll.; 306 Bibliothèque de l'Opéra/photo BN; 307-309 B. de J.; 310 Sem—S.P.A.D.E.M./photo B. de J.; 311 B. de J.; 312 coll. René Dazy; 313 priv. coll.; 314 B. de J.; 315 photo Reutlinger—S.P.A.D.E.M./B. de J.; 316, 317 B. de J.; 318 coll. Charles Hathaway; 319 B. de J.; 320 coll. M. Remy-Bieth; 321, 322 B. de J.; 323 Flammarion; 324 B. de J.; 325 photo BN; 326 B. de J.; 327 priv. coll.

IV Fetters (pages 172-223)

328 B. de J.; 329-331 photo Roger Schall; 332 coll. René Dazy; 333 photo Roger Schall; 334 B. de J.; 335, 336 B. de J.; 337 Rouveyre, copyright reserved, from *Visages des contemporains*, Paris, Mercure de France, 1913;

338 coll. M. Remy-Bieth; 339 Flammarion; 340-343 B. de J.; 344 Roger-Viollet; 345-349 B. de J.; 350 coll. G. Dormann; 351 B. de J.; 352-354 coll. G. Dormann; 355 priv. coll.; 356, 357 coll. J.L. Lécard; 358 B. de J.; 359, 360 coll. J.L. Lécard; 361 B. de J.; 362 coll. M. Remy-Bieth; 363 coll. Y. Bellon; 364-366 B. de J.; 367, 368 Flammarion; 369 priv. coll.; 370 René Carrère, copyright reserved/priv. coll.; 371 Flammarion; 372, 373 Vertès—A.D.A.G.P./photo B. de J.; 374, 375 priv. coll.; 376 B. de J.; 377 coll. J.L. Lécard; 378 coll. Sirot-Angel; 379 B. de J.; 380 coll. Sirot-Angel; 381 B. de J.; 382 Roger-Viollet; 383 Henry Bataille, copyright reserved/photo BN; 384, 385 Roger-Viollet; 386 Julhès, copyright reserved/coll. René Dazy; 387 coll. A. Khan

V The Ripening Seed (pages 236-249)

396, 397 B. de J.; 397 coll. J.L. Lécard; 398, 399 B. de J.; 400, 401 priv. coll.; 402 Vertès—A.D.A.G.P./coll. René Dazy; 403 Texcier, copyright reserved/Anacréon; 404 B. de J.; 405 Flammarion; 406 Andrée Sikorska, copyright reserved/coll. Michaux; 407 Flammarion; 408 priv. coll. 409 B. de J.; 410 photo Germaine Krull, © Galerie Wilde Köln; 411 Méheut—S.P.A.D.E.M./Editions Deschamps, 1929; 412 photo Edward Steichen, © International Museum of Photography, George Eastman House; 413 photo Piaz, copyright reserved

VI A Fine Autumn (pages 250-312)

414 Flammarion; 415, 416 B. de J.; 417 priv. coll.; 418 photo Germaine Krull, © Galerie Wilde Köln; 419 B. de J.; 420 coll. M. Remy-Bieth; 421, 422 Luc-Albert Moreau—A.D.A.G.P./coll. B. Villaret; 423 Dunoyer de Segonzac—S.P.A.D.E.M./photo Flammarion; 424 priv. coll.; 425 Dunoyer de Segonzac—S.P.A.D.E.M./photo priv. coll.; 426 Flammarion; 427 photo BN; 428 photo Jacques Henri Lartigue—S.P.A.D.E.M.; 429 B. de J.; 430 Luc-Albert Moreau—A.D.A.G.P./coll. B. Villaret; 431 photo André Kertesz; 432 B. de J.; 433-435 Flammarion; 436-438 B. de J.; 439, 440 coll. M. Remy-Bieth; 441 coll. Hermès; 442 Paul Colin, copyright reserved/coll. René Dazy; 443 Roger-Viollet; 444 priv. coll.; 445 B. de J.; 446 priv. coll.; 447, 448 Roger-Viollet; 449 coll. René Dazy; 450 Vertès—A.D.A.G.P./coll.. René Dazy; 451 B. de J.; 452 photo BN; 453 Roger-Viollet; 454 coll. J.L. Lécard; 455 Gallimard; 456 Flammarion; 457 photo Robert Doisneau—Rapho; 458 coll. René Dazy; 459 Vertès—A.D.A.G.P./priv. coll.; 460 B. de J.; 461 photo Gisèle Freund; 462-465 B. de J.; 466 coll. J.L. Lécard; 467 Christian Berard—S.P.A.D.E.M./priv. coll.; 468 B. de J.; 469 photo Serge Lido; 470 Jean Cocteau—S.P.A.D.E.M./coll. Edouard Dermit; 471 photo Serge Lido; 472 B. de J.; 473 photo Walter Carone—*Paris Match*; 474 F.J. Gould; 475 photo R. Landin; 476 photo Robert Doisneau—Rapho; 477 photo Cecil Beaton; 478 B. de J.; 479, 480 Flammarion; 481 photo Zalewski—Rapho; 482 priv. coll.; 483 B. de J.; 484 photo Gisèle Freund; 485 coll. Sirot-Angel; 486 photo by Ora; 487 photo Henri Cartier-Bresson—Magnum; 488 photo Jannine Niepce—Rapho.

Index

Numbers in *italic* type refer to illustrations and captions.